Black Bart Roberts

Black Bart Roberts

The Greatest Pirate of Them All

By Terry Breverton

PELICAN PUBLISHING COMPANY

Gretna 2004

For my family

*The word "Pelican" and the depiction of a pelican are trademarks
of Pelican Publishing Company, Inc., and are registered in the
U.S. Patent and Trademark Office.*

ISBN 1-58980-233-0

Printed in Canada
Published by Pelican Publishing Company, Inc.
1000 Burmaster Street, Gretna, Louisiana 70053

Contents

Terry Breverton is a Fellow of the Institute of Management Consultants and a Fellow of the Chartered Institute of Marketing. He studied in the universities of Manchester, Birmingham and Lancaster, has had a career in international management consultancy, and has been a board director of multinational companies. Returning with his family to live in Wales, he is a Senior Lecturer in marketing and management at UWIC Business School in Cardiff.

The author of 14 books and numerous articles, he was attracted to writing on piracy and buccaneers some years ago, upon seeing a small plaque in West Wales. It stated that nearby was born Black Bart Roberts, the most famous and successful pirate of all time. Knowing that Wales was the birthplace of the world's most successful buccaneer, Sir Henry Morgan, Breverton discovered that while more famous pirates such as Captain Kidd and Blackbeard took under 30 ships between them, Roberts took over 400 ships, and almost halted transatlantic shipping. He has been called by Time-Life, *'the last and most lethal pirate'*, and in his lifetime was called *'the great pirate'*, eclipsing all others in 'The Golden Age of Piracy'.

Roberts was a teetotal Christian, virtually forced into piracy when aged almost 40, and called *'the black Captain'* for his dark looks. A tall man for the times, he took over a successful pirate crew, whose senior members termed themselves *'The House of Lords'*, and turned them into a band feared by the navies of the major powers of that time – England, France, Holland, Spain and Portugal. His crews roamed the South American Coast, the Caribbean, the Atlantic Coast of the American Colonies and Canada, the Atlantic and the west coast of Africa. His is a fascinating story – that of the most successful and strange pirate of all time.

*The author at Black Bart's monument on
Little Newcastle Green*

INTRODUCTION -

'The Golden Age of Piracy' occurred in the first two decades of the 18th century, before the Royal Navy secured mastery of the seas. Gold, silver and jewels were systematically stripped out of South America and transported to Europe in great treasure fleets. Ships took goods and money from Europe to the Slave Coast of Africa. Slaves were then transported on the 'Middle Passage' to the Caribbean and American Colonies. On the third part of the voyage, the slave-ships, or 'blackbirders' returned to Europe with payment for the slaves. Thus the Atlantic and Caribbean were constantly being criss-crossed with ships holding precious booty. The wealth looted from South America built the great cathedrals of the Iberian Peninsula. Slavery built the great buildings of Bath and Bristol. As always, a surplus of money attracts a surplus of seekers of riches.

Peace between the great powers threw many seamen into penury, looking for alternative means to support themselves. The majority of the navy's crews had been forcibly 'impressed' into a life of unspeakable cruelty and discipline, and desertion was common. Deserters could not go home and lead a normal life, so were natural recruits for the booming trade of piracy. Many merchant seamen had also been 'pressed', and refused to fight off attacks, preferring to throw in their lot with the pirates. Merchant captains were often as vicious as their naval counterparts, and pirates always questioned the captured crew upon their treatment by the captain and officers. A 'bad' captain would normally be killed, but 'fair' captains allowed to go unharmed.

Every man was equal on a pirate ship – and the well-known phrase '*a short life and a merry one*' comes from the remarkable subject of the book, Black Bart. Compare this attractive life to that in the Royal Navy. The following passage is from Dava Sobel's brilliant 1995 book, '*Longitude*'.

'Dirty weather,' Admiral Sir Clowdisley Shovell called the fog that had dogged him for twelve days at sea. Returning home victorious from Gibraltar after skirmishes with the French Mediterranean forces, Sir Clowdisley could not beat the heavy autumn overcast. Fearing the ships might founder on coastal rocks, the admiral summoned all his navigators to put their heads together.

The consensus opinion placed the English fleet safely at Ile d'Ouessant, an island outpost of the Brittany peninsula. But as the sailors commenced north, they discovered to their horror that they had misgauged their longitude near the Scilly Isles. These tiny islands, about twenty miles from the Southwest tip of

England, point to Land's End like a path of stepping-stones. And on that foggy night of October 22, 1707, the Scillies became unmarked tombstones for two thousand of Sir Clowdisley's troops.

The flagship, the 'Association', struck first. She sank within minutes, drowning all hands. Before the rest of the vessels could react to the obvious danger, two more ships, the 'Eagle' and the 'Romney', pricked themselves on the rocks and went down like stones. In all, four of five warships were lost.

Only two men washed ashore alive. One of them was Sir Clowdisley himself, who may have watched the fifty-seven years of his life flash before his eyes as the waves carried him home. He had been approached by a sailor, a member of the Association's crew, who claimed to have kept his own reckoning of the fleet's location during the whole cloudy passage. Such subversive navigation by an inferior was forbidden in the Royal navy, as the unnamed seaman well knew. However, the danger appeared so enormous, by his calculations, that he risked his neck to make his concerns known to the officers. **Admiral Shovell had the man hanged for mutiny on the spot.**

No one was around to spit "I told you so!" into Sir Clowdisley's face as he nearly drowned. But as soon as the admiral collapsed on dry land, a local woman combing the beach purportedly found his body, and fell in love with the emerald ring on his finger. Between her desire and his depletion, she handily murdered him for it. Three decades later, on her deathbed, this same woman confessed the crime to her clergyman, producing the ring as proof of her guilt and contrition.

The demise of Sir Clowdisley's fleet capped a long saga in seafaring in the days before sailors could find their longitude. Page after page from this miserable history relates quintessential horror stories of death by scurvy and thirst, of ghosts in the rigging, and of landfalls in the form of shipwrecks, with hulls dashed on rocks and heaps of drowned corpses fouling the beaches. In literally hundreds of instances, a vessel's ignorance of longitude swiftly led to her destruction.'

This is the background to the days when Black Bart roamed across the Atlantic, from the age of 13 in 1695, to his death in 1722. We begin our story with the tale of the man who was responsible for Roberts becoming a pirate, Captain Howell Davies. Davies' capture of Captain Snelgrave is then recounted from the original 1734 publication, before the life of Black Bart Roberts is recounted. The book ends with the greatest pirate trial in history, and the life of one of Robert's crew, John Phillips.

CHAPTER I

CAPTAIN HOWELL DAVIS - 'THE CAVALIER PRINCE OF PIRATES' d. 1719

'Ah!' cried another voice, that of the youngest hand on board, and evidently full of admiration, 'he was the flower of the flock, was Flint!'

'Davis was a man, too, by all accounts,' said Silver. 'I never sailed along of him; first with England, then with Flint, that's my story; and now here on my own account, in a manner of speaking.' - 'Treasure Island', Robert Louis Stevenson, 1883.

"Howel Davis – the cavallier prince of pirates"

Milford Haven's Howell Davis was a Welsh pirate from Milford in Pembrokeshire, who preyed on shipping off the West African coast and in the Caribbean from July 1718 until June 1719. An expert in deception, Davis was killed in a skirmish with Portuguese troops on the West African Coast. Davis was virtually raised on a ship, coming to stature as chief mate of a slaver under Captain Skinner. In 1718, Davis was on Skinner's slaver snow *Cadogan* which was captured by Captain Edward England off the coast of Africa, en route from Nassau in the Bahamas to the island of Madagascar. Defoe wrote that England tried to get the good-natured, ever-smiling Davis to join his crew, but Davis *'resolutely answered that he would sooner be shot than sign the pirates' articles. Upon which England, pleased with his bravery, sent him and the rest of the men on board the snow (a small brig), appointing him captain in the room of Skinner (who had been shot) and commanding him to pursue his voyage. He also gave him a written paper sealed up, with orders to open it when he should come to a certain latitude..... This was an act of Grandeur like what princes practise to their admirals.... The paper contained a generous deed of gift of the ship and cargo to Davis and the crew, ordering him to go to Brazil, dispose of the lading to the best advantage and make a fair and equal dividend with the rest.'*

Skinner had been pelted with bottles by the pirates for being a brutal captain, before being put out of his misery by a musket-shot. Davis was a likeable, easy-going character, and easily had gained favour with England, and Davis wanted to sail on England's instructions to Brazil. However, most of the crew refused to follow this course of action, so Davis took the slaver on to Barbados, where he was charged with being a pirate and imprisoned for three months. Released for lack of proof, Davis found that his name had been blackened by the events, and could not get passage on any ship as a mate. He decided to head for the pirate stronghold of New Providence in the Bahamas, but Woodes Rogers had offered an 'Act of Grace' to the pirates at Nassau, and there was still no future for him. There were hundreds of former pirates now looking for 'honest' work there.

Governor Rogers took pity on him, and Davis sailed as an ordinary seaman on the *Buck*, a sloop full of New Providence's former pirates, with cargo for trading with Spanish and French possessions in the Indies. It sailed in consort with the *Mumvil Trader*. Rogers had few provisions, and the nearest island, Hispaniola, was in Spanish hands. He was surrounded by Spanish possessions which were not allowed to trade with him, and whose costagardas routinely tortured English seamen who fell into their hands. Rogers knew that if his expedition was stopped, it would have to fight the costagardas, so manned the ships *Buck* and *Samuel* with 'former' pirates, and filled the holds with barter goods. The Spanish colonists were willing to deal with pirates and merchants, as the Spanish monopoly of trade with them meant that they had to otherwise suffer high prices. The ships *Buck*, *Mumvil Trader* and *Samuel* left New Providence for Hispaniola in September 1718, anchored offshore and landed their cargo. Some sailors pretended to be filling casks with fresh water, so that any passing Spanish costagardas would possibly ignore them. Davis was still annoyed about his treatment - he knew that he would always be treated as a former pirate, with no chance of a mate's ticket.

Howell Davis, with former pirates Walter Kennedy, Dennis Topping, Thomas Anstis, Christopher Moody and William Magness, now saw their chance, and waited until Captain Brisk and the loyal members of his crew were asleep, then overpowered them. They transferred the remaining cargo from the *Mumvil Trader* onto the *Buck*, and sailed away to the north. The simmering and resentful Davis had started this mutiny at Martinique. There was no killing, merely a change of command, and most of the men who joined Davis were said to be Welsh and English. Davis was elected captain '*over a large bowl of punch.*' According to Defoe: '*as soon as he was possessed of command, he drew up Articles, which were signed by himself and the rest, then he made a short speech, the sum of which was a declaration of war against the whole world.*' He was voted captain with no opposition - the pirates thought the short, stocky Welshman '*pistol-proof*'. He is later said to have '*played the (pirate) game because he was given the name*'. The *Buck* was now careened with some difficulty at Coxon's Hole, a bay on the east of Cuba, as the pirates had no carpenter with them. With his crew of just thirty-five men, Davis then took a French ship. The *Buck* had followed the coast until Davis came across a 12-gun French ship at anchor in a sheltered creek. Davis fired a shot across the boat (not wishing to damage it), and some of its crew fled in a jolly-boat to the beach, there being no escape. While the vessel was being plundered, a larger, 24-gun French ship was spotted. Showing his native Welsh cunning, Davis then bluffed it into surrendering peacefully. He forced the prisoners on the first prize to pretend to be pirates and raised a dirty tarpaulin as a black flag. After a chase, the *Buck* caught up with the Frenchman, and after a couple of broadsides, the prize caught up with the action. Thinking it was outnumbered, the French ship struck its colours. Davis looted the two ships, transferring their equipment onto the *Buck*, then released them and their crews

Davis's sloops had only six light guns, and would find it difficult to capture a heavily-armed merchantman except by stealth, so the larger merchant ship was a fine acquisition, and they sailed into Privateer Bay, a hiding-place for pirates on the northern, uninhabited coast of Hispaniola. Impenetrable forests protected them from the Spanish settlers in the south of the island, and there were plenty of wild cattle for provisions. Now he decided to let the prisoners go. From the '*Buck*', Captain Brisk, his first and second mate, boatswain and two unfit seamen were put into Captain Porter's '*Samuel*'. A former pirate, Porter was also released, along with 17 of his crew who had families in New Providence. Porter sailed back to New Providence, and to the despair of Woodes Rogers, but other seamen were forced to stay with Davis, as he desperately needed crew members. One of those forced to stay was a young surgeon named Archibald Murray. Davis set sail for Cuba, where a Philadelphia ship was taken, then returned to Hispaniola. The busiest trade route in the West Indies was around Cape Franbarway, and more ships were captured. Upon one was a Welsh seaman called Richard Jones, who Davis wanted to join him, but who refused. A pirate gunner cut his leg, and the pirates repeatedly dropped him on a rope into the shark-infested seas, until Jones agreed to sign articles.

However, prizes were eluding the pirates, and Davis decided to cross the Atlantic and raid the African coast. He realised that his sloop needed to be properly careened. At a bay called Coxon's Hole in the east coast of Cuba, the 'forced men' like Jones cleaned the Buck, and stripped her ready for pirate action. One side of the hull was scraped of barnacles, seaweed and other accretions, then coated with sulphur and brimstone to kill the teredos worms and their eggs, then covered with a protective tallow. Then the boat was hauled over to treat the other side, making the boat safer and faster at sea. Davis also had prepared plenty of 'boucan', preserved strips of wild cattle meat, for the long voyage. A problem was that the 'Buck' was fitted for 15 men, whereas he had a crew of over 60, so the ship reeked of sweat and sulphur. For this reason, his pirates preferred to laze ashore rather than in the comparative safety of the sloop. Davis now tacked through the Windward Passage, along the coast of Florida, until in the latitude of the Bahamas he took the trade wind to the Portuguese Cape Verde Islands. His trusted lieutenants, known as 'the House of Lords' included the arrogant Walter Kennedy, the quartermaster John Taylor and the hot-tempered gunner Henry Dennis. These men were allowed privileges such as being on the quarterdeck, and had counselled Davis to set sail for Africa. Woodes Rogers had 'cleaned out' Nassau, and Blackbeard had been killed - the Guinea Coast was a safer place to operate for the time being.

After the long crossing, Davis flew the English flag to enter the port of Sao Nicolau in early 1719, and pretended to be an English privateer with a letter of marque to fight the Spanish. He was welcomed, indeed 'caressed by the Governor and inhabitants.' Davis had brought gold and goods in exchange for wine and apparel, and the Portuguese were only too happy to trade with the likeable 'merchant'. Davis was invited to meet the Governor. The fort only had 12 guns, and Davis had left his stinking pirate sloop, stripped for action, well out to sea, when he first visited the governor. He wore a maroon velvet coat, silver-buckled shoes and a lace cravat, and his small bodyguard from the House of Lords dressed almost as ostentatiously. For five blissful weeks the pirates enjoyed themselves – *'no diversion was wanting which the Portuguese could show or money could purchase.'* However, Richard Jones, when fetching water, tried to limp away and hide in the coconut groves. Quartermaster Taylor spied him attempting to escape and chased after him through the undergrowth. He could not allow Jones to divulge that the *Buck* was a pirate ship. Eventually he caught up with the unfortunate Jones and tied his hands to take him back to the ship. A Portuguese officer reported this to the governor, but Taylor, with a smattering of Portuguese, explained that Jones was a pirate who had been captured and had escaped. Jones, who spoke no Portuguese, was taken back to the *Buck*, tied to the mast, and whipped by every person in the crew. Davis decided it was time to leave the island, provisioned the boat, and sailed to the Isle of May, where there were supposed to be rich pickings. Five pirates stayed and settled on the island, including a Monmouthshire man, Charles Franklyn who married a local girl. Franklyn was said to be *'so charmed with the luxuries of the place and the free conversation of the Women'*.

Off the Isle of May (Maio, in the Cape Verde Islands), in February 1719, Davis sighted *'The Loyal Merchant'*, and sailing across its bows discharged chainshot at its crew, stopping the ship. Davis ordered its mate to come across to his ship, and questioned him on the sailing qualities of the merchantman, wishing to replace the small and slow *'Buck'*. Being slow to answer, the mate was badly beaten by the pirates, who hung him from the yardarm, and kept dropping him to the deck as he was about to pass out. *Lords* Dennis and Kennedy then *'woolded'* him and forced him to serve on the *Buck*. The *Buck* now took another seven Dutch and English prizes in the next few months, taking gold dust, ivory and slaves. One boat carried some welcome casks of rum, and one had a cargo of firearms. Eight heavy guns were taken off one merchantman, and used on a larger prize which they used to replace the *Buck*, which was now used as a consort ship. The new flagship was a two-masted brigantine with fore and aft rigging, which could take 26 cannon, and Davis named her the *Royal James*. Fore and aft rigging could be quickly altered to deal with different wind conditions.

Davis took the *Royal James* and the *Buck* to Gambia on February 23rd, and off Gallassee (later called Bathurst, and now Banjul) ran up merchant flags on the mastheads. He sailed past the Royal African Trading Company's fort of St James and its ship the *'Royal Ann'*, up the Gambia River, to see Orfeur, the company agent. Taking the guise of Liverpool traders, Captain Davis, the ship's master and the surgeon '*dressed like gentlemen*' instead of the normal pirate dress. They took dinner with '*the Governor of Gambia Castle*' (this was possibly Orfeur), saying that they were '*bound for the river of Senegal to trade for gum and elephant's teeth (ivory).*' Davis had taken a '*hamper of European liquor*' to dinner, as a present for the Governor. The pirates took the opportunity to study the fort's defences, and the disposition and effectiveness of the *Royal Ann*. The fort was being rebuilt at Gallassee, and in the meantime Orfeur was conducting the Company's business from the *Royal Ann*. Orfeur suspected that the traders were not normal merchantmen, as they were too well-dressed. Some reports stated that the pirates suddenly drew pistols on the governor and relieved him of £2000 in cash after tying him to his chair, but the facts are different.

That night the pirates lowered boats and attacked Orfeur's men, but were met by a cross-fire from portholes. However, when Orfeur was wounded, he surrendered to the 60 pirates. Two pirates were injured, and they set the fort ablaze, looted the *Royal Ann*, and took another company ship lying alongside it. One of the men sheltering in the Fort of St James was to become Governor Plunkett who was captured by Black Bart, after his Sierra Leone fort at Brent (or Bence) island was bombarded. The pirates loaded up with ivory and bars of gold. (It appears that Davis totally destroyed the trading post, because George Lowther sailed as second mate in March 1721 of the Royal Africa Company ship '*Gambia Castle*', under Captain Charles Russell. She was '*carrying stores and a company of soldiers to the river Gambia, on the African coast, to garrison a fort some time before captured and destroyed by Captain Howel (sic) Davis, the pirate*'.) The badly-treated Welshman Richard Jones had actively taken part in the assault upon the fort and *Royal Ann*, and half of Orfeur's 14-man garrison joined Davis's men. They were malnourished, with a short life-span in the Tropics, and treated terribly by the Company.

For two nights Davis's crew caroused, but then another sloop nosed up the river towards the smoking fort. The ship flew no flag, and Davis prepared to send a shot across it. Captain Olivier *La Bouse* was commanding a 14-gun French pirate ship with sixty-four crew members, half French and half former slaves. He had formerly pirated with Captains Bellamy and Williams. He hoisted his Black Flag, fired a shot and almost attacked Captain Howel Davis, who was resting with his crew. Seeing the pirate flag raised, Davis swiftly hoisted his own, and hostilities were averted. Oliver le Vasseur, also known as *la Bouche* or *la Buse (the Buzzard)*, apologised and the crews settled down to a week-long party. Both captains then agreed to sail down the coast together. On March 7th, they were guided by the master on the merchant vessel they had captured, through the treacherous channels of the River Gambia to the open ocean. The *Royal James* was followed by La Bouche's sloop, into the mists at the river's mouth. They came across Edward England's pirate ship, flying the black flag, but England declined to join their company and sailed on. Just a year later, La Bouche would join up with England on the account.

Davis allowed the merchantman to leave with its captain, but took his second mate, boatswain and five other crew. Two did not want to join and ran off into the forests, but Lord Taylor paid some Africans to find them. When they were hunted down they were brutally whipped by the pirates and thrown into the stinking hold. One who had suffered the same punishment, Richard Jones, was by now so highly thought of that he was elected boatswain by the pirates.

Arriving at Sierra Leone, they fired a broadside at a tall galley at anchor, which promptly hoisted its own Black Flag. The 'Mourroon' was commanded by pirate Captain Thomas Cocklyn (from New Providence). Davis was annoyed that another pirate would spoil their chances of booty, but when Cocklyn heard that la Bouche was aboard, he invited Davis and la Bouche aboard his ship. Captain La Bouche was at New Providence Island in 1718, and had served on the same ship as Cocklyn. When Davis stepped aboard, a forced seaman rushed up to him and told him the story of William Hall. Cocklyn was known as a cruel captain, and Hall had been taken prisoner the previous day, on the 'Edward and Steed'. Hall was ordered by Cocklyn to release the foretop-sailsheet, and had climbed the shrouds too slowly for Cocklyn's liking. The boatswain shot him, not fatally, then climbed up after Hall, to cut at him with his cutlass, and his body dropped into the sea. The rest of the 'Edward and Steed' crew feared the same fate, and Davis swore at Cocklyn, calling him a fool. The *law of the sea* was that those who surrendered without struggling would not be harmed. La Bouche intervened as the two pirate captains circled each other, holding their cutlasses out. He put his arms around both and led them to Cocklyn's cabin for a drink. The three captains now formed up for a joint cruise 'on the account.' Their crews drank together for two days and on the third day they decided to head upriver to where six merchantmen had fled from Cocklyn. He already had captured two ships off Sierra Leone, the 'Edward and Steed', and Captain Elliott's 'The 'Two Friends'', from Barbados.

Cocklyn was a vicious man, who had served with la Bouche under Christopher Moody. Moody had suspected Cocklyn of plotting against him, and had put him with other potential mutineers in a clapped-out galley, the 'Rising Sun', fully expecting it to sink. However, Cocklyn repaired it and renamed it the Mourroon. The rest of Moody's crew suspected that he had been withholding booty from them, deposed him and elected la Bouche as captain. Moody ended up in New Providence, where he joined Howell Davis's mutiny on the 'Buck'. Thus Moody was now in company with a man he had supported in mutiny (Davis), a man who had replaced him as captain (La Bouche), and a man whom he had thrown off his ship for plotting a mutiny (Cocklyn). Cocklyn suggested that he took the 'Two Friends' out for sea trials to see if it was suitable for replacing the 'Mourroon', while la Bouche and Davis stayed and blockaded the Royal African Company's Fort of Bence Island, in mid-river. (This location was later called Freetown, after British abolitionists settled freed slaves there in 1787). The two captains waited at sea, just out of the fort's gun range, to ensure that none of the merchantmen could slip away.

Suddenly, two cannon retorts were heard, and the pirates rushed to action stations. However, they soon began laughing - the shots had been fired by 'Crackers' John Leadstine, a private trader. He saluted each new pirate ship as he knew they would bring in cheap trade goods. His two brass cannon were surrounded by wooden cages in which he kept slaves for trade. La Bouche decided he did not wish to wait for Cocklyn, and despite Davis's protests, sailed toward Bence Island. Agent Plunkett organised cannon fire which tore through the mainsail and sprayed water over the sloop's decks, before la Bouche veered back to rejoin Davis. Davis's crew laughed at their efforts. Cocklyn now returned, with a boat that Davis had captured at Gambia, which he wanted to use as a store-ship. The pirate ships, all flying black flags, headed toward the fort, and the seamen abandoned the merchantmen for its relative safety. The abandoned merchantmen were secured and taken. They were the 'Jacob and Jael' under Captain Thompson and the 'Society' trading from London; the brig 'Robert and Jane' under Captain Bennet, out of Antigua; the snow 'Parnel' under Captain Morris, and the 'Nightingale', both out of Bristol; and the 'Queen Elizabeth' under Captain Creighton. Goods, provisions, sails and guns were stripped from the boats, and barter terms agreed for the boats themselves with four of the captains. The two other boats were burned.

However, the pirates needed more booty, and believed that the fort held gold and Company money. At dawn the pirate ships began bombarding the fort, whose largest guns had rusted up. Davis sent Plunkett a cheeky message, asking if he had any spare gunpowder, ammunition or gold to lend him, and Plunkett retorted that he had no gold, but plenty of gunpowder and shot if Davis would care to come and collect it. However, Plunkett soon ran out of ammunition in the burning fort, and one wall had been smashed in. He tried to take his men in canoes off the island but they were captured, and a furious Cocklyn put his pistol to Plunkett's head, cursing him. Plunkett responded with such a vile stream of invective at Cocklyn that the pirate was non-plussed and his men burst out laughing. Even the evil Cocklyn saw the funny side of this exchange, and spared Plunkett's life. The pirates stripped the fort of all its valuables, and forced some men to join them. Many did so willingly. There was an enormous party, and Plunkett was allowed to go back to his ruined fort. In the next few days, three more ships were taken as they sailed into the port, including the '*Sarah*', which Cocklyn wanted to replace the *Mourroon*. The pirates spent their time selling off their loot to local traders, including '*Old Crackers*'. Two men from the '*Mourroon*' escaped into the local forests, and for a day the pirates searched for them, but Davis counselled that they would either return or die anyway. After three days, one was dead and the carpenter Henry Thrixton returned, starving and lacerated from the thorny jungle. Cocklyn wanted to torture and kill him, but Davis put him in safety on the *Royal James* to serve under him.

The three captains now agreed to leave Sierra Leone - pickings were slim as more and more ships knew that '*a new gang*' of pirates was operating in the area. La Bouche and Davis allowed Cocklyn to refit the '*Sarah*' with his guns and equipment from the *Mourroon*, and it was decided to split up the joint booty, which was kept in Cocklyn's store-ship. The other captains were afraid of Cocklyn making a '*soft farewell*', leaving at night with all the accumulated loot. However, the pirates spotted a ship unexpectedly approaching, Captain Snelgrave's '*Bird*', a London galley which had not heard of the pirate take-over of the port. The pirates hastily took their ships up-river, out of sight of Snelgrave, in order to entice him into port. By the time they had rigged ready for sailing out to sea, they might have lost their prey. In the calamitous rush to get up-river, they omitted putting out their camp-fires on the beach, and Snelgrave became suspicious. In the gathering dusk, he sent a pinnace to investigate, but the crew reported back that it was too dark to discover what had been happening. (Snelgrave's remarkable account of the capture, from his wonderful '*A New Account of some Parts of Guinea*, *and the Slave-Trade*', published in 1734, is appended to this chapter. He recounts Davis as brave, '*my generous Friend*', and humane, and records his death with some sadness).

Snelgrave took supper while pondering the findings of the search-party, and anchored off-shore. However, the officer of the watch rushed to him, reporting the sounds of rowing. Two boats containing 12 of Cocklyn's men, armed to the teeth, were close to the 16-cannon ship. Snelgrave ordered that 20 of his 45-man crew be woken and sent to the quarter-deck, and he hailed the two boats, asking who they were and what they wanted. The pirates shouted back that they were from Captain Elliott's '*Two Friends*', out of Barbados. Snelgrave's crew had refused to arm themselves and go on deck, and the pirates shot at Snelgrave and began to board his ship. Snelgrave charged below to get help, but only a couple of loyal crewmen accompanied him, and they ran back up onto the deck, where one was shot. A grenade exploded, and his crew implored the unarmed Snelgrave to surrender, which he was forced to do.

Cocklyn's quartermaster was incensed by Snelgrave's decision to fight, for which the penalty was death, and he held a pistol against him. Snelgrave impulsively pushed the firearm away, but was shot in the arm. He turned to run, and was pistol-clubbed to the ground, and the situation looked bleak for him. The pirate boatswain said '*No quarter shall be given to any captain that offers to defend his ship*', and lashed out with his cutlass, breaking its blade on the deck-rail. Luckily, Snelgrave's crew implored the boatswain to spare Snelgrave, one member crying '*For God's sake, don't kill our captain, for we were never with a better man.*' Just then the pirate quartermaster returned from a quick inspection of the '*Bird's*' splendid cargo, and announced that it was a fine prize. In the general exultation, Snelgrave was unusually spared, and the pirates fired their pistols into the night sky to celebrate. Snelgrave later wrote that Davis claimed that '*their reasons for going a pirating were to revenge themselves on base merchants and cruel commanders of ships*'.

However, Cocklyn had brought the *Mourroon* out to back up the assault by his men, and thought that the *Bird's* crew was firing. He ordered a broadside fired at the *Bird*, which unfortunately smashed its masts and sails, before he realised his mistake. Cocklyn next questioned Snelgrave upon the sailing qualities of the *Bird*, and requisitioned it, while boatloads of goods were ferried to the port's private traders, which included the Welshman Henry Glynn, an old friend of Snelgrave's. Snelgrave also told the pirates that Edward England, who had captured

Davis and sailed with la Bouche, was still taking ships off the Gambia coast. Each of the boarding-party was given a fresh suit of clothes, and the look-out who first spotted the *Bird* was given a pair of pistols, while the three pirate quartermasters divided up the rest of the booty. Captain Snelgrave later wrote in his '*A New Account of Some parts of Guinea, and the Slave Trade*' that when Howell Davis captured his ship, his men drank the looted claret and brandy from bowls before throwing bucketfuls of the precious alcohol at each other, and ended up by swabbing the decks with the drink. (As Bart Roberts commented later, a pirate's life was to be a short and happy one.) Snelgrave also reported that '*Captain Howell Davis came in the river (Gambia) with a Black Flag showing, which said flag is intended to frighten honest merchantmen into surrender on penalty of being murdered if they do not*'

An 18 year-old who served under Davis tried to break open a chest when the quartermasters were assessing the spoils, but Cocklyn's quartermaster swung at him with a broadsword. The youth ran to the safety of Davis, who was sitting drinking in the *Bird's* captain's cabin with Cocklyn and la Bouche. The quartermaster swung again at the youngster, cutting him on the thumb, but also Davis on the hand. Davis was furious at this latest insult from Cocklyn or his crew. The youngster may have been at fault, but it was Davis's right to punish him. Back on the *Royal James*, he ordered that the guns were run out, and trained on the *Mourroon*. Cocklyn frantically sent his quartermaster on a boat from the *Bird* to apologise profusely to Davis.

It had been decided that la Bouche could replace his sloop with the *Bird*, and that Cocklyn could take the *Sarah* and leave the leaking *Mourroon*. Cocklyn renamed his new galley the '*Speakwell*', and stripped the below-decks to allow 30 cannon to be installed. La Bouch renamed his new ship the '*Wyndham Galley*', and fitted it with 24 guns. The apportioning of loot was finished, and quartermaster Taylor took the *Royal James'* share, but there was some ill-feeling, as Davis had more men that la Bouche or Cocklyn, who each received the same amount for their smaller crews. Each crew member had a single share of the ship's booty, officers took a share and a quarter, the quartermaster took a share and a half, and the captain two shares. A French ship was taken, and Cocklyn took such a dislike to its captain that he put a rope around his neck and repeatedly hung him from the yardarm and dropped him to the floor. The enraged la Bouche rescued his fellow-countryman, and Cocklyn pacified him by giving him the captain and ship. Meanwhile Davis, Dennis and

Taylor discussed provisioning, weaponry and munitions as they prepared to leave the port.

Davis, Cocklyn and la Bouche first decided to visit the local harlots, and took three of Snelgrave's finest embroidered outfits to wear. Their crews were angry that they had taken the finery without asking, and stripped them off their backs. La Bouche's Welsh quartermaster, Williams, blamed Snelgrave for the presumption and wished to kill him, but Snelgrave wheedled his way out by flattery, addressing Williams as *Captain* Williams. Davis decided to calm tempers among the inebriated, bored crews by throwing a huge final party on board the *Royal James*. The revellers were so drunken during the feast that they did not notice a fire, which began with a dropped lamp near the rum stores. The sober Snelgrave organised a chain gang to work the pump and take buckets down the hold, and luckily doused the raging fires. There were 18 tons of gunpowder stored on the *Royal James*, and the pirates were so grateful for Snelgrave's efficiency and management that they wanted to take him with them as a pilot. Snelgrave argued piteously at this fate, and Davis spared him, giving him la Bouche's old sloop to sail home.

Howell Davis was now elected commodore by the pirates, with three pirate ships - the *Royal James*, the *Speakwell* and the Wyndham *Galley*, Cocklyn's store-ship the *Two Friends* and the captured 'Guinea Hen' in his fleet. The ships left Sierra Leone at the end of April, heading south and keeping near the shore. Cocklyn allowed its captain to sail off in the *Guinea Hen*, because it was slower than the rest of the fleet. Davis sailed around Cape Palmas, along the Ivory Coast, and on towards the Gold Coast. There were rich pickings there, with many ships carrying money and goods to four Royal African Company forts, to buy slaves for the Americas.

In the extreme heat, the pirates needed fresh water, but because of the lack of landing places and the heavy Atlantic rollers, relied upon native fishermen to supply them. Davis sent a longboat ashore with some men, guided by natives in their canoes, to whom he gave some old muskets. However, the natives eventually returned to the *Royal James*, with no white men among them. They said that the pirates had run off into the jungle. As one of the pirates had been with Davis since the *Buck* Mutiny, he knew this to be a lie, and that the men had been murdered for their weapons, but his crews were desperately short of water. Davis used his quartermaster, Taylor, as an interpreter to tell the native leader that they would need a second party to be led ashore. He then told Taylor in English to get heavily armed, take the best men, and force the natives to return to the *Royal James* with them. Casks were filled with fresh water by the natives at gunpoint, and they were forced back to the ship.

Taylor interrogated them as to the fate of the pirates, but could get no answer, so decided to use the blacks as target practice. In pairs they were hoisted in the air, with two teams competing for rum, to kill each swinging target first. Howell Davis watched thoughtfully, seeing how the men followed Taylor in his lust for blood, and knew that his time as captain was limited. Two days later another prize was taken, but with little booty, and his fate was sealed. One of Taylor's supporters proposed him as captain and Davis was deposed within minutes. However, he was then elected quartermaster in Taylor's place. Luckily for Davis, Taylor was another Cocklyn, a vindictive, vicious brute, and the crew soon tired of his bullying, capricious ways. Within a few days, they had voted again, and Davis was re-elected captain. In a fit of pique, Taylor joined Cocklyn's ship, with some of his supporters. The young Irishman, Walter Kennedy, was elected quartermaster on the *Royal James*.

La Bouche renamed his ship the *Duke of Ormond*, and Cocklyn's storeship, the *Two Friends*, sailed off one night in a '*soft farewell*'. At the end of May another ship was taken, but Davis now disagreed on the destination of the fleet with the other two captains. He wished to sail east to Principe, and as '*strong liquor stirring up a spirit of discord, they quarrelled*'. Howell Davis defused the situation, saying '*Hark ye, Cocklyn and la Bouche. I find by strengthening you, I have put a rod into your hands to whip myself. But I am still able to deal with you both. Since we met in love, let us part in love, for I find that three of a trade can never agree.*' Cocklyn, la Bouche and Taylor sailed off (- see the notes at the end of this chapter).

Davis now came upon the *Marquis del Campo*, formerly a British naval ship, out of Ostend with 30 guns, anchored off Cape Three Points. Pirates usually kept away from Dutch merchantmen because of their fighting reputation, but Davis probably felt he had something to prove after being deposed by his men recently. The first Dutch broadside killed nine pirates, and dozens more died in battle of their injuries. The fighting, in late May, lasted from noon until next morning. Both ships suffered severely. On capturing the Dutch ship, he made repairs and put 32 cannon and 27 swivel guns aboard and renamed it the *Royal Rover*.

Unusually, none of the Dutch sailors were hurt when they surrendered. This was contrary to the pirate practice of 'no quarter' for those who dared to fight them. The wounded were taken ashore and tended by the surgeon Archibald Murray, while the *Royal Rover* was stripped to make a better fighting ship. Davis let the *Buck* go, and now had two very powerful ships to rove the seas. They passed the Royal African Company stronghold of Cape Coast Castle, heading towards Accra, towards another of its forts and ports, 15 miles away. Annambo (Anamabu) was not as important a slave-trading centre, and consequently was less well-defended.

On June 6th 1719, the *Royal Rover* and *King James* nosed into the slaving harbour of Annambo on the Gold Coast, flying the black flags, drums beating and trumpets blaring. The three English slave ships moored there, the 'Morris', the 'Royal Hynde' and the 'Princess of London' immediately struck their colours. The merchant captains were on shore, bartering for slaves, and the members of crew who did not escape in boats had no thoughts of bloody resistance. Davis took their cargoes of slaves, gold and ivory – like most pirates he always tried to avoid a fight and consequent damage to his ship, crew and the precious booty of the prize ships. Also there was always the chance of obtaining fresh crew members and 'sea-artists', or a better ship. Equally, merchant traders, although often well-armed, knew that if they surrendered immediately, quarter was nearly always given. They had no real desire to fight for the ship's owner or a hated captain. As a former merchant seaman and captain, Davis knew this, and had therefore deliberately drawn up his Ship's Articles to give quarter when it was asked for, that is when a *ship struck her colours* (lowered her flag). The Royal Africa Company's fort opened fire on the ships but its cannon were designed for short-range work against attacking natives. Pirate attacks were rare off this coast. The shot fell harmlessly out of range. Davis ordered his cannon to fire back, and the fort's guns fell silent, knowing the futility of the task. Davis leisurely finished looting the three slave vessels, and later gave one of them to the captain of the Dutch ship, releasing him and his crew.

One of the English ships captured was the *Princess of London*, a slaver whose third mate was a man of Pembrokeshire, like Davis. Something about the tall, dark John Roberts captured Davis' imagination, but he was proud of never having 'forced' a man to become a pirate. Davis had brought the *Royal Rover* up alongside the *Princess*, and its second mate, Stephenson, asked what he wanted. Captain Plumb and the first mate were hiding ashore. Davis told Stephenson to bring the carpenter

Eastwell, the gunner John Jessup, John Owen, Thomas Rogers, James Bradshaw, William Gittus, and the third mate John Roberts on to the *Royal Rover*. Davis told them that some of them would be '*forced*' to become pirates if there were not enough volunteers to replace the men he had lost in the fight against the *Marquis del Campo*. He sent the sailors back to the *Princess*, to allow them time to make a decision whether to join the pirate crew or not. ('*Black Bart*' Roberts soon became the most successful and feared pirate of them all). Eastwell decided to change sides, and the other men looked on as the three merchant captains, Plumb, Hall and Fenn, rowed back to their ships to negotiate with the pirates. They wanted to stop their ships being burnt, and to be left with enough crew to sail them back home.

Captain Blunt found that his *Princess of London* had been stripped bare. What Davis's new quartermaster Walter Kennedy could not find, Eastwell had eagerly directed him towards. Eastwell personally took Stephenson's hats and money from him, and threatened to shoot the mate if he did not tell him the whereabouts of 40 ounces of missing gold dust. Some slaves were also taken off the ships, to carry out menial labour on the pirate ships. Two Welshmen on the *Princess*, John Owen and Thomas Rogers, tried to take the ship towards the fort by hoisting sails, and were brought before Davis. He admired their bravery and made them join his crew. Davis now met the three merchant captains and asked for some of their crew members, as only Eastwell had volunteered his services, apart from the unfortunate Rogers and Owen. Fenn protested strongly, and in response Davis impressed all his crew except a cripple. He then gave Fenn's ship, the '*Morris*' to his thirty captured Dutch sailors from the *Marquis del Campo*, but kept a Scotsman, John Stewart from their crew.

Among the sailors forced to join from the *Morris* and the *Royal Hynde* was James Sail, who tried to escape, but was captured and taken on the *Royal James*. He again escaped, to the *Princess of London*, and upon this recapture was tied to the mainmast and whipped by crew members. Bradshaw, Jessup, Stephenson and Roberts were among those others taken from the *Princess* for Davis's crew. Sailing east, the next day the pirates plundered another Dutch ship bound for Holland. After just one broadside from the *Royal Rover*, it surrendered. It was a great prize, with the '*Governor of Accra on board, with all his effects.*' Apart from merchandise, there was over £15,000 in coin aboard. Davis now rid himself of the other two captured slavers, and let those that wanted leave his ships. However, Roberts and thirty-four other merchant seamen had to stay with Davis, who needed skilled seamen for his two great ships. Fenn and Plumb went with the *Royal Hynde* to Cape Coast Castle, and the Dutchmen sailed the *Morris* to Accra. Black Bart Roberts must have been bemused how easy the pirate life was, and he had heard of the bloodless trickery of Howell Davis in his past exploits. *'The Weekly Journal'* reported (April 9, 1720), *'The pyrates off the coast of Guinea in Africa have taken goods to the value of £204,000'*.

Davis seems to have been drawn towards Roberts, and consulted with him on sailing rigs and courses. Roberts, in his late 30's, had massive experience of the Americas and Africa and the *Slave Triangle*. Without accurate longitude in these times, experience and intuition could keep a ship on the Trade Routes and out of the *Doldrums*. Davis decided to head for the Portuguese island of Principe, a wealthy colony around 600 miles east-South-East of Annambo. More ships were taken on the Guinea Coast, but off Cameroon the *King James* was seen to be trailing about a mile behind. Davis immediately suspected Kennedy of plotting a *'soft farewell'*, but soon discovered that the ship was listing and the sailors working the pumps. Roberts suggested careening it in Cameroon Bay and repairing the rotting hull with fresh timber. However, the damage was so extensive that the *Royal James* had to be abandoned, and its rigging, cargo, provisions, guns, and men transferred to the *Royal Rover*.

"The death of Captain Davis".

The *Royal Rover* now sailed south to the Isle of Princes (Principe), where Davis hoisted navy flags and claimed to be captain of an English man-of-war sent to bring piracy to a halt in the area. Kennedy and Jones had wanted to attack by force rather than ruse, but were outvoted by the other pirates. A small sloop sailed up to the *Royal Rover* asking its business, and Davis responded that they were chasing the pirates which had been devastating the Guinea Coast. They were given permission to enter Principe's harbour. The Portuguese Governor officially welcomed Davis, and the pirates found a sandy cove to careen the ship. Davis was escorted on his pinnace to meet the governor by nine men in fresh white linen shirts and black trousers, and he dressed in a maroon velvet coat. Escorted by soldiers to see the Governor, he was granted the freedom of the island, while Davis in return promised that King George would reimburse any expenses.

In the evenings, the pirates spent their booty on women and drink in the little settlement on the main harbour. Because of their free-spending ways, the Governor must have soon known that they were pirates rather than the poverty-struck and impressed men of His Majesty's Navy. His suspicions must have been raised when the *Royal Rover* blocked a French ship's entry into the harbour, and Kennedy's boarding-party swarmed over it, looking for plunder. Davis explained to the Governor that the French ship had been trading with pirates, and that it had been seized in reparation by the English Crown. After another fortnight, during which the pirates became increasingly difficult to control, Davis and fourteen other men including his Lords, walked inland to a native village, upon hearing that some women might be available there. The women fled to the woods, and their chief complained to the Governor. To placate him, Davis invited the Governor to lunch on the Royal Rover, which was still anchored near the harbour entrance.

No-one knows whether Davis intended to repeat his feat at Gambia, when he attempted to trick the Governor, or just rest and carouse a while, as at the Cape Verde Islands under its Portuguese Governor. It appears that the latter was the case – he would not have allowed his men to get out of hand if his motive had been to capture the Governor of Prince's Island by subterfuge. Tragedy now happened for Davis. Esquemeling recounts that a Portuguese negro swam ashore and told the Governor that he was to be invited on Davis' *Royal Rover* and held to ransom. It seems more likely however that the Governor was afraid of being reported to Portugal for consorting with, and profiting from pirates, on his poor little island. The Governor accepted the invitation, and invited Davis for a glass of wine at the fort before they were rowed to lunch on the ship.

Davis was called to the Government House on Sunday, the day before he was due to sail off. He took his ship's surgeon and several of the leading officers of the ship. (Esquemeling categorically states that he was going to capture the Governor, but this is unlikely, as this would mean risking the leadership of the *Royal Rover*). Davis took Kennedy, and nine other men. John Roberts was left in command of the *Royal Rover*, and Jones in charge of the pinnace, which would take the governor and his colleagues back to the *Royal Rover*. The building was empty, so Davis decided to return to his ship, but the party was ambushed by musketeers half-way down the hill. All but two of the party were killed, but it took five bullets and a cut throat to despatch Davis. He fired both pistols as he lay dying, so he died *'like a game-cock, giving a dying blow, that he might not fall unavenged.'*

Kennedy managed to escape to the waiting boats, and another pirate jumped off the cliffs and was luckily picked up by the pirates' longboat, just returning from a fishing expedition and alerted by the sound of musketry. The pirate escape and their revenge is described in the next chapter, upon Black Bart Roberts. The baton of captaincy now passed to his fellow Pembrokeshire man John Roberts, soon to become the most feared pirate in history, *Black Bart*. Howell Davis was known as *'the cavalier prince of pirates'*, and according to Howard Pyle; *'The name of Capt. Howel Davis stands high among his fellows. He was the Ulysses of pirates, the beloved not only of Mercury, but of Minerva. He it was who hoodwinked the captain of a French ship of double the size and strength of his own, and fairly cheated him into the surrender of his craft without the firing of a single pistol or the striking of a single blow; he it was who sailed boldly into the port of Gambia, on the coast of Guinea, and under the guns of the castle, proclaiming himself as a merchant trading for slaves.*

The cheat was kept up until the fruit of mischief was ripe for the picking; then, when the governor and the guards of the castle were lulled into entire security, and when Davis's band was scattered about wherever each man could do the most good, it was out pistol, up cutlass, and death if a finger moved. They tied the soldiers back to back, and the governor to his own armchair, and then rifled wherever it pleased them. After that they sailed away, and though they had not made the fortune they had hoped to glean, it was a good snug round sum that they shared among them.

Their courage growing high with success, they determined to attempt the island of Del Principe - a prosperous Portuguese settlement on the coast. The plan for taking the place was cleverly laid, and would have succeeded, only that a Portuguese negro among the pirate crew turned traitor and carried the news ashore to the governor of the fort. Accordingly, the next day, when Captain Davis came ashore, he found there a good strong guard drawn up as though to honour his coming. But after he and those with him were fairly out of their boat, and well away from the water side, there was a sudden rattle of musketry, a cloud of smoke, and a dull groan or two. Only one man ran out from under that pungent cloud, jumped into the boat, and rowed away; and when it lifted, there lay Captain Davis and his companions all of a heap, like a pile of old clothes.

Capt. Bartholomew Roberts was the particular and especial pupil of Davis, and when that worthy met his death so suddenly and so unexpectedly in the unfortunate manner above narrated, he was chosen unanimously as the captain of the fleet, and he was a worthy pupil of a worthy master. Many were the poor fluttering merchant ducks that this sea hawk swooped upon and struck; and cleanly and cleverly were they plucked before his savage clutch loosened its hold upon them.'

CHAPTER II

CAPTAIN SNELGRAVE'S ACCOUNT

The following is the full text of the report by Captain Snelgrave on his captivity under Howell Davis:

A New Account of some Parts of Guinea, and the Slave Trade

by Captain William Snelgrave, 1734

BOOK III

Containing an Account of the Author's being taken by Pirates, on the North part of the Coast of Guinea, in the Bird Galley of London, belonging to the late Humphrey Morrice Esq: who was sole owner of the said Ship. Interspersed with several Instances of the Author's many Deliverances, and narrow Escapes from Death, during the time he was detained Prisoner by the Pirates.

"In the beginning of November, in the year 1718, the late Humphrey Morrice Esq; Merchant of London, appointed me Commander of the Bird Galley, and gave me Orders to go to Holland, to take on board a cargo for the coast of Africa: having so done, we were unfortunately detained by contrary Winds, at Helvoet-Sluys, till the 10th day of December, when a violent storm arose, and in the night following forced our ship on shore, with several others. The ship, by the strength of the wind, and the height of the tide, was carried with a great force against the Dyke, or bank that secures the land from being overflowed by such high tides, which frightened the inhabitants thereabouts not a little. Moreover, the waves made her work so much on the ground where she was stranded, that when the tide had left her, we found she had set seven feet abaft (towards the stem of the ship) in the strand; but had the satisfaction to find, on examination, the ship had received no damage in her bottom. Having unloaded, and hired many Boers or peasants, to dig a trench of near 300 foot in length to the low water mark, we waited some time for a high tide; and then getting the ship off, carried her into Helvoet-Sluys pier.

Having refitted and loaded again, we proceeded on the voyage the latter end of January; but the wind changing by the time we were off the isle of Wight, and rising to a great storm westerly, we were forced into Spithead; where having lain some time, we sailed again with a fair wind, which carried us above 70 leagues to the westward of the Lizard. Here such a severe storm of wind coming up at southwest, obliged us to lie by, under a reefed mainsail; and it increased to such a violent degree, that we expected to be swallowed up every minute, by the great sea which ran mountains high; but it pleased God, that after 24 hours, it began to abate, and we received no other damage, than the loss of the ship's cut-water, which was washed away by the sea.

The wind (after this storm) remaining contrary a long time, with frequent hard gales, obliged us at last to go for Kingsale (Kinsale) in Ireland: Where having lain a few days, and repaired the ship's head, with other things that were out of order, we sailed from that place, with a northerly wind, the 10th day of March 1718-1719, and had a short and fine passage to the River Sierraleon; on the north coast of Guinea, in the latitude of 8 degrees 30 minutes, where we arrived the first day of April 1719: We met with nothing remarkable in our passage, except, that near the Canary Islands, we were chased by a ship whom we judged to be a Sallee-Rover; but our ship outsailing her, they soon gave over the chase.

There were, at the time of our unfortunate arrival in the above-mentioned river, three Pirate Ships, who had then taken ten English ships in that place. As it is necessary for illustrating this story, to give an account of how these three ships came to meet there, I must observe, that the first of them which arrived in the river, was called the Rising Sun, one Cocklyn commander, who had with him above 25 men. There having been one Captain Moody, a famous pirate, some months before, in a brigantine, which sailed very well, and took the Rising Sun, they were *marooned* by him, (as they call it) that is forced to board the ship, and deprived of their share of the plunder, taken formerly by the brigantine. These people being obliged to go away in her, with little provision and ammunition, chose Cocklyn for their commander, and made for the River Sierraleon; where arriving, they surprised in his sloop, one Segnor Joseph, a black Gentleman, who had formerly been in England, and was a person of good account in this country. This man's ransom procured the pirates a sufficient supply of provision and ammunition. Moreover, several Bristol and other ships arriving soon after, were likewise taken; and many of their people entering with the pirates, they had, when I fell into their hands, near 80 men in all.

The crew of the brigantine, who, with their Captain Moody, had thus forced their companions away in the Rising Sun, soon after repenting of that action, it bred great discontentment amongst them; so that they quarrelled with their captain and some others, whom they thought the chief promoters of it, and at last forced him, with twelve others, into an open boat, which they had taken a few days before, from the Spaniards of the Canary Islands; and they were never heard of afterwards, doubtless they perished in the ocean. After this, they chose one La Bouse a Frenchman for their commander, who carried them to the River Sierraleon, where they arrived about a month after their parting from the Rising Sun.

At the first appearance, of this brigantine, Cocklyn and his crew were under a great surprise; but when they understood how Moody and some others had been served by them, they cheerfully joined their Brethren in Iniquity.

On the same day also arrived one Captain Davis, who had been pirating in a sloop, and had taken a large ship at the Cape Verde Islands. He coming into Sierraleon with her, it put the other two pirates in some fear, believing at first it was a Man of War: But upon discovering her black flag at the Main-top-mast-head, which Pirate Ships usually hoist to terrify Merchant-Men; they were easy in their minds, and a little time later, saluted one another with their cannon.

This Davis was a generous man, and kept his crew, which consisted of near 150 men, in good order; neither had he consorted or agreed to join with the others, when I was taken by Cocklyn; which proved a great Misfortune to me, as will appear afterwards. For I found Cocklyn and his crew, to be a set of the basest and most cruel villains that ever were. And indeed they told me, after I was taken, *'That they chose him for their Commander, on account of his Brutality and Ignorance; having resolved never to have again a Gentleman-like Commander, as, they said, Moody was.'*

Upon mentioning this, I think it necessary to observe in this place, that the Captain of a Pirate Ship, is chiefly chosen to fight the vessels they may meet with. Besides him, they choose another principal Officer, whom they call Quarter-Master, who has the general inspection of all affairs, and often controls the Captain's Orders: This person is also said to be the first man in boarding any ship they shall attack; or go in the boat on any desperate enterprise. Besides the captain and the Quartermaster, the pirates had all other officers as is usual on board Men of War.

I come now to give an account of how I was taken by them. The day that I made the land, when I was within three leagues of the river's mouth, it became calm in the afternoon. Seeing a smoke on shore, I sent for my first mate Mr Simon Jones, who had been formerly at Sierraleon, where I had not; *'Bidding him take the pinnace, and go where the smoke was, to enquire of the natives, how affairs stood up the river.'* But he replied *'it would be to little purpose, for no people lived there: As to the smoke we saw, he believed it might be made by some travellers who were roasting oysters on the shore, and would be gone before he could get a mile from the ship. Moreover, as night drew on, it would be difficult for him to find the ship again.'* Thinking this answer reasonable, I did not press him further, though I understood afterwards, there was a town where the smoke appeared. But I did not then in the least suspect that Mr Jones would have proved such a Villain as he did afterwards.

About five o'clock in the afternoon, a small breeze arising from the sea, and the tide of flood setting strong, we stood for the river's mouth. At sun-setting we perceived a ship at anchor, a great way up the river; which was the Pirate that took us soon after. The other two pirate ships, with their prizes, were hid from our sight by a Point of Land.

It becoming calm about seven o'clock, and growing dark, we anchored in the river's mouth; soon after which I went to supper, with the officers that usually eat with me. About eight o'clock the Officer of the Watch upon deck, sent me word, *'He heard the rowing of a boat.'* Whereupon we all went immediately upon deck; and the night being very dark, I ordered Lanthorns (lanterns) and Candles to be got ready, supposing that the boat might come from the shore with some white gentlemen, that lived there as free Merchants; or else from the ship we had seen up the river a little while before we came into anchor. I ordered also, by way of Precaution, the First Mate to go into the steerage, to put all things in order, and to send me forthwith twenty men of the quarter-deck with fire-arms and cutlaces (cutlasses), which I though he went about.

As it was dark, I could not yet see the boat, but heard the noise of the rowing very plain: Whereupon I ordered the second mate to hail the boat, to which the people in it answered, *'They belonged to the Two Friends, Captain Eliot of Barbadoes.'* At this one of the Officers, who stood by me, said, *'He knew the Captain very well, and that he commanded a vessel of that name.'* I replied, *'It might be so; but I would not trust any boat in such a place;'* and ordered him to hasten the First Mate (Jones), with the people and the arms upon deck, as I had just ordered. By this time our lanthorns and candles were brought up, and I ordered the boat to be hailed again; To which the people in it answered *'They were from America:'* And at the same time fired a volley of small shot at the ship, though they were then above a pistol shot from us; which showed the Boldness of these Villains: For there was in the boat only twelve of them, as I understood afterwards, who knew nothing of the strength of our ship; which was indeed considerable, we having 16 guns, and 45 men on board. But as they told me after we were taken, *'They judged we were a small vessel of little force. Moreover, they depended on the same good fortune as in the other ships they had taken; having met with no resistance: For the people were generally glad of an opportunity of entering with them:'* Which last (sentence) was but too true.

When they first began to fire, I called aloud to the First Mate, to fire at the Boat out of the Steerage Port-holes; which not being done, and the people I had ordered on deck with small arms not appearing, I was extremely surprised; and the more, when an Officer came and told me, *'The People would not take Arms.'* I went thereupon down into the Steerage, where I saw a great many of them looking at one another. Little thinking that my First Mate had prevented them from taking Arms, I asked them with some roughness *'Why had they not obeyed my Orders?'* Calling upon some brisk Fellows by name, that had gone a former Voyage with me, to defend the Ship; saying, *'It would be the greatest reproach in the World to us all, if we should be taken by a Boat.'* Some of them replied, *'They would have taken Arms, but the Chest they were kept in could not be found.'* The reason for this will be related hereafter.

By this time the Boat was along the Ship's Side, and there being no body to oppose them, the Pirates immediately boarded us; and coming on the Quarter-deck, fired their Pieces several times down into the Steerage, and shot a Sailor in the Reins (shoulders), of which Wound he died afterwards. They likewise threw several Granado-shells (grenades), which burst amongst us, so that 'tis a great wonder several of us were not killed by them, or by their Shot.

At last some of our People bethought themselves to call out for Quarter; which the Pirates granting, the Quarter-Master came down into the Steerage, enquiring, *'Where the Captain was?'* I told him, *'I had been so till now.'* Upon that he asked me, *'How I dared order my People to fire at their Boat out of the Steerage?, saying, that they had heard me repeat it several times.'* I answered, *'I thought it my Duty to defend the Ship, if my People would have fought.'* Upon that, he presented a Pistol to my Breast, which

I had but just time to parry before it went off; so that the Bullet passed between my side and arm. The Rogue finding he had not shot me, he turned the Butt-end of the Pistol, and gave me such a Blow on the Head as stunned me; so that I fell upon my knees, but immediately recovering myself, I forthwith jumped out of the Steerage upon the Quarter-deck, where the Pirate Boatswain was.

He was a bloody Villain, having a few days before killed a poor Sailor, because he did not do something so soon as he had ordered him. This cruel Monster was asking some of my People, *'Where their Captain was.'* So at my coming upon Deck, one of them, pointing to me, said, *'There he is.'* Though the light was very dark, yet there being four lanthorns with candles, he had full sight of me: Whereupon lifting up his broad Sword, he swore, *'No Quarter should be given to any Captain that offered to defend his Ship,'* aiming at the same time a full stroke at my Head. To avoid it I stooped so low, that the Quarter-deck Rail received the blow, and was cut in at least an inch deep: Which happily saved my Head from being cleft asunder: And the Sword breaking at the same time, with the force of the blow on the rail, it prevented his cutting me to pieces.

By good Fortune his Pistols, that hung at his Girdle, were all discharged; otherwise he doubtless would have shot me. But he took one of them, and with the Butt-end endeavoured to beat out my Brains, which some of my People that were then on the Quarter-deck observing, cried out aloud, *For God's sake, don't kill our Captain, for we never were with a better Man!'* This turned the Rage of him and two other Pirates on my People, and saved my Life: But they cruelly used my poor Men, cutting and beating them unmercifully. One of them had his Chin almost cut off; and another received such a Wound on his Head, that he fell on the Deck as dead; but afterwards, by the care of our Surgeon he recovered.

All this happened in a few minutes, and the Quarter-master then coming up, ordered the Pirates to tie our People's hands, and told me, *'That when they boarded us, they let their Boat go adrift, and I must send an Officer, with some of my People in our Boat to look for theirs.'* Whereupon my First Mate, Mr Simon Jones, who stood by, offered to go: and the Quarter-master telling him, *'He must return quickly, otherwise he should judge that they had run away with the Boat, in order to go on Shore; and if they did so he would cut me to pieces.'* Mr Jones replied, *'He would not stay above a quarter of an hour, but return whether he found the Boat or not.'* Happily for me he soon found her, and returned (though it was very dark) in less time than he had promised.

Then the Quarter-master took me by the hand, and told me, *'My Life was safe provided none of my People complained against me.'* I replied, *'I was sure none of them could.'*

The Pirates next, loaded all their small Arms, and fired several Vollies for Joy that they had taken us: Which their Comrades on board their Ship hearing, it being then very near us, though we could not see it for the darkness of the night, they concluded we had made Resistance and Destroyed their People.

It will be proper to observe here, that soon after we had anchored in the mouth of the River Sierraleon, it became calm; and the Tide of Ebb beginning to come down, the Pirates cut their Cable, and let their ship drive down with the Tide towards us, from the place where we had seen her at anchor; having sometime before sent their Boat against the Tide of Flood, to discover us. The Ship being by that means come near us, and seeing our lights, without asking any questions, gave us a Broad-side with their great Guns; verily believing we had destroyed their Boat and People. This put the Pirates on board us into Confusion, which I observing, asked the Quarter-master, *'Why he did not call with the speaking Trumpet, and tell their Ship they had taken us?* Upon that he asked me angrily *'Whether I was afraid of going to the Devil by a great Shot? For, as to his part, he hoped I would be sent to Hell one of these days by a Cannon Ball.'* I answered *'I hoped that would not be my Road.'* However, he followed my Advice, and informed their Ship, *'They had taken a brave Prize, with all manner of good Liquors and fresh Provisions on board.'*

Just after this, Cocklyn, the Pirate Captain, ordered them to dress a quantity of these Victuals; so they took many Geese, Turkeys, Fowls and Ducks, making our People cut their Heads off, and pull the great Feathers out of their Wings: but they would not stay until the other Feathers were picked off. All these they would put into our great Furnace, which would boil Victuals for 500 Negroes, together with several Westphalia Hams, and a large Sow with Pig, which they only (disem)bowelled, leaving the Hair on, This strange medley filled the Furnace, and the Cook was ordered to boil them out of Hand.

As soon as the Pirate-ship had done firing, I asked the Quarter-master's leave, for our Surgeon to dress my poop People who had been wounded; and I likewise went into the Steerage, to have my Arm dressed, it being very much bruised by the Blow given me by the Pirate-boatswain. Just after that, a person came to me from the Quarter-master, desiring to know, *'What a Clock it was by my watch?'* Which judging to be a civil way of demanding it, I sent it to him immediately: desiring the messenger to tell him, it was a very good going Gold Watch. When it was delivered to the Quarter-master, he held it up by the Chain, and presently laid it down upon the Deck, giving it a kick with his Foot, saying, *'It was a pretty Foot-ball'*: On which, one of the Pirates caught it up, saying, *'He would put it in the common Chest to be sold at the Mast.'*

I would not mention such trifling *Circumstances*, but that I judge they serve to show the Humours and Temper of these sort of People.

By this time I was loudly called upon to go on board the Pirate-ship. As soon as I came upon Deck, they hurried me over our Ship's side into the Boat; but when we arrived along the side of the Pirate-Vessel, I told them, *'I was disabled in my Arm, and so desired their help to get me into their Ship:'* Which was readily done. Then I was ordered to go on the Quarter-deck to meet their Commander, who saluted me in this manner. *'I am sorry you have met with bad usage after Quarter given, but 'tis Fortune of War sometimes. I expect you will answer truly to all such Questions as I shall ask you: otherwise you shall be cut to pieces; but if you tell the Truth, and your Men make no Complaints against you, you shall be kindly used; and this shall be the best Voyage you ever made in your Life, as you shall find by what shall be given you.'* I thanked him for his good Intentions, telling him, *'I was content to stand on the footing he had proposed to me.'*

Having answered all his Questions, one of which was, *'How our Ship sailed, both large, and on a wind?'* I replying, *'Very well:'* He then threw up his Hat, saying *'She would make a fine Pirate man of War.'* When I heard that, I must own that I could not but be so concerned for having answered so truly in that particular: But then considering, that some of my People would no doubt have told them the same, and moreover, my Journal, when they looked into it, would have made it plainly appear, which might have proved my Destruction, I satisfied my Mind with these Reflections.

As, in this whole Affair, I greatly experienced the Providence of Almighty God, in his Goodness delivering me from the hands of these Villains, and from many Dangers; so the same good Providence gave me such a presence of Mind, that when I believed I was upon the Point of being killed, such Terrors did not arise, as I had formerly experienced, when in danger of Shipwrack (wreck). And though I fared very hard, and endured great Fatigues during the time I was there Prisoner; yet praised be God, I enjoyed my Health: Submitting with that Resignation to the Will of the Almighty, as a Man ought to do in such severe Misfortunes.

But to return to my Narrative, which the Remembrance of my past Dangers hath interrupted.

As soon as I had done answering the Captain's Questions, a tall Man, with four Pistols in his Girdle, and a broad Sword in his hand, came to me on the Quarter-deck, telling me, *'His name was James Griffin, and that we had been School-fellows.'* Tho' I remembered him very well; yet having formerly heard, it had proved fatal to some who had been taken by Pirates, to own any Knowledge of them; I replied, *'I could not remember any such Person by name.'* Upon that he remembered some boyish Pranks that had formerly passed between us. But I still denying any Knowledge of him, he told me, *'He supposed I took him to be one of the Pirate's Crew, because I saw him armed in that manner; but that he was a forced Man, and had lately been Chief Mate to Captain James Crichton of Bristol; who was then, with his Ship, in the Possession of the Pirates in the River, and had not been destroyed by them, at his earnest entreaty: That since being forced, they had obliged him to act as Master of the Pirate-ship; and the reason of his being so armed, was to prevent their imposing on him; for there was hardly any amongst the Crew of Pirates belonging to Captain Cocklyn, but what were cruel Villains; misusing much better Men than themselves, only for having the Misfortune to fall into their hands, as I had already experienced, and might find hereafter; but he would himself take care of me that night, in which would be my greatest Danger; because many of their People would soon get drunk with the good Liquors found in my Ship.'*

This generous Declaration was very acceptable to me, and I then readily owned my former acquaintance with him. Then he turned to Captain Cocklyn, and desired a Bowl of Punch be made. Which being done, the Captain desired Mr Griffin my Schoolfellow to show me the way to the great Cabin, and he followed himself.

There was not in the Cabin either Chair, or anything else to sit on; for they always kept a clear Ship ready for an Engagement: so a Carpet was spread on the Deck, upon which we sat down cross-legged. Captain Cocklyn drank my Health, desiring, *'I would not be cast down at my Misfortune, for one of the Boat's crew who had taken us had told him, My Ship's Company in general spoke well of me; and they had Goods enough left in the Ships they had taken to make a man of me.'* Then he drank several other Healths, amongst which was that of the *Pretender*, by the name of

King *James the Third*, and thereby I found that they were doubly on the side of the Gallows, both as Traitors and Pirates.

It being by this time Midnight, my Schoolfellow desired the Captain, *'To have a Hammock hung up for me to sleep in,'* for it seems that every one lay rough, as they called it, that is, on the Deck; the Captain himself not being allowed a Bed. This being granted, I took leave of the Captain, and got into the Hammock, tho' I could not sleep in my melancholy Circumstances. Moreover, the execrable Oaths and Blasphemies I heard among the Ship's Company, shocked me to such a degree, that in Hell its self I thought there could not be worse; for though many Seafaring Men are given to swearing and taking God's Name in vain, yet I could not have imagined, human Nature could ever so far degenerate, as to talk in the manner those abandoned Wretches did.

After I was got into the Hammock, Mr Griffin, according to his Promise, walked by me, with his broad Sword in his Hand, to protect me from Insults. Some time after, it being about two a clock in the morning, the Pirate Boatswain (that attempted to kill me when taken) came on board very drunk, and being told I was in a Hammock, he came with his Cutlace (cutlass) near me. My generous Schoolfellow asked him what he wanted. He answered *'To slice my liver, for I was a vile Dog, for ordering my People to fire on their Boat; neither would I deliver my Watch when the Quartermaster first demanded it.'* Upon hearing that, I told Mr Griffin, *'The last was false, for I had immediately sent it by a Messenger, who only asked "what a clock it was?" supposing the Quartermaster expected it.'* Then Griffin bid the Boatswain keep his Distance, or else he would cleave his head asunder with his Broad Sword. Nevertheless, that bloody-minded Villain came on to kill me; but Mr Griffin struck at him with his Sword, from which he had a narrow escape, and then ran away. So I lay unmolested till day light. By that time the Fumes of the Liquor being gone off by Sleep amongst most of the Pirates, Mr Griffin complained to the Quartermaster and the Company, of the cruel Intentions towards me; representing, *'They ought to observe strictly that Maxim established amongst them, not to permit any ill usage to Prisoners after Quarter given.'* At the hearing of this, many of them voted for his being whipped, though he was a great favourite of several others. But though I wished him hanged in my Mind, yet I thought it prudent to plead for him, saying, *'I believed it was his being in Liquor that was the cause of his using me in that manner.'* So he received a general Order, not to give me the least Offence afterwards: Yet did that vile Wretch attempt once more to kill me, as shall be related in its due place.

I come now to relate, how Mr Simon Jones, my First Mate, and ten of my Men entered with the Pirates. The Morning after we were taken, he came to me, and said, *'His Circumstances were bad at home: Moreover, he had a Wife whom he could not love; and for these Reasons he had entered with the Pirates, and signed their Articles.'* I was greatly surprised at this Declaration, and told him, *'I was very sorry to hear it, for I believed he would repent when too late; and as he had taken this Resolution rashly, without communicating it to me, all I could say now would be to no Purpose; neither would it be proper for me, in the future, to have any Discourse with him in private.'* I saw this poor Man afterwards despised by his Brethren in Iniquity: and have since been informed, he died a few months after they left the River Sierraleon. However, I must do him the Justice to own, He never showed any Disrespect to me; and the ten People he persuaded to enter with him, remained very civil to me, and of their own accord, always manned the side for me, whenever I went on board any Ship they belonged to.

Several of these unhappy People soon after repented, and desired me to intercede for them, that they might be cleared again; for they durst (dared) not themselves mention it to the Quarter-master, it being death by their Articles: but it was too nice a matter for me to deal in; and therefore I refused them.

Some days after this, one of these poor Men, whose name was Thomas Wilders, discovered things to me, of which I only had a suspicion before. After cursing Mr Jones for persuading him to join with the Pirates, he said to me, *'That several times in the Night-Watch, before we came to Sierraleon, he had heard him say, "That he hopes we should meet with Pirates when we came to that River"*; which he then thought to have been spoken only in jest; but now he found it too true. As I seemed not to believe this, he called another of our People, who confirmed what he had told me. Then I asked them the Reason why the Chest of Arms was put out of the place where it usually stood at the Steerage; and where it was hid in the time we were taken. They answered, *'I might remember, that the Morning we made Land, I ordered the Steerage to be cleaned, to do which all the Chests there were carried between the Decks; and after the Steerage was cleaned, all the Chests were brought back into their places, except the Chest of Arms, which was left behind by the Mate's Order: That when I called to the People in the Steerage to fire on the Pirate-boat, supposing Mr Jones had delivered them Arms according to my Order, many of the Men would have broken the Chest open, but he prevented them, by declaring. "This was an opportunity he had wished for; and that if they fired a Musket, they would all be cut to pieces."*

And they further assured me, that to induce them to enter with the Pirates, he had declared to them, *'That I had promised him to enter my self.'* Putting all this together, with what several of the Pirates told me afterwards, namely, *That he had been the chief occasion of their keeping my Ship*, it was a wonder that I escaped so well, having such a base Wretch for my principal Officer.

But to resume the thread of my Story.

As soon as the Fumes of the Liquor were gone out of the Pirates' heads, they all went on board the Prize, as they called my Ship, about eight a clock in the morning, it being the second day of April. Mr Jones, who had been my First Mate, went with them; and he having confirmed them in their intention of keeping the Ship for their own use, all hands went to work to clear the Ship, by throwing overboard Bales of Woollen Goods, Cases of India Goods; with many other things of great Value: So that before night they had destroyed between three and four thousand pounds worth of the Cargo. For they had little regard for these things, Money and Necessaries being what they chiefly wanted. The sight of this much grieved me, but I was obliged in prudence to be silent. For my Schoolfellow told me, I was still under the displeasure of many of them, on account of my ordering my People to fire on their Boat when they took me.

There were then residing at Sierraleon, several Englishmen who traded on their own accounts; and among the rest, one Captain Henry Glynn, who was since Governor for the Royal African Company at Gambia, and died there. This Gentleman was an honest generous Person, and of so much Integrity, that though he had suffered by the Pirates when they first landed, yet he would never accept any Goods from them, which they had often pressed him to receive for his own use. This Conduct, with an engaging deportment, so gained him the Good-will of the Pirates, that they were ready to oblige him in whatever he requested. Captain Glynn and myself having formerly been acquainted, as soon as he heard of my being taken, he engaged Captain Davis and Le Boose, the Commanders of the two other Pirate Ships, who were then on Shore at his House, to come on board with him to see me. I was very agreeably surprised with his coming that Afternoon, and both the Pirate captains that came with him saluted me civilly.

Captain Davis told me, *'He knew me'*, though I never could recollect where I had seen him; and I found, he did not care to tell, where he had seen me.

Soon after this, Captain Cocklyn with his Quarter-master and others, came from the Prize on board their old Ship, to compliment Captain Davis and the rest that came with him. After the Compliments were over, Captain Davis generously said, '*He was ashamed to hear how I had been used by them. That they should remember, their Reasons for going a pirating were to revenge themselves on base Merchants, and cruel Commanders of Ships. That as for the Owner of the Prize, he had not his fellow in London for Generosity and Goodness to poor Sailors, as he had formerly heard from others, and now from Captain Glynn: That as for my part, no-one of my People, even those that had entered with them, gave me the least ill Character: But by their respect since shown me, it was plain they loved me. That he indeed had heard the occasion of my ill usage, and of the ill-will some still bore me, was, because I had ordered my People to defend the Ship: Which he blamed them exceedingly for, saying, If he had the good fortune to have taken me, and I had defended my Ship against him, he should have doubly valued me for it: That as he was not in Partnership with them, he would say no more at present; but that he hoped they would now use me kindly, and give me some Necessaries, with what remained undestroyed of my pirate Adventure.*' This was by no means relished by this pack of Miscreants; for in their hearts they hated Captain Davis, because he kept his Ship's Company in good order, they dreaded his Resentment. However Cocklyn, and the chief of his People putting a good face on the matter, invited him and Captain Glynn on board the Prize; and they two desiring I might accompany them, it was readily granted.

Soon after we were on board, we all went into the great Cabin, where we found nothing but Destruction. Two Scrutores (escritoires, or desks) I had there were broke into pieces; and all the fine Goods and Necessaries in them were all gone. Moreover two large Chests that had Books in them were empty; and I was afterwards informed, they had been all thrown overboard; for one of the Pirates, upon opening them, swore, '*There was Jaw-work enough (as he called it) to serve a Nation, and proposed they might be cast into the Sea; for he feared, there might be some Books amongst them, that might breed Mischief enough; and prevent some of their Comrades from going on in their Voyage to Hell, whither they were all bound.*' Upon which the Books were all flung out of the Cabin-windows into the River.

After the Company were all sat down in the Cabin, they were treated with all sorts of Liquors, and other things, that had once been mine: By this means the chief Pirates being put into a good humour, my friend Captain Glynn took the opportunity of begging the Quarter-master several Necessaries for me: Which being readily granted, they were tied up in Bundles, and Captain Glynn designed to take them on Shore with him to his House for me. But an unlucky accident happened, which made me lose them all again.

For some of Captain Davis's People were coming on Board at that time; one of them, a pert young fellow of eighteen, broke a Chest open to plunder it. The Quarter-master hearing of it, goes out of the Cabin, and asks the reason for his so doing; the young Man replied, '*As they were all Pirates, he thought he did what was right.*' On that the Quarter-master strikes at him with his broad Sword, but the young man running away, escaped the Blow, and fled for protection into the great Cabin to his Master Captain Davis. The Quarter-master pursues him in a great Passion; and there not being room amongst so many of us, to make a stroke at him, he made a thrust with his Sword, and slit the Ball of one of the young Man's Thumbs, and at the same time Captain Davis upon the back of one of his Hands. Davis, upon that, was all on Fire, and vowed Revenge, saying, '*That though his Man had offended, he ought to have been first acquainted with it; for no other Person had a right to punish him in his Presence;*' and immediately goes on board his own Ship. Where telling the Story to his Ship's Company, they all resolve to revenge this great injury done to one of their Comrades, and the Indignity shown their Captain. Upon that they slip one of their Cables, and began to heave on the other, in order to come and board Cocklyn's Ship, and destroy such a set of vile Fellows, and they called him and his Crew.

When Captain Davis went from the Prize, Cocklyn soon followed, and went on board his own Ship, to get all things in readiness to defend himself. Captain Glynn and myself only remained behind, and hoped quickly to have seen hot work between them; but Cocklyn having consulted his People, and judging they should be in no way able to cope with Captain Davis, hastily came on board the Prize again, and desired Captain Glynn to go on board Davis with him, in order to make up matters. My Friend would have refused this unpleasant Office, if he durst; but on his not readily complying, Cocklyn grew enraged. I, fearing the consequences, persuaded him to go: Which Cocklyn was so well pleased with, that he often spoke after of it to my advantage.

By the time they came on board Davis, his Ship was just on Cocklyn's Anchor; and though Captain Glynn was a well-spoken ingenious Man, he found it very difficult to compromise the Matter: which at last was done on these Terms; '*That Captain Davis and his Ship's Company, should have their share of Liquors and Necessities on board the Prize; and, That the Quarter-master, who had wounded the young Man belonging to Davis, should before all his Crew acknowledge his fault, and ask Pardon for the same.'*

Night now approaching, Captain Glynn was obliged to go on Shore, without calling upon me for the Things he had begged, intending to come next day for them. Being thus left on board the Prize, with only three or four of the Pirates, amongst whom the bloody-minded Boatswain (formerly mentioned) was one; and there being no Boat along the side at that time, I resolved to stay where I was all night, and not hail their Pirate-Ship to send their Boat for me.

The Pirate-Carpenter was then lying on my Bed in the State-Room; so I sat some time by myself in the Cabin, having a Candle by me on a Table. When he awoke, he civilly desired me to go and take some rest, saying, *'He feared I had not any since I was taken.'* I returned him thanks, saying, *'I would sit up till eight a clock:'* Whereupon he came and sat down by me on the Lockers, abaft in the Cabin.

The Boatswain came down soon afterwards, and being a little in Liquor, began to abuse me. On that the Carpenter told him, *'He was a base Villain,'* and turned him out of the Cabin. Soon after, a puff of Wind coming in at one of the Cabin Windows, put our Candle out; and the Carpenter and I rising up together, to blow the Candle in again, (but not being able to do it) we accidentally shifted places in the dark, he seating himself just over against the Cabin Door, where I sat before: and having no Tinder-Box, we were at a great loss how to light the Candle again.

While we were considering how to do it, the Boatswain came into the Steerage, and finding the Candle out, began to swear and rant, saying, *'I had put it out purposely, with design to go into the Powder-room undiscovered, and blow the Ship up.'* But the Carpenter told him, *'It was done by accident, and that I still sat by him on the Locker.'* So he came to the Cabin Door, and by the Star-light that came in at the Windows, perceived us sitting; but could not distinguish our Faces. Thinking I sat still in the Place where he had seen me before, he presented a Pistol, and drew the Trigger, swearing, *'At that instant, he would blow my Brains out.'* But by good fortune the Pistol did not go off, but only flashed in the Pan: by the Light of which the Carpenter observing that he should have been shot instead of me, it so provoked him, that he ran in the dark to the Boatswain: and having wrenched the Pistol out of his hand, he beat him, with that and his Fist, to such a Degree, that he almost killed him.

The noise that was made in this Fray (affray) being heard on board the Pirate-ship that lay close to us, a Boat was sent from her; and they being informed of the Truth of the matter, the Officer that was in her, thought fit to carry away this wicked Villain, who had three times attempted to murder me.

After this I slept soundly, having been much fatigued; but I was awaked early in the Morning by a great number of Captain Davis's Crew, who came on board to take part of the Liquors and Necessaries, according to Agreement. It was very surprising to see the Actions of these People. They and Cocklyn's Crew (for Le Boose's were not yet admitted) made such Waste and Destruction, that I am sure a numerous set of such Villains would in a short time, have ruined a great City. They hoisted upon Deck a great many half-Hogsheads of Claret, and French Brandy; knocked their Heads (bungs) out, and dipped cans and bowls into them to drink out of: And in their Wantonness threw full Buckets of each sort upon one another. As soon as they had emptied what was on the Deck, they hoisted up more: and in the evening washed the Decks with what remained in the Casks. As to bottled Liquor of many sorts, they made such havoc of it, that in a few days they had not one Bottle left: For they would not give themselves the trouble of drawing the Cork out, but nicked the Bottles, as they called it, that is, struck their necks off with a Cutlace (cutlass); by which means one in three was generally broke: Neither was there any Cask-liquor left in a short time, but a little French Brandy.

As to Eatables, such as Cheese, Butter, Sugar, and many other things, they were as soon gone. For the Pirates being all in a drunken Fit, which held as long as the Liquor lasted, no care was taken by any one to prevent this Destruction: Which they repented of when too late.

As for my things, which the Quarter-master had given my at Captain Glynn's Request, and which were accordingly bundled up; a company of drunken Pirates coming into the Cabin, and stumbling over some goods that lay on the Floor, they took them, with three of my Bundles, and threw them overboard; swearing, '*They had like to have broken their Necks by those things lying in their way.*'

I had then but one Bundle left, in which was a black suit of Clothes, and other things which this Gang had spared. They being gone out of the Cabin, a Pirate, who was tolerably sober, came in soon after, and seeing my Bundle, said, '*He would see what was in it;*' which in prudence I did not oppose. He then took out my black Cloth Clothes, a good Hat and Wig, and some other Things. Whereupon I told him, *Captain Cocklyn's Quarter-master had given them to me, and I hoped he would not deprive me of them, for they were of no service to him in so hot a Country. But would be of great use to me, as I should soon return to England.'* I had hardly done speaking, when he lifted up his broad Sword, and gave me a Blow on the Shoulder with the flat side of it; whispering at the same time these Words in my Ear, *'I will give you this Caution, never to dispute the Will of a Pirate: For, supposing I had cleft your skull asunder for your Impudence, what would you have got by it but Destruction? Indeed you may flatter yourself, I should have been put to death for killing a Prisoner in cold Blood; but assure yourself my Friends would have brought me off on such an Occasion.'* I gave him thanks for his Admonition, and soon after he put on the Clothes, which in less than half an hour after, I saw him take off and throw overboard. For some of the Pirates seeing him dressed in that manner, had thrown several Buckets of Claret upon him. This Person's true name was Francis Kennedy. He was afterwards hanged at Execution-Dock, but he told me at the time he put my Clothes on, that his name was Sun; asking me, *'If I did not know his Father, who was the Commander of a Ship that used the Barbados Trade; and that if ever the old Dog fell in his way, he would kill him.'* To which I answered, *'I knew no such Person.'*

When night came on, I had nothing left of what had been bundled up, but a Hat and Wig. I must own, that whenever they plundered me, no Affront was offered to my Person; but several brought me Liquor, and Slices of Ham broiled, a Biscuit being my Plate; saying, *'They pitied my condition.'* The Hat and Wig I had left, being hung on Pins in the Cabin, a person half-drunk came in about eight a clock a night, telling me, *'He was a great Merchant on Shore, and that his name was Hogbin.'* But supposing him to be a Pirate, I said little to him. By this time these was a great Quietness in the Ship, most of the Pirates being dead drunk. After a little conversation, as Mr Hogbin was going out of the Cabin with my Hat and Wig on, he met Cocklyn's Quarter-master; who knowing him not to be one of the Crew, asked him, *'How he came by the things he had on?'* To which the Fellow not returning a direct answer, the Quarter-master beat him very severely, for taking things he had no Right to: Then coming to me, he asked in a kind manner, *'How I had fared in the hurly burly of that Day?'* When I told him, *'I had lost all the Necessaries he had given my the Day before,'* he expressed much concern, and said, *'He would take care the next day to recover what he could for me.'* But he did not prove so good as his word.

The next day, which was the third since my being taken, Le Boose's Crew were permitted to come on board the Prize: Where they finished what was left of the Liquors and Necessaries; acting in the same destructive manner as their vile Brethren in Iniquity had done before.

Being quite weary of such Company, and understanding that the three Pirate Captains were on Shore at my Friend Captain Glynn's House, I asked leave of the Quartermaster to go to them; which he readily granted. On this I got into a Canoe, and as we rowed towards the Shore, we had like to be overset, through the drunkenness of the Pirates that was with us. If Providence had not prevented this Accident, we should undoubtedly have all been lost; for the Tide ran very strong, and several voracious Sharks were then near us.

When I came to Captain Glynn's, he and the Pirate Captains received me in a very civil manner; and upon telling them *'How I had lost all my Necessaries that had been given me;'* the Captains promised, That the next day they would do all they could, to recover some of them again for me. Then I begged a Shirt of my Friend Captain Glynn; for I had been three days without shifting (changing clothes), which is very uneasy in so hot a Country, where people sweat so much.

Being greatly refreshed with that clean Shirt, and having stayed all night with him, where I had more rest than I before had for a good while; next day I went on board, in company with the Pirate-Captains. Captain Davis desired Cocklyn to order all his People on the Quarter-deck, and made a Speech to them on my behalf; which they relished better that the one he had formerly made, It was resolved to give me the Ship they designed to leave, in order to go into the Prize, with the Remains of my Cargo which was undestroyed. And there being a large quantity of Goods likewise remaining in the several prizes, they concluded to give me them also: Which, with my own, were worth several thousand Pounds. One of the leading Pirates proposed to the rest, *'That they could take me along with them down the Coast of Guinea; where I might exchange the Goods for Gold: And if in order to make a quick Sale, I sold them at prime cost, I should get Money enough by them: That, no doubt, as they went down the Coast, they should take some French and Portuguese Vessels, and then they might give me as many of their best Slaves, as would fill the Ship: That then he would advise me to go for the Island of St Thomas in the West Indies, a Freeport belonging to the Danes, and sell them there, with the Vessel: And after rewarding my People in a handsome manner, I might return with a large sum of Money to London, and bid the Merchants defiance.'*

This proposal was unanimously approved of by them: But it struck me with a sudden damp (sweat), apprehending it would be fatal to me. So I began to insinuate, *'It would not be proper for me to accept of such a quantity of other Peoples' Goods, as they had so generously voted for me:'* And going on to give my reasons, I was immediately interrupted by several of the Pirates, who began to be very angry, that I did not readily accept of what had been proposed, so much to my advantage, as they thought; for many of them were so ignorant, as to think their Gift would have been legal.

On this, Captain Davis said, *'I know this Man, and can easily guess his thoughts concerning this matter; for he thinks, if he should act in the manner you have proposed, he shall ever lose his Reputation. Now I am for allowing every body to go to the Devil their own way; so desire you will give him the Remains of his Cargo, with what is left of his private Adventure, and let him do with it what he thinks fitting.'*

This was readily granted, and they advised me to take Le Boose's Brigantine, which he had then just quitted, (having fitted one of the Prizes for a Pirate-ship for him and his Crew) and carry her along the side of my Ship, in order to save the Goods then left undestroyed in her; allowing me some of my own people to do it. By this means we saved a considerable part of the Cargo, but of my private Adventure not above thirty Pounds Sterling: for that chiefly consisting in Necessaries and Liquors, with fine Goods, was soon destroyed by them: One instance out of many I shall give. The Pirates took several pieces of fine Holland, and opening them, spread them on the Deck; and being almost drunk, lay down on them: Then others came and threw Buckets of Claret upon them, which rousing them up, and the Hollands being thereby stained, they flung the Pieces overboard.

Captain Davis likewise obtained for me, that I might lie on board the 'Two Friends' Captain Elliott of Barbados; whom they had taken and forced to be their Store Ship; and that I might go on shore when I pleased, to my Friend Captain Glynn's house, on condition I should return whenever they sent for me.

And now, the Tide being turned, they were as kind to me, as they had been at first severe. So we got the Brigantine the side of the Prize, and as Bale-goods and cases came to hand, we got them into her; only now and then we lost some, by the ill-nature of two or three leading Pirates: For if we could not receive the Goods so fast as they expected, with the few People I had of my own then with me, they would let them drop overboard.

The same they did by a quantity of Irish Beef, the first day after I was taken; for they despised it, having found so much English, in the several Prizes they had met with in the River. This sight moved me to entreat Captain Cocklyn to give me the Irish Beef they were going to throw overboard; for the use of my poor People that had not entered with them. But I being then under the high Displeasure of him and his crew, he brutishly replied, *'There is Horse-beans enough in the Prize to serve you and your People six months.'* To which I answered, *'It was coarse diet.'* But answering thus put him into a Passion, and I held my Tongue, and the Beef was cast into the Sea.

In this place I think it is proper to acquaint the Reader, What danger all the Prisoners were in by a false Report brought on board the Prize Ships that afternoon. For it was confidently averred by some Negroes, *'That one of their Crew was murdered, by two Captains, whose names were Bennet and Thompson, who had been obliged to fly into the woods from the rage of the Pirates.'* And they added, *'That these two Gentlemen, coming to the House of one Mr Jones (who lived a great way up the River) to seek for Provisions, they there met with the person whom they had killed.'* Upon this report the Pirates resolved to revenge themselves on us who were their prisoners. *'Which obliged me to argue with them, and observe how great a cruelty it would be, to punish us who were wholly innocent, for the faults of others.'* Moreover I said, *'The report might be false, it coming from the Shore-Negroes; and I hoped at least they would defer their resentment against us, till they had a more certain account of the matter.'* This calmed their Rage a little, when, to our great Joy, the Person who was reported to be killed, came on board soon after; and told his Comrades, that he had met with Captain Bennet and Thompson at Mr Jones' House, who threatened him; from which the report arose that they had killed him; but that they had not otherwise misused him: So on this their passion was calmed.

As I have mentioned these two Captains Bennet and Thompson, I shall give an account of their Misfortunes, which I had afterwards from their own Mouths. Captain John Bennet, being bound from Antegoa (Antigua) to the Coast of Guinea, was taken at Cape de Verd Islands by Davis. Who, after plundering him, restored him his Ship; and he went into the River Sierra Leon, where Captain Thompson was arrived before him. Upon Cocklyn the Pirate's coming into the River, they carried their Ships a good way up, to a place called Brent's-Island, being the Settlement of the Royal Africa Company; where one Mr Plunket was Governor. Having got their Ships very near the Shore, they made a Battery thereon, and having landed Ammunition, resolved with their

People to defend themselves to the utmost; thinking at that time they would remain faithful. Le Boose being arrived in his Brigantine, and hearing that several Ships were up the River, he resolved to have one of them for his use; so he went up to attack them, and they bravely defended themselves against him: But, soon after, Cocklyn coming with his Ship to the assistance of Le Boose, their People began to falter; and these gallant Captains were, for saving their Lives, obliged, with Mr Plunket, and several of their Officers, to fly into the Woods: Where, for many Weeks, they remained, having nothing to subsist on but Rice, with now and then some Oysters, which they got by night from the River side: neither durst they appear near the place where the Pirates were (as long as they remained there) for they had vowed to cut them to pieces, if ever they fell into their hands. Moreover, their Ships were burned, and Le Boose took for his own use, one Captain Lamb's Ship, which at that time lay farther up River. I thought proper to relate this, in order to set the story in a better light, though it happened some weeks before I was taken.

But now, to return to my Subject, I was relating, how we were employed in saving what Goods we could. This took us up four days; and I slept every night on board the 'Tender' commanded by Captain Elliot, who was very kind to me, and had a great ascendant over the leading Pirates: so that he seldom had the Company of the common sort, having orders to drive them away, whenever they came on board him. And I have often been amazed, to hear and see what he has done to some of them when they have been impudent; beating some of them, and saying, *'He was sure he would see them hanged in due time at Execution-dock.'* However, by this means we were generally easy on board him, which was no little satisfaction to me in my Circumstances.

About this time the Quarter-master, who took me, fell sick of a Fever; which increasing, he sent to speak with me: And having desired all present, except myself, to withdraw, he told me, *'That at the time I was taken, he designed to have killed me, when he presented the Pistol to my breast; begging I would forgive him his cruel Intention:'* Which I readily doing, he further said, *'That he was a most wicked Wretch, having been guilty of all manner of abominable Crimes; and that now believing he should die, his Conscience sadly tormented him, fearing he would be punished, as he deserved, in Hell-fire, which so often in their vile discourse he had made light of.'* Upon hearing that, *'I exhorted him to sincere Repentance; telling him, the Christian Religion assured us of God's Mercies, if we are truly penitent; and I instanced the goodness of God to myself, in that he was graciously pleased to preserve me, the night I was taken, from being murdered by him and others; which great*

Mercies I believed were shown me, because I put my Hope and Trust in Almighty God; and exhorted him to do the same.' But he replied, *'O, Sir, my heart is hardened; however I will endeavour to follow your good counsel.'* As he was going on, expressing his sorrow for his former course of Life, some of the Pirates broke in upon us, to ask him, *'How he did?'* So he called his Boy, and, as a mark of his Good-will towards me, ordered him to take the Key of his Chest, and let me take out what Necessaries I would. Accordingly I took that opportunity of providing myself with Shirts, Stockings, and several other things. As I was taking them out, a Pirate coming from the Deck, and knowing nothing of the Quarter-master's order, called out aloud; *'See how that Dog is thieving there: He does it as cleverly as any Rogue of us all.'* But being told, *'It was with the Quarter-master's leave,'* he came and helped me bundle the things up, and I sent them on board the Tender. These were the first Necessaries which I could call my own, since my Misfortune.

The Quarter-master that evening falling into a Delirium, died before morning in terrible Agonies; cursing his Maker in so shocking a manner, that it made a great Impression on several new entered Men: and they afterwards came privately to me, begging, *'*that I would advise them how to get off from so vile a Course of Life, which led them into Destruction of both Body and Soul. Some of them proposed to fly into the Woods, and remain there till their Ships were gone, if I would promise to protect them afterwards; but this being too nice (i.e. tricky) a matter for me to meddle with at that Juncture, I declined it; Exhorting them in general, Not to be Guilty of Murder, or any other Cruelty to those they should take. For if ever they should, by a general consent, resolve to embrace the King's Pardon, it would be a great Advantage to them, to have the unfortunate people they had taken to give them a good Character in that respect.*'*

Having mentioned the King's Pardon, I shall here relate what I before omitted, with relation to his late majesty's Proclamation, for a *Pardon to Pirates, that should surrender themselves at any of the British Plantations, by the first of July 1719.* This Proclamation I had on board, with a Declaration of War against Spain. The Quarter-master finding them amongst my Papers, and not being able to read, he brought them to me, the next day after I was taken, and *'*bid me read them aloud to all present;*'* which I did: But there being Rewards offered in the proclamation, to those that should take or destroy Pirates; so much for a Captain; and in proportion so much for the other Officers and common Pirates; this put them into such a Rage, that I began to apprehend myself in some Danger. But Captain Cocklyn ordering silence to be made, bid me read the other Paper, which was *The Declaration of War against Spain.* When I had read it, some of them said, 'They wished they had known it before they left the West Indies.' From thence I took occasion to observe to them, 'That if they thought fit to embrace his Majesty's most gracious Pardon, there was not only time enough for them to return to the West Indies, (there still being three Months to come of the time limited in the Proclamation) but now that War was declared against Spain, they would have an opportunity of enriching themselves in a legal way, by going a privateering, which many of them had privately done.' This seemed to be relished by many: but several old Buccaneers, who had been guilty of Murder and other barbarous Crimes, being no ways inclined to it, they used the King's Proclamation with great contempt, and tore it in pieces. I thought myself well off, that no Resentment or ill-usage was shown me on this occasion.

Amongst the several Pirates, that came to consult me, 'How they should get off.' There was one Ambrose Curtis, who was in a bad state of Health, and generally walked the Deck in a Silk Night-gown. This person finding me shy in answering his Questions, he told me, 'Though I had forgotten him, yet he had not me; for he was eleven years ago at Sea with my Father, who had used him severely for being an unlucky Boy: That I might remember, my Father died in Virginia, and I commanded the Ship afterwards, and brought her home to England; having been very kind to him, except in one thing, which was, That he having confessed to me, he was a Servant, and run away from his Master, I refused to pay him his Wages, till he brought a person who gave me Security that I should not pay them twice; and then he had his Wages to a farthing: Adding, 'he had told this to several leading Pirates, who had persuaded him to revenge himself on me; but as I had been kind to him, and in his Conscience he believed I was in the right, to demand Security when I paid him his Wages, so he bore no ill-will to me on that account; and when my necessaries came to be sold at the Mast, he would buy some of them for me;' in which he proved as good as his word.

But as to his Questions about getting off, I replied as I had done to others; 'Assuring him, if ever it came into my power to serve him, I would not spare for Money or Pains to do it.' But this poor fellow died, before the Pirates left Sierraleon.

I hope the Reader will pardon me for mentioning several things, which are not so coherent as I should wish; as also several little incidents.

The reason why I mention them is, because I think they display the true humours and ways of these Miscreants.

Amongst my Adventure of Goods, I had in a Box three second-hand embroidered Coats. One day the three Captains, coming on board the Prize together, enquired for them, saying, 'They understood by my Book such Clothes were in my Ship.' I told them, 'They were in a Box under the bed place in the State-room. So they ordered them to be taken out, and immediately put them on. But the longest Coat falling to Cocklyn's share, who was a very short Man, it almost reached as low as his ankles. This very much displeased him, and he would fain have changed with Le Boose, or Davis: But they refused, telling him, 'As they were going on Shore amongst the Negroe-Ladies, who did not know the white Men's fashions, it was no matter. Moreover, as his Coat was Scarlet embroidered with Silver, they believed he would have the preference of them, (whose Coats were not so showy) in the opinion of their Mistresses. This making him easy, they all went on Shore together.

It is a Rule amongst the Pirates, not to allow Women on board their Ships, when in Harbour. And if they should take a Prize at sea, that has any Women on board, no one dares, on pain of death, to force them against their inclinations. This being a good political Rule to prevent disturbances amongst them, it is strictly observed. So now being in a Harbour, they went on Shore to the Negroe-women, who were very fond of their Company, for the sake of the great presents they gave them. Nay, some white Men that lived there, did not scruple to lend their black Wives to the Pirates, purely on account of the great Rewards they gave.

The Pirate Captains having taken these Clothes without leave from the Quarter-master, it gave great Offence to all the Crew; who alleged, 'If they suffered such things, the Captains would in future assume a Power, to take whatever they liked for themselves.' So, upon their returning on board next Morning, the Coats were taken from them, and put into the common Chest, to be sold at the Mast. And it having been reported, 'That I had a hand on advising the Captains to put on these Coats,' it gained me ill-will in particular of one Williams, who was Quarter-master of Le Boose's Ship. He seeing me in the Tender's Boat, going on board a French Ship lately taken, where he then was, he swore, 'That if I came there, he would cut me to pieces, for the advice I had given to the Captains.' But Captain Elliott, who was then in the Boat, whispered me, saying, 'Don't be afraid of him, for it is his usual way of talking. But be sure you call him Captain, as soon as you get on board.' It seems this

Villain had been Commander of a Pirate Sloop; who, with a Brigantine, two years before, took Captain Laurence Prince in the Whidaw Galley near Jamaica; and now being Quarter-master, which he did not like, he loved to have the Title of Captain given him. So when I came into the French Ship, I addressed myself to him, saying, 'Captain Williams, pray hear me upon the point you are so offended at.' Upon that he gave me a slight Blow on the Shoulder, with the flat of his Cutlace, swearing at the same time, 'he had not the heart to hurt me;' When I told him how the affair had really happened, which he had been so angry about, he gave me a Keg of Wine, and was my Friend ever after.

The French Ship just now mentioned, fell into their hands about a fortnight after I was taken by them, in this manner. It was not bound for Sierraleon, but having not had an Observation for several days, because the Sun was near their Zenith, they made land unexpectedly; and not knowing whereabouts they were, but seeing several Ships in the River at an Anchor, they came boldly towards them.

I was then on board Captain Cocklyn's old Ship; for they had not quite fitted mine for their use, not having at that time any Guns mounted; so I saw the great fear and confusion that was amongst them. My Mate, who had entered with them, said, 'He believed, by the Ship's coming in so boldly, it was the Launceston Man of War of forty Guns, whom we had left in Holland. For he had heard me say, she was to follow us to the Coast of Guinea.'

Happy it would have been for us and many more, if it had been so. For had that, or even a smaller Ship of twenty Guns, with the King's Commission, come in at that time, or any other, whilst I was in their hands, I am persuaded they would have easily destroyed them. For the new-entered-men had little Courage; and the far greater part of both old and new Pirates, were so much in drink, that there could have been no Order of Conduct amongst them in an Engagement. So that it would have been very easy to have subdued them, and prevented that terrible Destruction, which happened to above one hundred Sail of Ships, that fell afterwards into their Hands, in their going down the Coast of Guinea: Together with those Damages that happened a good while after in the East Indies, by some of this Gang; and the great Ravage made by Roberts (who rose out of Davis's Ashes) till he was happily destroyed by Sir Chaloner Ogle in the Swallow Man of War. But the reason why no timely care was taken to prevent so great a Destruction, is not proper for me to mention in this place.

As I had no business to be on board the Pirate Ship in time of Action, I asked Captain Cocklyn's leave to go on board their Tender, which he readily granted. Just as I was going, several of my people who had entered with him, said, 'They would go along with me, for they had never seen a Gun fired in anger.' Cocklyn hearing that, told them, 'That now they should learn to smell Gunpowder, and caned them heartily.

So I went on board Captain Elliot, where I soon saw the French Ship taken. For coming so unexpectedly into the Pirates' hands, they made no Resistance: And because their Captain did not strike (his colours) on their first firing, they put a Rope around his Neck, and hoisted him up and down several times to the Main-yard-arm, till he was almost dead. Captain Le Boose coming at that instant, luckily saved his Life: And highly resenting this their cruel usage to his Countryman, he protested, 'he would remain no longer in Partnership with such barbarous Villains.' So, to pacify him, they left the Frenchmen with the Ship in his care; and after the Cargoe was destroyed, they cut the Ship's Masts by the board, and run her on Shore, for she was very old, and not fit for their purpose.

After the affair of the French Ship was over, I was employed for several days, in landing out of the Brigantine the Goods that had been given me, out of my own Ship's Cargoe, and carrying them to my Friend Captain Glynn's House; in which both he and I worked very hard. For my own People that did not enter with the Pirates, were mostly obliged to work on board the Prize, in fitting her for them; and the Natives who served Captain Glynne at his House, were grown so insolent by the large quantity of Goods given them by the Pirates, that they would do nothing but what they pleased. However, at last, with much trouble we got them housed.'

By this time, which was about the 20th of April, the Ship the had taken from me was completely fitted, and the next day was appointed to name her, to which Ceremony I was invited. When I came on board, the Pirate Captains told me, 'It was not out of Disrespect they had sent for me, but to partake of the good Cheer provided on this occasion:' So they desired I would be cheerful, and go with them into the great Cabin. When I came there, Bumpers of Punch were put into our Hands, and on Captain Cocklyn's saying aloud, 'God bless the Windham Galley, we drank our Liquor, broke the Glasses, and the Guns fired.

The Ship being Galley-built, with only two flush Decks, the Cover of the Scuttle of the Powder-room was in the great Cabin, and happened at that time to be open. One of the after-most Guns blowing at the Touch-hole, set fire to some Cartouch-boxes, that had Cartridges in them for small Arms, the Shot and Fire of which flew about us, and made a great smother. When it was over, Captain Davis observed, there had been great Danger to us from the Scuttle's being open; there being under, in a Room, above twenty thousand weight of Gunpowder. Cocklyn replied, 'He wished it had taken fire, for it would have been a noble blast, to have gone to hell with.'

Then all going upon Deck, three Prizes that remained undestroyed, were ordered to be burned; upon hearing that, I privately represented to Captain Davis, 'How hard it would be upon us who were Prisoners, to remain in that Country, without necessaries, and without Food to subsist on: Besides, there was no manner of Prospect of our getting away quickly; That to the many Obligations I owed him, I hoped he would add one more, and by his Interest, at least save one of the Vessels, for us to return to London in: That as he had several times hinted to me, how much he disliked that course of Life, hoping he should have an opportunity of leaving it in a short time; so I wished he would put it in my power, to report to his Advantage, the good deed I then requested of him; for, in my Opinion, next to Murder and Cruelty, too often practised by Pirates, nothing could make them more odious to the World, than their destroying, out of mere Wantonness, so many Ships and Cargoes, as had been done by Cocklyn and Le Boose's Crews; in which I knew he had no hand: And if he would be pleased to secure my entire Liberty, at the same time that he pleaded for one of the Vessels for us, it would be a double Obligation on me to Gratitude, in case it ever fell into my power to serve him.'

This he readily promised, and by his Management the Ships were saved from being burned, and they made a Bonfire only of the old Rising Sun, being the Ship they had quitted for mine: And now obtaining, through Captain Davis's means, my entire Liberty, I went on Shore to my friend Captain Glynn's House again.

Two days after this Captain Elliot sent his Boat for me, desiring I would forthwith come on board his Ship, because he wanted much to speak with me. I had too many obligations to this Gentleman to refuse going, (tho' I had a sort of aversion). Upon coming on board, he privately represented to me, 'That I knew he had been obliged against his will by the Pirates, to receive into his Ship a great quantity of other People's Goods; for which he might hereafter be called to an account; therefore he desired I would give him a Certificate, testifying the Truth of it.' Knowing this to be true, I readily complied; for he was a very honest Man, as appeared soon after. For the Pirates compelling him to go to go out of the River with them, as their Tender, he took the first opportunity of getting away from them, which he did in a Tornado, or sudden Gust of Wind, that arose in the Night; and having the good fortune to succeed in his attempt, he made a good Voyage for his Owners, with Slaves to Barbadoes; where he fell sick and died.

While I was in his Ship, the three Pirate captains called along the side. Not expecting to see me there, they seemed very glad of it, and invited me to go and sup with them on board Captain Davis. This I declined, being desirous of going on Shore to Captain Glynn's. But Captain Davis insisting on it, I thought it prudent to comply; that I might not lose that gentleman's Good-will, who had been so kind to me.

After we had been some time on board his Ship, Supper was brought about eight a clock in the Evening; and the Musick was ordered to play, amongst which was a Trumpeter, that had been forced to enter out of one of the Prizes. About the middle of Supper, we heard upon Deck an outcry of 'Fire!', and instantly a Person came to us, and said, 'The Main-hatchway was all in a Flame'; so we all went upon Deck.

At that time, besides the Pirate Ship's Crew, who were mostly drunk, there was on board at least fifty Prisoners; and several Boats along the side, into which many People jumped, and put off. I being then on the Quarter-deck, with the Captains, observed this to them; but they all in confusion said, 'We know not what to do in the matter:' Upon that I told them, 'If the sober People were allowed to go away with the Boats, no one would endeavour to save the Ship; and we that were left should be lost, (for the other Ships were a Mile from us, and the Tide of Flood then ran so strong, that their Boats could not row against it to save us:) So I proposed to them, 'to fire the Quarter-deck Guns at the Boats which had just put off, to oblige them to come on board again;' which being instantly done, it so frightened the People in them, that they forthwith came back; and all that were able, and not drunk, lent their helping hand to put out the Fire; which by this time was come to a great head in the Ship's hold.

After this I went down into the Steerage, where I saw one Goulding, who was Gunner's mate, and a brisk active Fellow, put his head up the After-hatch-way, calling for Blankets and Water; 'which if not brought immediately, (he said) the Bulk-head of the Powder-room would be fired, and the Ship soon blown up.' Observing the Stupidity of the People about me, who stood looking on one another, I caught up several

Blankets and Rugs which lay scattered about, and flung them to him, and so did others by my example. Then I ran out of the Steerage upon Deck, where meeting with some People who were sober, I got them to go over the side, and draw up Buckets of Water; And others handing them to Goulding, who had by this time placed the Blankets and Rugs against the Bulk-head of the Powder-room, he flung this Water on them, and thereby prevented the Flames from catching the Powder, and consequently from blowing up the Ship, which must otherwise have happened: For there was on board as least thirty thousand pounds of Gunpowder, which had been taken out of several Prizes, it being a Commodity much in request amongst the Negroes.

There was still great Confusion amongst us, occasioned by the darkness of the Night, and the many drunken People, who were not sensible of the great danger we were in: Moreover, the People in the Hold gave us as yet no Hopes of their getting the Mastery of the Fire. So I went again on the Quarter-deck, and considered with myself, if the fire could not be conquered, as I could not swim, I should have no chance of being saved: and even those that could, would, I knew, be exposed to be torn to pieces by voracious Sharks, which abound in that River: So I took one of the (wooden) Quarter-deck Gratings, and lowered it by a Rope over the Ship's side, designing to get on that, if I should be forced to quit the Ship. For tho' the Boats had been once obliged to come back, yet it being a dark Night, some People, unperceived, had slipped again away with them, and were quite gone away.

Whilst I stood musing with myself on the Quarter-deck, I heard a loud shout upon the Main-deck, with a Huzza, 'For a brave blast to go to Hell with', which was repeated several times. This not only much surprised me, but also many of the new entered Pirates; who were struck with a Panic Fright, believing that the Ship was just blowing up, so that several of them came running on the Quarter-deck, and accidentally threw me down, it being very dark. As soon as I got upon my Legs again, I heard these poor Wretches say, in a lamentable Voice, one to another; 'Oh, that we should be so foolish as to enter this vile course of Life! The Ship will be immediately blown up, and we shall suffer for our Villainies in hell Fire.' So that when the old hardened Rogues on the Main-deck, wished for a blast to go to hell with, the other poor wretches were at the same time under the greatest Consternation at the thoughts of it.

The Apprehension of the Ship's being just ready to blow up, was so universal, that above fifty People got on the Bolt-sprit, and the Sprit-sail-yard, thinking they should have there a better chance for their Lives: But they much deceived themselves, so had so great a quantity of Powder as was at that time on board, been fired, it would have blown them up to Atoms.

There was one Taylor, master of this Pirate Ship, as brisk and courageous a Man as ever I saw; (who afterwards commanded the Cassandra, and English East India Ship, and carried her to New Spain, where he and his Crew separated). This Person, with fifteen more, spared no pains to extinguish the Fire in the Hold; and tho' they were scalded in a sad manner by the Flames, yet they never shrunk till it was conquered; which was not till near ten a clock at night, when they came upon Deck, declaring the Danger was over: So the Surgeons were called to dress their Burns. This was joyful News to us all on Deck, for we little expected to escape.

I shall now relate how this Fire happened, from which our Deliverance was almost miraculous. About half an hour after eight a clock in the evening, a Negroe Man went into the Hold, to pump some Rum out of a Cask; and imprudently holding his Candle too near the Bung-hole, a Spark fell into the hogshead, and set the Rum on fire. This immediately fired another cask of the same Liquor, whose Bung had been, through carelessness, left open: And both the Heads of the hogsheads immediately flying out, with a report equal to that of a small cannon, the fire ran about the Hold. There were twenty casks of Rum, with as many Barrels of Pitch and Tar, very near the place where the Rum lay that was fired; yet it pleased God none of these took fire, otherwise it would have been impossible for us to escape.

After this was over, I was obliged to stay on board till Morning, all the Boats being run away with. In that time Goulding, the Gunner's Mate, told the Pirate's Crew several things to my Advantage: 'How I had handed the Blankets to him, and ordered Water to be thrown on them; which saved the Bulk-head, where the Powder lay, from being fired, and consequently the Ship from being blown up.' So now I was more than ever in their favour: For several of them desired me to come on board the Windham Galley, the day things were sold there at the mast, and then they would be kind to me. Likewise Captain Davis pressed me to come, asking me, 'Whether the gold watch that was taken from me was a good one?' To which I answering 'It was very good, at that time.' He then said, 'He would buy it for his own use at any rate.'

While he and I were talking thus, one of the Mates came half drunk, on the Quarter-deck, saying to him, 'I propose on behalf of the Ship's Company, that this Man shall be obliged to go down the Coast of Guinea with us; for I am told we cannot have a better Pilot.' This was a great surprise to me; but my generous Friend Davis soon put me out of pain. For he told him, 'They wanted no Pilot:' and the fellow still insisting on my going, Captain Davis caned him off the Quarter-deck, and I heard no more of it: For soon after I went on Shore to my Friend Captain Glynn's House.

Two days after this, a small Vessel came into the River, and was taken by them. It was called the Dispatch Captain Wilson, belonging to the Royal Africa Company. Mr Simon Jones, formerly my First Mate, who had entered with the Pirates (as I have before related) told them, on this occasion, 'That he had once commanded a Ship, which was hired and freighted by the Royal Africa Company; and that he had been very unjustly used by them; so he desired the Dispatch might be burned, that he might be revenged of them.' This being immediately consented to, and forthwith ordered to be executed, one John Stubbs, a witty brisk Fellow, stood up, and desired to be heard first; saying, 'Pray, Gentlemen, hold a little, and I will prove to you, if this Ship is burnt, you will thereby greatly serve the Company's Interest.' This drawing everyone's attention, they bid him go on: Then he said, 'The Vessel has been out these two years on her Voyage, being old and crazy, and almost eaten to pieces by the Worms; besides, her Stores are worth little; and as to her Cargoe, it consists only of a little Redwood and Melegette-pepper; so if she should be burned, the Company will lose little; but the poor People that now belong to her, and have been so long on the Voyage, will lose all their Wages, which, I am sure, is three times the value of the vessel, and of her trifling Cargoe; so that the Company will be greatly obliged to you for destroying her.' The rest of the Crew being convinced by these Reasons, the Vessel was spared, and delivered again to Captain Wilson and his People, who afterwards came safe to England in it.

The 29th of April, such of the Pirates as were my Friends, sent me word on Shore, 'That the Sale of Necessaries was to begin that day in the afternoon, in the Windham-galley, Captain Cocklyn.' So I went on board in a large Cannoe, belonging to two Men who lived ashore, who went at the same time with me. At the Sale, several of the Pirates bought many Necessaries that had been mine, and gave them to me. Likewise, Mr James Griffin, my Schoolfellow, was so civil as to beg from those who were not so kind to me, as he hoped they would have been. The two white Men that went with me in the Cannoe, minded their own business so well, that they got several great Bundles of Clothes and Goods, which they put into the Cannoe with mine.

By this time several Pirates being half drunk with Brandy, looked over the side, and seeing so many Bundles in the Cannoe, which they supposed to be all mine, they swore, 'I was insatiable, and that it would be a good deed to throw them overboard.' This my kind Schoolfellow hearing, he came and told me of it; advising me, to go immediately on Shore, which I accordingly did; and it proved very happy for me. For soon after my Watch was put up for sale, and many bidding for it, some of them out of Spite to Captain Davis, it was run up to one hundred pounds, which he paid down. One of the Pirates being greatly vexed at it, said, 'He believed the Cases of the Watch were not good Gold'; and calling for a Touch-stone, he tried them on it. The Touch looking of a copperish Colour, (as indeed all the Gold-cases of Watches do on the touch, by reason of the quantity of Alloy put in to harden them) this pretence served the turn of this Villain; who thereupon exclaimed against me, saying, 'I was a greater Rogue than any of them, who openly professed Piracy; since I was so sly, as to bring a base Metal Watch, and endeavour to put it off for a gold one.'

This Speech procured me the Anger of many, who knew no better; they believing every word of what he said to be true. And tho' Captain Davis laughed at it, yet several swore, 'If I had not been gone on Shore, they would have whipped me.' And as their Drunkenness increased, they talked of sending for me to be punished for so great a Villainy, as they called it. But my Schoolfellow apprehending they would really offer me some Violence, was so kind as to send me word of what had passed, by a white Man living on Shore, who was then on board; advising me to go into the Woods, for they should sail quickly out of the River.

The next morning early, which was the last day of April, as I was just going to follow his advice, I was agreeably surprised by the arrival of one Mr James Bleau, my Surgeon, whom they designed to take by force with them. This honest Man had been very cast down at it, and had often desired me to intercede for his liberty. Accordingly I had done it, representing, 'That he grieved himself so much, that if he did not die quickly, yet he would be of no use to them.' But this had no effect. However, at last, a fortunate Accident cleared him, when he least expected it; for that very evening, after I was come on Shore, the

Surgeon of the French Ship entered with them; whereupon they gave Mr Bleau his Liberty the next morning.

Mr Bleau brought us the agreeable News, that the three Pirate Ships, with their Tender, were under sail, going out of the River. This gave us all on Shore the highest Satisfaction; for I had been in their hands a Month, and many others much longer. Mr Bleau, whom I have here mentioned, lives now at Woodford-Row on Epping Forest, where he follows his Business.

I shall now inform the Reader, what became of my kind Schoolfellow Griffin, and my generous Friend Davis. The first took an opportunity of getting out of the hands of the Pirates, by taking away in a Boat from the Stern of the Ship he was in, when off the Road of Annamaboe, on the Coast of Guinea. He was driven on Shore there, unperceived in the night time; and from thence went to Cape Coast Castle, belonging to the Royal Africa Company; from which place he went Passenger to Barbadoes, in an English Ship, where he was taken with a violent Fever and died.

As to Davis, having discovered, a few days after they left the River Sierraeon, a Conspiracy to deprive him of his Command, which was carried on by one Taylor, that was the Master of the Ship under him, he timely prevented it: But he and some others left their Ship, and went on board the Windham Galley, Captain Cocklyn, by whom he found Taylor had been set on to displace him. This causing him to leave their partnership, he took a few days after one Captain Plumb in the Princess of London, whose second mate Roberts, so famous afterwards for his Villainies, entered with him; and Davis's Crew, after plundering the Ship, restored her to Captain Plumb again. After this captain Davis went to the Island Princess, belonging to the Portuguese, which lay in the Bay of Guinea. Here the Pirates gave out, 'They were a King's Ship'; but the People soon discovered what they were by their lavishness, in purchasing fresh Provisions with Goods; but the Governor winked at it, on account of the great Gains he, and others of the Chief of his People made by them. But at last putting him in mind, 'That if this Affair should come to the King of Portugal's ear, it might prove his ruin'; he plotted how to destroy Davis and his Crew, in order to colour over what he had so basely permitted, in allowing them a free trade, after discovering they were Pirates.

Captain Davis being one day on Shore with the Governor, he told him, ' They designed to sail from the Island in three Days, and that he would come, and take his leave of him the day before.' Accordingly he went on a Sunday morning, taking with him his first Surgeon, the Trumpeter, and some others, besides the Boat's Crew. At their coming into the Governor's House, they saw no body to receive them; so they went on, till they came to a long Gallery fronting the Street. Here the Governor's Major-Domo presently came to them, saying, 'His Master was at his Country-House, but he had sent a Messenger to him, when they saw Captain Davis coming on Shore, and no doubt he would soon be in Town. But the Surgeon observing, that many People had got together in the Street, with Arms in their hands, he said to his Captain, 'I am sure we shall see no Governor today', and advised him immediately to go away. So Davis and the Surgeon went out of the House; whereupon the Major-Domo called to the people in the Street, to fire at them. The Surgeon and two more were killed on the spot, and the Trumpeter was wounded in the Arm, who seeing two Capuchin Friars (from whom I had this Account at the Island Princess) fled to them. One of them took him in his Arms to save him, but a Portuguese came, and shot him dead without any regard to the Friar's Protection. Captain Davis, tho' he had four Shots in divers Parts of his Body, yet continued running towards the Boat: But being closely pursued, a fifth Shot made him fall, and the Portuguese being amazed at his great Strength and Courage, cut his Throat, that they might be sure of him.

The Boat's Crew hearing the firing, put off in good time at some distance from the Shore; and seeing the Portuguese advancing to fire at them, they rowed on board their Ship; where relating what had happened, as they supposed, to their Captain, and to the rest on Shore, it set the Pirates all in a flame; and they directly chose Roberts as their Commander, vowing a severe revenge on the Portuguese.

The Water was so shallow, that they could not get their Ship near the Town; so they prepared a Raft, on which they mounted several Pieces of Cannon, with which they fired at the place: but the Inhabitants having quitted it, and all the Houses being of Timber, they did little damage to the Town. Neither durst they land to burn the Place, for fear of the great number of People, whom they perceived in the Bushes with small Arms: So, they returned to their Ship, and the next day sailed out of the Harbour.

Thus fell Captain Davis, who (allowing for the Course of Life he had been unhappily engaged in) was a most generous humane Person. And thus Roberts arose, who proved the reverse of him, and did afterwards a great deal of mischief in the West Indies, and on the Coast of Guinea; till he and his Crew were happily suppressed by Sir Chaloner Ogle, in the Swallow Man of War, and in the Engagement, Roberts, and several of his People were killed. But as there is 'An Account of the Pirates' published, in which the principal Actions of Roberts are related, I shall say nothing more of him here; but go on to relate what is not mentioned in the aforesaid Book.

As soon as it was commonly known, that the Pirates were sailed from Sierraleon, Captain Bennet and Thompson, with several others that had been obliged to keep in the Woods, as I have formerly related, came to Captain Glynn's Hose. There we all consulted about preparing the Bristol Snow, which the Pirates had spared at my entreaty, so as to make it fit for us to return to London in. There was with us one Captain David Creichton, in the Elizabeth of London, laden with dyeing wood; whom the Pirates had taken not long before me. Him they plundered, and would have destroyed, but by the Interest of Mr James Griffin, who had been chief Mate with the Captain's Brother, the Ship was spared. In this Ship Captain Creichton took as many People as he possibly could, in order to spare our Provisions, and sailed a few days after the Pirates left the River Sierraleon, for London: We that were left behind, sent notice by him to our Owners of the great Misfortunes that had befallen us.

Then applying ourselves to fit the Bristol Snow, whom a worthy Person, one Captain John Morris, commanded, we found we should be in very great want of Provisions, considering how many poor People desired to go home with us. Upon that Captain Glynn sent a small Sloop belonging to him, to fetch Provisions from the River Sherberow, where the destroying Pirates had not been. From thence she returned in a few days, with a good quantity; and one Captain Nisbet having found under his Ship's Ballast in the Hold, several Casks of Beef; which had not come to the knowledge of the Pirates (otherwise it would no doubt have been destroyed, as most part of his Cargoe was) he was so kind as to spare me as much of this Beef as he possibly could; and I drew a Bill on my Owner for the value of it.

Lastly, knowing that large quantities of Goods had been given by the Pirates, to all the white Men residing on Shore upon their own Accounts, we all went in a body to demand them. Messieurs Mead and Pearce, who were in Partnership, very readily and honourably delivered up all they were possessed of: But others did not follow their Example, for they only showed us what Goods they thought proper, of which I allowed them one third part for salvage.

So I shipped what I had recovered from them, with the other Goods the Pirates had given me formerly out of Captain Morris's Vessel; and then we embarked in her, being above sixty Passengers, besides six Masters of Ships, whose Vessels had been destroyed, or fitted for the use of the Pirates. We left the River Sierraleon the 10th of May and, after a tedious Passage, occasioned by the Ship's bad sailing, we came safe to Bristol, the first of August 1719.

On my landing at the Key (quay), Mr Casamajor, Merchant of that City, delivered me a Letter from my Owner, the late Humphrey Morrice Esq; who had received mine by Captain Creichton, with the account of my Misfortune, a few days before we arrived at Bristol. Mr Morrice, in his Letter, was pleased to comfort me under so severe a Trial, as I had undergone, assuring me, 'He would immediately give me the Command of another Ship; (which accordingly he most generously did soon after) and that he had ordered Mr Casamajor, his Correspondent, to supply me with Money, to distribute amongst my poor Sailors, who had returned with me to Bristol; in order to enable them to go to their several Habitations' which was in several Parts of England.

.... This ends the narrative of Snelgrave, the final third book in its entirety, in which the account of Howel Davis's death is probably the truest account we have. Humphrey Morrice was a founder-member of the New Royal Africa Company, on September 27th, 1672, so had a long history of slave-dealing. Other founders were Charles II's brother, James, Duke of York (later James II), Prince Rupert, the Earls of Shaftesbury, Craven and Arlington, and the Welshmen Henry Griffith, Thomas Lewis, Simon Lewis, Richard Middleton, John Middleton, Robert Morris, John Morgan, Lord Powis, William Roberts, Gabriel Roberts, Henry Richards and Godfrey Richards.

NOTES ON THE OTHER PIRATES WHO APPEAR IN THE ACCOUNT OF HOWELL DAVIS

(notes on Thomas Anstis appear under the Bartholomew Roberts chapter)

EDWARD ENGLAND

Jasper Seagar (Edward England) was mate on a sloop from Jamaica to Providence which was taken by Captain Christopher Winter in 1717. His sailing skills and friendliness were such that he was given his own sloop, sailing out of New Providence. However, after Woodes Rogers' amnesty there, he sailed off to the coast of Africa, where he took Howell Davis in the snow *Cadogan*. After his crew tortured Captain Skinner, as recounted above, he gave the *Cadogan* to Davis. England next took the *Pearl*, and exchanged it for his sloop, renaming her the *Royal James*. Several ships were taken off the African coast, then off the Azores and Cape Verde Islands. Returning to Africa in 1719, England took ten ships between the River Gambia and the Cape Coast. Four were burned, four released after being plundered, and the *Mercury* and *Elizabeth and Katherine* were fitted out as pirate ships. Renamed the *Queen Anne's Revenge* and the *Flying King*, they were given to Captain Lane and Captain Robert Sample, who took them to the Caribbean. England now took the galley *Peterborough*, which he kept, and the *Victory*, which he released. At Cape Coast castle, he tried to take the *Wida* and the *John*, but they sailed under the protection of the fort's guns. On Whydah roadstead, he discovered that Olivier la Bouche had been taking any plunder available. He then careened his ships, renaming the *Peterborough* as the *Victory*. It was captained by John Taylor, one of Howell Davis's former pirates. In an isolated bay in Ghana, Johnson says '*they lived there wantonly for several Weeks, making free with Negroe Women, and committing such outrageous Acts, that they came to open Rupture with the natives.*' After of month's roistering, the two ships sailed around the Cape of Good Hope, and arrived at Madagascar in January 1720. Off the Malabar coast several Indian vessels were captured, and a Dutch vessel taken and used as a 34-gun pirate ship renamed the *Fancy*. The *Royal James* was given to the Dutch captain.

At Johanna Island (Juanna), the *Victory* and *Fancy* came across Captain James Macrae's *Cassandra* and the *Greenwich* from England and a Dutch East Indiaman from Ostend. The *Cassandra* fought back strongly while the other ships fled. The *Cassandra* and *Fancy* were both grounded, and pounded each other with broadsides for several hours. Macrae suffered 37 casualties, and more than 90 pirates were killed before Macrae escaped to the shore, leaving £37,000 worth of booty. Macrae hid for 10 days, and then took a chance. He went aboard the *Victory* and asked for mercy. In the Great Cabin, England pleaded for Macrae's life, but Taylor was adamant that he had to die. However, England plied Taylor with more and more rum, until Taylor agreed. The *Fancy* was so badly damaged that she was given to the English captain, which further annoyed Taylor. (Macrae with his 47 surviving crew had a terrible 7-week journey in the semi-derelict ship before they reached the safety of

Bombay). England was seen as weak, and in early 1721 he was marooned on Mauritius with three other crewmen. John Taylor sailed off as the new pirate captain. One of the men marooned with him was the model for Long John Silver, being *'a man with a terrible pair of whiskers and a wooden leg, being stuck around with pistols.'* Fashioning a small boat out of driftwood, the marooned men managed to sail to St Augustine Bay, Mauritius. England lived for a short time off the charity of others, before dying in late 1720 or early 1721.

JOHN TAYLOR

A fierce member of Howell Davis's *'House of Lords'*, he was in Edward England's crew which took a 30-gun vessel off Africa in 1719. He was given command of the *Victory*, and after some success off India with England, he marooned him for the clemency that he showed to Captain Macrae of the *Cassandra*. Taylor now took some Indian, Arab and European prizes. Taylor paid the Dutch governor of Cochin a huge bribe in order to stay there, and he and his men spent the entire month of December 1720 carousing in relative safety. He then went to careen the fleet at Mauritius and St Mary's Island, and Olivier la Bouche took over as captain of the *Victory*. Taylor in the *Cassandra* and La Bouche moved on to Reunion, where they captured a Portuguese carrack which had put in for repairs. *Nostra Senhora de Cabo* was carrying the retiring viceroy of Goa with all his accumulated treasure, diamonds valued at £500,000, and £375,000 in value of rare oriental products. This was a huge windfall, and the two pirate ships and the Portuguese prize sailed back to Madagascar, where 240 pirates shared about a million pounds in accumulated plunder. Johnson wrote that each man received up to 42 diamonds. The *Nostra Senhora de Cabo* was renamed the *Victory*, and the old *Victory* was burned.

Being informed that a Royal Navy squadron was being sent to Madagascar, Taylor and La Bouche spent some time in East Africa, deciding to split up in December 1722. Some pirates returned to Madagascar and burned the *Victory* (the former *Nostra Senhora de Cabo*), to destroy evidence, before vanishing into the townships with their loot. Taylor took the *Cassandra* and 140 pirates to Panama in May 1723, and exchanged the *Cassandra* with the governor in exchange for pardons. Each pirate still had around £1200 in gold and silver, plus his diamonds. It seems that Taylor became a captain in the Panamanian costa-garda. Interestingly, Captain Christopher Winter, originally responsible for Edward England's pirate career, was also a captain of the Hispaniola

(Cuba) costa-garda in 1723, and was accused of robbing English ships and taking Jamaican slaves off the plantations.

OLIVIER LE VASSEUR, LA BOUZE, LA BUSE (THE BUZZARD) LA BOUCHE (The Mouth)

Possibly from Calais, La Bouche was a small man with a limp, who sailed from the pirates' nest of New Providence in 1716, cruising with another pirate ships commanded by Benjamin Hornigold and later by Samuel Bellamy (q.v.) With Bellamy and Paul Williams, he captured English and French ships off the Virgin Islands, but their ships were separated by a great storm early in 1717. In July 1717 Captain John Frost was chased by La Bouse for 12 hours, who caught up with him at 9 in the evening, in a ship of 20 guns and with a crew of 170 men. To force Frost to surrender, La Bouse fired a broadside of *'double round and cartridges, and a volley of small shot'*, so each of 10 guns was loaded with two cannon balls and a bag of partridge shot. The bombardment, combined with the firing of muskets and landing of grenades, forced Frost to surrender his wrecked ship.

La Bouse left his New Providence base when Woodes Rogers became governor of the Bahamas in July 1718, although he accepted the King's Pardon. *The Buzzard* then made for the easier targets of the coast of West Africa. Edward England found thin pickings at this time along the coast, because La Bouche had scared away much of the merchant shipping. In Spring 1719, La Bouche joined up with Howell Davis and Thomas Cocklyn, as recounted in the entry on Howell Davis. He had borne down on Davis, only to see Davis also raise the black flag. They met Thomas Cocklyn a few weeks later. The three pirates took the galley *Bird* at Sierra Leone, which was given to La Bouche to replace his brig, but the three captains argued and parted. Cocklyn, Taylor and la Bouche joined up with Edward England's pirates, and took some merchantmen off the Cape Coast, then sailed a hundred miles west to the Portuguese fort at Ouidah. There they took the English *'Heroine'*, two Portuguese and a French ship. Later in 1719, they all sailed to Madagascar. In 1720 La Bouche commanded the 250 ton *'Indian Queen'* with twenty-eight guns and ninety crew. He was still sailing with Taylor in 1722, on the other side of Africa, around Madagascar.

Making from the Guinea Coast for the Red Sea, he was wrecked on Mayotte in the Comoros Islands in 1720. Early in 1721, La Bouche met up again with Taylor when he landed at St Mary's Island to careen, and

Taylor gave him command of the *Victory*. Off Reunion, the took vast treasure off a Portuguese carrack (see the entry on Taylor), and divided up the booty back at St Mary's. His capture of *Virgen del Cabo* (*La Vierge du Cap*) with Taylor is noted above, and during his ten-year pirate career it is said that he took spoils estimated at £300 million in today's money. In the Bishop of Goa's treasure ship, they found '*rivers of diamonds, a large quantity of gold bars, cascades of gold coins and cases and chests of sacred church vessels.*' It included the diamond-encrusted, golden '*Fiery Cross of Goa*', an opulent crucifix which, it is said, took three men to lift.

Some of the crew stayed at St Mary's, but La Bouche and Taylor sailed on, in 1722 plundering the Dutch garrison at Fort Lagoa. Le Vasseur was supposed to have hidden his share of the treasure on an island in the Indian Ocean. On sailing from Guinea Coast to the East Indies, Captain La Bouche lost his ship near Madagascar on the Island of Mayotta. La Bouche and about forty of his men started building a new ship and the rest of the crew left in canoes and joined pirates led by Captain England at Johanna. Olivier la Bouche retired on the islet of Bel Ombre near Mahe in the Seychelles. He seems to have been offered an amnesty by the French government. However, he realised that he would have to give up his booty, and the Buzzard turned them down. He carried on sporadic piracy, until captured by the French man-of-war *Meduse* off Fort Dauphin. He was trapped, tried and sentenced to death after resuming piracy. On the scaffold on the French island of Reunion, he flung a coded message into the crowd, crying '*Find my treasure he who can!*' La Bouche was hanged at Reunion Island or Mahe on July 17th, 1730.

The Buzzard's code seems to have surfaced in the Seychelles, the French islands 1,100 miles north of Reunion, soon after WWI. In 1948 Reginald Cruise-Wilkins, a former British army officer, bought the cryptogram, believing that it showed La Bouche's treasure to be buried at Bel Ombre Bay on Mahe, the main island in the Seychelles. He spent the rest of his years searching for the booty, finding what he thought was an 18th century pirates' graveyard and dozens of artefacts contemporary with la Bouche. He presumed that a group of up to 250 men stayed there between 1725 and 1729, a time when the Buzzard apparently vanished from history. The Seychelles were uninhabited until the middle of the 18th century. On his death-bed in 1977, Cruise-Wilkins claimed that he was only 6 yards or so from finding the loot. In 1988, his son John resumed the search, upon hearing that a metal object the size of a table had been traced by a remote survey of Bel Ombre. At the bay, there is a series of carvings of birds, snakes, female genitalia and a human nose.

Reginald Cruise-Wilkins thought that these were related to the cryptogram, but others believe that it is indecipherable or a fraud.

'Seychelle Nation' Report
Hunter prepares to enter tunnel he believes holds treasure worth £100 million

Treasure hunter John Cruise-Wilkins Thursday blasted an eight-foot tall rock of similar length at Bel Ombre, which he said stood at the entrance to a tunnel where pirates hid treasure worth £100 million around the year 1721.

He told Nation that once the rubble from the now-broken, formerly turtle-shaped rock was cleared, he would gain access to the treasure, which he hoped included the *golden Sacred Fiery Cross of Goa*, stolen by buccaneer Olivier Le Vasseur, better known as *La Buse*, and another pirate, from a Portuguese ship in April 1721.

He said that following Greek mythology and signs at the site, and going by "known" practices of pirates, he was convinced that the rock had been deliberately placed on that spot to block the entrance to the tunnel by the pirates, who were executed in 1730 in Reunion for their theft.

Mr Cruise-Wilkins said it appeared that the search his late father started in 1949 would soon be over, adding that a German firm was funding his exploration which had ran into hundreds of thousands of rupees.

The Treasure Islands of The Indian Ocean - website information

These islands, located some one-thousand miles east of the African mainland, were so named after a Minister of Finance during the reign of Louis XV, Vicomte Moreau de Seychelles. There is some evidence that these islands may have been known about or visited in the Middle Ages by Arab traders from the Arabian peninsula and Persian Gulf, sailing to and from ports in East Africa before the Monsoons. The period of Portuguese exploration in the Indian Ocean records the sighting of the Amirantes group by Vasco da Gama on his second voyage to India in 1502 or 1503. Previously, in 1501 or 1502, the island of Farquhar, formerly called John de Novo, may have been discovered by the Portuguese explorer of that name. 1501 is also the date on the first map showing what are believed to be the main group of islands. On the morning of January 19, 1609, twenty-eight days out of Zanzibar, boatswain Jones of the brig Ascension under the command of General Alexander Sharpleigh passed the word *"land ... one point off the starboard bow."* This British expedition financed by private merchants was known as `The Fourth Voyage of The East India Company'. Two company traders, John Jourdain and William Revett were on board ship. Their orders were to sail around Africa's Cape of Good Hope with the object of establishing trade relations with Aden and Surat. The ship was attacked by natives near the Portuguese island of Pemba. The aim of the natives was to capture the ship and turn it over to the Portuguese. On escaping from Pemba, the brig ran straight into the northeast monsoon. The prevailing winds made it virtually impossible to steer the Ascension to the next port-of-call, Aden and Surat. It was during this off-course stretch that land was sighted. Looking for fresh water, they sailed among a "cluster of islands" at the time mistaken for the Amirantes, but clearly identifiable by log and journal entries as Mahe and adjacent islands. First landings were made on North Island and Silhouette. On North Island, the men found many giant land tortoises, the larger ones weighing between five and six hundred pounds. The men took eight tortoises for the purpose as recorded by boatswain, Mr. Jones, in the ships log: *"The tortells were good meate, as good as fresh beefe, but after two or three meales our men would not eate them, because they did looke soe uglie before they were boyled."* William Revett recorded in his journal: *"we fownde land turtles of such bignes which men would think incredible; of which our company had small lust to eat of, being such huge deformed creatures and footed with five claws lyke a beare."* On the morning of the third day, January 22, the ship dropped anchor in a bay sheltered from the monsoon winds on the leeward side of the largest island. The next day, the ship's skiff was lowered and the crew, in charge of boatswain Jones and accompanied by John Jourdain and William Revett, went ashore. The description of their landing place as recorded in their journal entries fits the bay of present day Port Victoria. The bay teemed with fish and sea turtles, and they spotted some crocodiles. An account of this shore excursion was recorded in the 'Journal of John Jourdain', published by the Hakluyt Society. He wrote: *"within a pistol shot of the shore where we rode as in a pond from the 22nd to the 30th ditto; in which time wee watred and wooded at our pleasure with much ease; where wee found many coker nutts, both ripe and greene, of all sorts, and much fishe and fowle and tortells and many soates with other fishe. As alsoe aboute the rivers there are many allagartes (crocodiles); our men fishinge for scates tooke one of them and drewe him aland alive with a rope fastened within his gills. Within two miles where we roade, there is a good tymber as ever I sawe of length and bignes, and a very firme timber. You shall have many trees of 60 and 70 feete without spriggs except at the topp, very bigge and straight as an arrowe. It is a very good refreshing place for wood, water, cooker nutts, fish and fowle, without any feare or danger except the allagartes for you cannot discerne that ever any people had bene there before us."* The Ascension left the islands on February 1, arriving in Aden April 7. The ship's log and Jourdain and Revett's journals are the first record of Europeans landing in the Seychelles. With the departure of the Ascension, the islands remained dormant among the warm waters of the Indian Ocean. Located outside the usual spice trading routes to India and the Far East, they remained unexplored and barren of human habitation for more than a hundred years. Although visited by pirates in the 18th century, the islands continued in their isolation from the rest of the world.

Towards the end of the 17th century the British Navy cracked down on the many pirates, who had been active in the West Indies and the Spanish Main, driving them into new territory for the practice of their nefarious trade. Tales of the wealth of the Orient seems to have taken them into the Indian Ocean where an abundant scattering of uninhabited islands provided ideal refuge and hiding places from the law. Between 1700 and 1720 no less than eleven of their ships that used to sail in the Caribbean were identified in Indian Ocean waters. It was highly unlikely that the archipelago, with its ample supply of fresh water, magnificent trees for masts and spars, and safe anchorages would escape their notice. It was in 1721 that the notorious pirate **Olivier Le Vasseur**, also known as La Buse (The Mouth) visited the islands in his ship *Le Victorieux*. He was accompanied by the equally infamous English pirate Taylor in his ship *Defence*. Other pirates, such as Kidd and Conduit, may also have been visitors. More than likely, the islands were only used as a temporary refuge from the law or as a hiding place for plundered loot. The pirates' main centre of operation continued to be Madagascar. It was there that the middlemen from New York were ready to buy the loot at bargain prices. The era of the Indian Ocean Buccaneer came to an end shortly after La Buse was captured by the French Navy and hanged from the yard-arm of a ship in Reunion harbour on July 7, 1730. There is nothing as fascinating as a historical mystery. There is a beach on the south coast of Mahe that is named Anse Fourbans (Pirate's Cove). The north-east coast of Praslin is known as Cote d'Or (Gold Coast). These places were so named by the colonists who arrived 30 to 40 years after the pirates ceased their operations in the Indian Ocean. Cote d'Or is primarily associated with La Buse and Anse Fourbans with pirates in general. Pirates, treasure, and islands are ingredients in the minds of many people that conjure up fantasies of high adventure in exotic places.

It is rumoured amongst the Seychellois that the fortunes of at least two island families can be attributed to the accidental unearthing of wine jars filled with coins. One was purportedly found on Therese Island and the other near the site of St. Elizabeth Convent in Victoria. There is also a rumour that during the construction of the Seychelles International Airport, a treasure chest full of gold and jewels was unearthed by the contractor. What happened to it? No one knows. But these cases are insignificant compared to, what some believe, is a treasure worth millions of pounds that La Buse is said to have buried at Bel Ombre on Mahe. There was one man who had searched for this treasure for more than a quarter century, with no reward except for the excitement of the search. The adventure of seeking with hope and expectation is a reward in itself. The only authentic find so far that has been documented has been 107 silver coins, a few forks and spoons, two shoe buckles and a boatswain's whistle. Those items were found on Astove Island in 1911. Since then, even the government's share has been mysteriously pirated away with only the written record remaining as proof of the find.

CHAPTER III

JOHN ROBERT - BARTHOLOMEW ROBERTS - BARTI DDU – BLACK BART
'THE GREAT PYRATE', 'THE BLACK CAPTAIN', 'THE LAST AND MOST LETHAL PIRATE'

WHAT I HEARD IN THE APPLE BARREL

'No, not I,' said Silver. 'Flint was cap'n; I was quarter-master, along of my timber leg. The same broadside I lost my leg, old Pew lost his daylights. It was a master surgeon, him that ampytated me – out of college and all – Latin by the bucket, and what not; but he was hanged like a dog, and sun-dried like the rest, at Corso Castle. That was Roberts' men, that was, and comed of changing names of their ships – Royal Fortune and so on. Now, what a ship is christened, let her stay, I says.'

- 'Treasure Island' by Robert Louis Stevenson, 1883.

(Roberts moved his ship's name at least 5 times. He took over Davis's *Rover*, then the *Rover* was lost as Kennedy sailed it away from the African coast. Off the Newfoundland coast Roberts then took a Bristol galley, mounting 16 guns and naming her the *Fortune*. Then he swapped her for a French ship of 26 guns, which he also named the *Fortune*. In 1720, the Fortune was replaced with a captured French ship of 42 guns, named the *Royal Fortune*, and then off the African coast he took the *Onslow* and refitted her as the *Royal Fortune*.)

Only three real pirate captains were mentioned in *Treasure Island* – Captain England and the two Welsh captains, Bart Roberts and Howell Davis. Gosse, in his 1932 'The History of Piracy' notes that Black Bart Roberts *'seems to attain most nearly to the popular pirate of fiction'*. He paints a pen-picture of the Welshman thus: *'He was remarkable, even among his remarkable companions, for several things. First of all, he only drank tea, thus being the only recorded teetotaller known to the fraternity (of pirates). Also he was a strict disciplinarian and on board his ships all lights had to be out by 8pm. Any of the crew who wished to continue drinking after that*

Black Bart –
"The last and most
lethal pirate".

hour had to do so upon the open deck. But try as he would this ardent apostle of abstemiousness was unable to put down drinking entirely.

If Roberts had lived today, he would probably have been the leading light on the council of a local vigilance society. He would allow no women aboard his ships; in fact he made a law by which any man who brought a woman on board disguised as a man was to suffer death. Nor did he permit games of cards or dice to be played for money, as he strongly disapproved of gambling. Being a strict Sabbatarian, he allowed the musicians to have a rest on the seventh day. This was as well, for the post of musician on a pirate ship was no sinecure, since every pirate had the right to demand a tune at any hour of the day or night. He used to place a guard to protect all his women prisoners and it is sadly suspicious that there was always the greatest competition amongst the worst characters in the ship to be appointed sentry over a good-looking woman prisoner. No fighting was permitted amongst his crew on board ship. All guards had to be settled on shore, the duellists standing back-to-back armed with pistol and cutlass, pirate fashion.

Bartholomew dressed for action, surprisingly, was the very beau of pirates. A tall, dark man, he used to wear a rich damask waistcoat and breeches, a red feather in his cap, a gold chain round his neck with a large diamond cross dangling from it, a sword in his hand and two pairs of pistols hanging at the end of a silk sling flung over his shoulders.' This is the picture of the **most successful pirate of all time.**

In 1924, in his 'The Pirate's Who's Who', Gosse had written *'If a pirate is to be reckoned by the amount of damage he does and the number of ships he takes there can be no doubt that Captain Roberts should be placed at the very head of his profession, for he is said to have taken over 400 vessels. The only man who can rival him is Sir Henry Morgan, but Morgan, although in some ways an unmitigated blackguard, was a man of much greater outlook than Roberts ever was, and, moreover, was a buccaneer rather than a pirate.'*

And Patrick Pringle, in 'Jolly Roger', puts the Welshman's 'career' as a pirate into true perspective: *'Most of the Guinea pirates were exceptionally daring, and one of them was possibly the most daring pirate who ever lived. His name was Bartholomew Roberts, and he bestraddles the Age of Piracy like a colossus. A Welsh poet has honoured "Black Barty", but he has never become a household name like Kidd or Blackbeard. I cannot imagine why. Not only was he immeasurably bolder, braver, and more successful - not only is his story far more exciting and dramatic - but in his lifetime he achieved a far greater fame. For nearly three years he was feared more than any other man at sea. Moreover, Johnson, on whose history most popular pirate books are based, did*

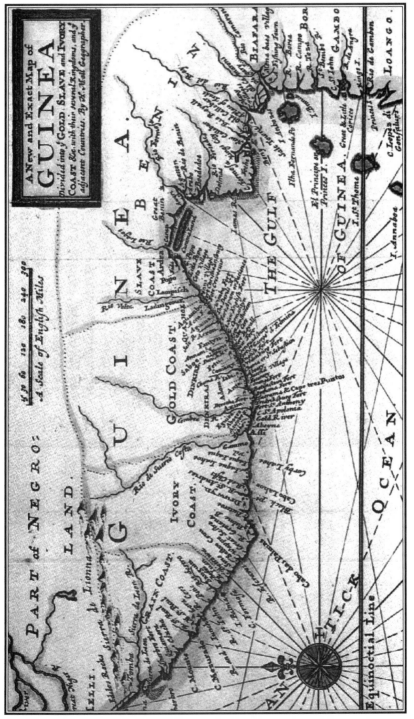

The Guinea Coast in Roberts' time

Roberts full justice, giving him five times as much space as Blackbeard or any other pirate ... the story of Roberts (is) one of the best documented in pirate history. This is very fortunate, for Roberts was of considerable historical as well as personal importance. **He was not only the greatest of the pirates, but he was virtually the last.** *...Captain Ogle was knighted for destroying Roberts. I think this is the only case of such an honour being granted for taking pirates, and it is a measure of the importance that was attached to the event. Bartholomew Roberts was indeed the terror of the seas, and the news of his death was acclaimed by Governors in places as far apart as New York, Port Royal, and even Bombay.... It was said that the end of "the great pirate" would be the end of the great days of piracy. It was, too.'*

John Robert was born in the peaceful hamlet of Little Newcastle (Casnewydd Bach, which Daniel Defoe described as *'Newybagh'*), a few miles south of Fishguard (Abergwaun), Pembrokeshire, in 1682. His father was probably George Robert, noted in the Pembrokeshire Hearth Tax list of 1670. A metal memorial on an old stone on the village green reads:

CAS NEWYDD BACH	LITTLE NEWCASTLE
Yn y pentref yma y ganed	In this village was born
BARTI DDU	**BLACK BARTY**
y mor-leidr enwog	the famous pirate
1682-1722	1682-1722

(Mor-leidr literally means *'sea-robber'*)

John Robert went to sea aged 13, in 1695, but vanished from history, until we find him working as mate on a Barbados sloop in 1718. He probably served in the Royal Navy during the years 1702 to 1713, when the War of Spanish Succession brought hostilities between Britain and Spain. From 1713, he then served on slave-ships, signing on in Barbados, one of thousands of seamen left jobless when the wars ended.

1718

Our first real record is that John Robert is mate of a sloop in Barbados. These were times of pirate mayhem in the Caribbean, with the notorious Edward Teach, Blackbeard, in the fore. The pirate John Plantain maintained that he sailed from Rhode Island on the privateer sloop *Terrible*, with the Welshman John Williams as captain, and Bart Roberts as mate. On the way to West Africa, and off its coast, several prizes were taken. A Dutch slave ship, the *Fancy*, was taken and given to Edward England, who was an experienced ship's mate. England now wanted the squadron to sail to the Indian Ocean, but Roberts strongly disagreed. There was a meeting, and some pirates voted to stay with Roberts in Africa, while others went with England on the Fancy and Victory. Only Plantain gives this account, but it may well be that Roberts was known as a former pirate when he was captured by Howell Davis.

1719
THE SLAVE TRADE

It is in Spring 1719, that John Robert, later known as John Roberts, explodes into maritime history. Under Captain Abraham Plumb, he had sailed to the Guinea Coast of West Africa, as third mate on the galley *Princess of London*. His ship left England in November, 1718, sailing in consort with Captain Snelgrave's *Bird* (captured by Howell Davis), and traded along the Guinea coast. His wage was less than £3 a month, and he had no chance of promotion to his own ship's captaincy in the Merchant Navy. A superb navigator and handler of men, he was condemned to roam the seas working for fools, risking his life on every voyage, in terrible conditions on slave ships. One of the reasons for his going on the account was *'to get rid of the disagreeable Superiority of some masters he was acquainted with — and the Love of Novelty and Change.'* Since the peace with Spain in 1713, many English ships were licensed by the Royal African Company of London to carry slaves from Africa to the Spanish colonies in the New World. (The Asiento Clause in the Treaty of Utrecht gave Britain this *'right'*). The Royal Africa Company, with its President King George 1, was granted the monopoly on trade in both goods and *'black ivory'* by the Crown in 1718.

The *Princess* had discharged its trade goods in Annambo on the Gold Coast in the Gulf of Guinea. Annambo was one of a number of forts along this coast which also acted as trading stations. It was also the main slaving depot of the Royal Africa Company. The Company received a 10% tax off the owners of the *Princess* for the right to sell goods and buy slaves, gold and ivory. In early June Captain Plumb and John Robert were supervising the taking on of slaves to replace the trade goods they had disposed of. The slaves were destined for the islands of the West Indies and possibly for the Spanish settlements in the New World. There were two other slave ships at harbour with it, when two pirate ships approached bearing black flags.

THE TAKING OF ROBERTS

The three merchant ships immediately lowered their colours. The pirate ships were full of armed men, and they could expect quarter for not resisting. Merchant seamen had no affection for their owners anyway – most had been impressed into service, or driven into it by poverty, and a life at sea was generally short and unpleasant. The pirates were led by Captain Howell Davis, a Welsh Jacobite from Milford Haven, a few miles from John Robert's home. His ship was the *King James* (because of his Jacobite leanings), with 26 guns. His consort was a recently captured Dutch ship, now called the *Royal Rover*, with 32 cannon and 27 swivel guns. Davis looted the three slave ships, then gave one to the captain of the Dutch ship he had overcome. Michael Mare of Ghent joined from the Dutch ship. He then sailed out to sea with Roberts' *Princess* and the other slave ship.

The next day, Davis gave chase to, and captured an extremely rich Dutch ship, which surrendered after one broadside. Davis gave quarter to the enemy, as he had stipulated in his Ship's Articles. Roberts must have watched bemused at the ease with which this pirate seemed to take prizes. Davis sold off the three captured ships, and asked all those who wanted to join his crew to say so. Roberts demurred for a while, but Davis was keen to have a fellow-Pembrokeshire man and expert sailing-master with him. Roberts was almost exactly the opposite of the happy-go-lucky extrovert Davis, although he came from only a few miles away from Davis's home town of Milford. Davis was a typical short, stocky Welshman, but Roberts was taller than all his colleagues, lean and brooding, black hair and clean-shaven, with a '*black*' or sombre aspect, according to Defoe. Eventually Roberts and 34 other crewmen from the slavers joined. The *Princess's* second mate Stephenson joined with Roberts. Davis boasted that he forced no man to join him. Roberts' reluctance could have been because he wanted to be seen to be '*forced*' to join the pirates – then there was some hope of mitigation of sentence if captured. John Jessup of Wisbech also voluntarily joined from the *Princess* (another John Jessup later joined the crew).

THE DEATH OF DAVIS

Travelling down the Guinea Coast, past the Bight of Biafra and the Bight of Benin, Davis took more ships, but off Cameroon the *Royal James* was leaking badly, still damaged by battling with the first Dutch ship a few weeks earlier. The *King James* was abandoned, and the crew transferred to the *Rover*, which Davis renamed the *Royal Rover*. They had to careen the ship in Prince's Island, in the Gulf of Guinea, off Spanish Guinea. With just one ship, it had to be fast and seaworthy. Besides, there were women and drinking dens in this Portuguese enclave. Howell Davis claimed that he was captain of an English man-of-war, chasing pirates out of the local seas. His ship was saluted by the fort's twelve cannons overlooking the harbour, and Davis was greeted personally by the Governor of Prince's Island.

No one really knows whether Davis intended just to careen his ship, spend his loot, or attack the island, as in his previous raids. Careening was a laborious, and necessary process, carried out every three months or so. On a sandy beach, the topmasts were taken down (and perhaps replaced) and all the guns removed. By blocks and tackles, the ship was attached to trees (or another ship) and pulled over onto her side. The hull was then cleared of debris, repairs made, and coated with tallow and pitch. The process was repeated on the other side. This hard work was often accompanied by evenings of whoring, gambling and drinking.

The Governor probably suspected Howell Davis was a pirate, but there were huge profits to be made from trade with such a ship. Pirates had few outlets for their stolen merchandise, accepted low prices, and usually spent the proceeds very quickly. The Royal Rover was to leave harbour after a few weeks, on a Monday morning. Davis had promised to pay the Governor a farewell visit on the Sunday morning, and went with his chief surgeon and a handful of other crew. There was no-one at the Government House, and on his return the party was ambushed. Three were immediately killed, including the surgeon. Davis was shot four times but still fought back. After the fifth bullet wound he fell to the ground, but still managed to shoot and kill two Portuguese soldiers. The Portuguese swarmed over his dying body and cut his throat to ensure he was dead.

Just two pirates managed to escape the ambush. The fearless quartermaster, Walter Kennedy, managed to flee to the waiting boat, which was rowed quickly to the *Royal Rover*. Without a captain, there had to be an election of someone agreed by the whole crew. However, Davis' ship was very different from other pirate vessels. The hardest and most experienced pirates, such as Thomas Anstis (who later captained his own pirate ship), and Valentine Ashplant (the former captain of a brig), had formed themselves into what they called *The House of Lords*. *Lord* Christopher Moody had already captained a pirate crew. They had assumed powers not available to the rest of the crew, or *Commoners*. They could go ashore at will, walk the quarter-deck and parley with the captains of prize ships. They referred to each other as '*my fellow noble*' and greeted others as '*my noble lord*'. It was this *House of Lords* which first debated who among them should be the new captain. In all other pirate ships, the crew were not by-passed in this manner in such important discussions.

ROBERTS MADE PIRATE CAPTAIN

The *Lords* were furious and wanted revenge – Davis had been an intelligent leader and had led some profitable voyages, with very little bloodshed. Kennedy was discussed as a captain, but he was a hard taskmaster, and the merits of *Lords* Henry Dennis and Thomas Anstis were also debated. *Lords* Ashplant, Moody, Topping, Phillips and Sutton also could have claims to be the next captain, but the over-riding quality apart from bravery in a captain had to be navigational skills. Daniel Defoe gives us the text of the speech that Lord Dennis made to the assembled Lords in their Council: '*It is not of any great significance who is dignified with the title of commander, for really, and in truth, all good governments have, like ours, the supreme power lodged with the community, who might doubtless revoke and depute authority as suited interest or humour. We are the original holders of this claim and should a captain be so saucy as to exceed prescription at any time, why, down with him! It will be a caution after he is dead to his successors of what fatal consequences any sort of assuming may be. However, it is my advice, that, while we are sober, we pitch upon a man of courage, and skilled in navigation; one who by his counsel and bravery seems best able to defend this commonwealth, and ward us from the dangers and tempests of an unsuitable element, the sea, and the fatal consequences of anarchy; and such a one I take Roberts to be. A fellow, I think, in all respects worth your esteem and favour.*' Only Lord Simpson, known as '*Little David*', did not applaud – he wanted the captaincy himself. This West countryman grumbled: '*I do not care whom we choose captain so he is not a Papist, for against them I have conceived an irreconcilable hatred, for my father was a sufferer in Monmouth's Rebellion.*' (This is Defoe's version but David Simpson did not join until 1720).

Roberts had only been aboard for six weeks, but must have tremendously impressed the *House of Lords*. They knew that Davis had desperately wanted Roberts to join them, and an outside candidate from the *House of Commons* kept the *House of Lords* as it was. Anyway, any captain could be deposed by popular vote at any time, so they had little to lose if Roberts did not prove *'pistol-proof.'* Lord Dennis referred to this fact at the start of his speech. The *House of Commons* unanimously agreed, and Roberts accepted with this short speech:

'Since I have dipped my hands in muddy water and must be a pirate, it is better to be a commander than a common man.' He was also sure to tell his new crew that *'he neither feared nor valued any of them'*. They soon found out that he did not suffer fools gladly - his rages at ineptitude, inefficiency drunkenness or poor seamanship became legendary. However, he was forced to tread easily with the *Lords* in the first few months of his captaincy. He became more autocratic with them as time went on and success bred their complacency.

Captain Roberts later justified his going *'on the account'*: *'In an honest service said he, there is thin commons (poor food and drink), low wages and hard labour; but in a pirate life there is plenty and satiety, pleasure and ease, liberty and power, and who would not balance creditor on this side when all the hazard that is run for it, at worst, is only a fore-look or two at choking (dying). No, **a merry life and a short one** shall be my motto…. Damnation to him who ever lived to wear a halter.'* (This seems to be the origin of the phrase, *'a short life and a merry one'*).

THE ATTACK ON PRINCE'S ISLAND

The new ship's surgeon and other officers were next appointed to replace those lost at Prince's Island. After this it was down to the serious business of avenging the death of Howell Davis. Some pirates had wished to leave the island, but the fort's guns covered the harbour exit, although they did not cover the harbour itself. The Governor expected the pirates to flee, and their guns would be primed, and trained upon the harbour exit. Roberts counselled prudence, stating that they could bombard the fort from where they were, with no fear of retaliation. The *Royal Rover* swung around and its cannonade started pounding the fort. One of the *Lords*, Walter Kennedy, had been voted as one of Roberts' lieutenants, and he now led a band of thirty men up the hill to attack the fort. The settlement on Prince's Island was only a couple of streets with wooden shacks, and the fort guarded both this and the harbour. The *Royal Rover* fired broadsides at the fort, while the pirates attacked under this cover, but the Portuguese fled before they reached the walls. The fort was fired, and its 12 cannon thrown into the sea. Kennedy's band returned, as agreed to the ship.

The Pirate Council then decided that it wanted to take the town as well. Roberts, being the captain only in times of aggression (or being chased) agreed, but only on condition that the town could be taken at minimum risk. To get to the settlement on land would mean passing through dense forest, perfect for an ambush. The Royal Rover could not sail into the shallow inner harbour without stripping itself of goods and armaments, leaving the pirates defenceless if things went wrong. He therefore took a French sloop which had been captured by Kennedy, stripped it of everything removable and mounted three cannon and two swivels on it. He put seven other guns on rafts which the French ship towed towards the town. Once in the harbour, the town was bombarded at length, until it had been virtually levelled and the remains were burning. For good measure, two Portuguese ships in the harbour were also ransacked and set alight. Roberts restored the French ship to her captain and sailed southwards, away from 'The Isle of Princes' and its burning settlement. Davis had been revenged. It was the second week of July, 1719. Roberts took the *Royal Rover* into an inlet near Cape Lopez for refitting, where a forced man named Rogers attempted to escape and was clapped in irons and then soundly whipped.

MORE PRIZES

Almost immediately after leaving the inlet, on July 27th, off the Bight of Biafra Roberts came upon a Dutch merchantman, the '*Experiment*', sailing from London under Captain Cornet. This was a slaver, or '*blackbirder*', of the Royal Africa Company like the *Princess* that Roberts had been serving on, just eight weeks earlier. Seamen hated working on these ships, and sickness was rife in the Bight of Benin and the Gulf of Guinea. Black Bart fired a couple of shots across the '*Experiment's*' bows, then hauled up the black flag. The *Experiment* struck its colours. Kennedy now shouted at the sailing-master, Thomas Grant, to row across to board the *Royal Rover*. When on board, Kennedy began furiously shouting at Grant, asking him where the valuables were. Grant answered quite reasonably that they were still aboard the *Experiment*. He hit and threatened to kill Grant, whose life was saved from the quartermaster by other pirates. The hot-headed Kennedy supervised the ransacking of the merchant, and found little - Captain Cornet had handed over 50 ounces of gold and some coin. Roberts now wanted to keep the *Experiment* as a storeship, but Kennedy, after burning the *Experiment's* yawl in a fit of pique, then set fire to the ship as well. Most of its crew joined Roberts, and the others including Cornet and Grant imprisoned on the *Rover*.

Black Bart Roberts

The next day, a small Portuguese merchantman was plundered, and just two days later Roberts took the *'Temperance'* under Captain Sharman. It still had a cargo of British pots and pans that Sharman had been trying to barter for slaves. Roberts gave him the Portuguese ship, and kept the *Temperance*. There was now a pirate council about the next destination. Roberts knew that Edward England, and probably la Bouche and Cocklyn were still operating off Africa, so decided to head for Brazil where there would be less competition. Some men wanted to head for Madagascar, and the pirates headed down to the island of St Thomas (Sao Tome), but found no new prizes. They now carried on south-west to the island of Annabona for fresh water and provisions. The Council met again, to decide whether to go to the East Indies (Java, Sumatra, etc.), or west across the Atlantic to Brazil. Roberts won the vote. The long voyage to the coast of Portuguese Brazil on the Southern Trades was taken in August 1719. In just three weeks Roberts, by use of the cross-staff, long-staff, quadrant, hourglass and logline, landed exactly where he wanted in Brazil. In these days when there was no way of calculating longitude, it was a superb example of seamanship, and Roberts further earned the crew's respect. At a small, uninhabited island off its coast, Fernando de Noronha (Ferninadino), they quickly boot-topped (partially careened) the *Royal Rover*. For weeks they cruised the shore, unaware that the Portuguese trade with Brazil was very minor, and that other pirates had been active along this coast, scaring off any potential shipping. In this climate, Roberts began to lose his aura as a *'lucky'* captain amongst his bored crew.

THE PORTUGUESE TREASURE FLEET

Roberts had kept the ship away from sight of land, but simply cruised the Brazilian coast for several weeks. He did not want to alert the Portuguese that he was in the area. With no luck, the pirates then agreed to head for the far busier waters of the Caribbean, the international cross-roads of Atlantic traffic. In September, they came upon the Lisbon Fleet of 32 ships laden with gold, silver, hides, tobacco and sugar. These armed merchantmen were lying-to at Bahia de Todos dos Santos (the Bay of All Saints) in Brazil. The fleet was waiting for its escort to Lisbon, two Portuguese men-of-war with seventy guns apiece, to finish their preparations for the Atlantic Crossing. Two forts trained their guns over the fleet, which had over 500 cannon and over 1000 men. The *Lords* decided to turn tail before they were spotted by the Portuguese. Roberts, conscious of the murmurings of discontent, stated that they would attack. He seemed to know that his days as captain would have been numbered, without a quick success. There followed an attack which for sheer audacity rivalled that of Francis Drake on Cadiz or of Henry Morgan on Portobello.

Black Bart quietly outlined his plan to the disbelieving pirates. Roberts sent a party in a boat to capture some Portuguese pilots to assist him, and then ordered his men to stay quiet and below decks. It was a moonless, dark night, which would assist their endeavours. Because of Roberts' incredible track-record, although short, the crew must have agreed to this outrageous attack. Once attack was under way, all decisions were the captain's until his death in action. *Lord* Henry Dennis, who had also been Howell Davis's gunner, inspected and prepared each cannon for action. Dennis stayed as Roberts' gunnery expert throughout his career. The pirates prepared their weapons and grappling-hooks and ropes. However, Captain Roberts knew he could not take on all forty-two ships. He had to find the most wealthy ship, take it quickly and flee before the other merchantmen, or the men-of-war, trapped him. Kennedy guided the *Royal Rover* slowly to the nearest heavily-laden vessel. Once alongside, all the pirates came up on deck with their cutlasses and muskets, and threatened to give no quarter, unless the captain told them which was the richest ship. Anstis had led the party and took the captain back to Roberts. The frightened captain took the easy option and pointed to the biggest ship, the *Sagrada Familia* (*Holy Family*). As yet no-one suspected that a pirate ship was in the harbour. Roberts coolly and calmly took the Portuguese captain and crew upon his ship, bound them and sailed on, towards the *Sagrada Familia*, its Vice-Admiral and its forty cannon.

THE TAKING OF THE *SAGRADA FAMILIA*
In hailing distance of the treasure galleon, Roberts ordered the Portuguese Captain to ask the Vice-Admiral to come aboard the ship for urgent news. The response was that he would, but obviously the captured captain had given a warning, as the Portuguese crew made ready for action. Roberts immediately ordered a full broadside, sailed quickly within grappling distance and boarded the prize. The boarding party was again led by the Irishman, Lieutenant Kennedy, who lost just two men in a brief but bloody battle. A tow-line was attached to the 36-gun *Sagrada*, and Kennedy then towed the slow and unwieldy treasure galleon out of the bay. All over the fleet, guns were firing, and one of the men-of-war began closing with the slow, unwieldy *Rover* and *Sagrada*. Roberts fired at

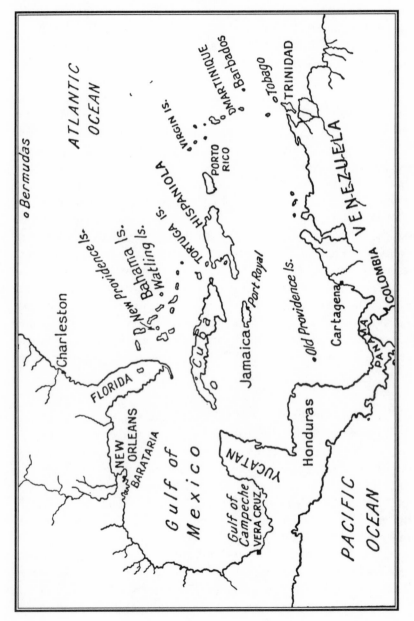

The West Indies

it from the *Royal Rover*, and the man-of-war amazingly stopped its pursuit. Eastwell shouted from the crow's-nest that it was waiting for the other man-of-war to catch up, which was stationed on the other side of the fleet. With dawn breaking, Roberts escaped out to the open sea. The *Weekly Journal* reported in 1720 on the action *'The Lisbon Fleet from the Bay of All Saints, Brazil, has arrived. But one vessel of 36 guns was taken by a pyrate ship (formerly an English hog-boat) and two others plundered.'* The third boat's identity is unknown. The rest of the Spanish fleet had arrived in Lisbon on the 21st January 1720, carrying 759,000 octaves of gold dust, 164,000 moidores of gold (plus unspecified amounts of gold, including some for the king), 164 slaves, 205 raw hides, 11,000 rolls of tobacco, 950 chests of sugar, 92 barrels of honey, 22,000 hides, unspecified amounts of hardwoods, 128 baskets of cake-sugar and 7,800 chests of sugar.

The pirates made off with the galleon plus 40,000 *moidores* (*moeda d'oura, money of gold*), jewellery, sugar, skins, tobacco, silver plate and the diamond-studded gold cross designed for the King of Portugal. Roberts now started wearing two brace of pistols in a red silk sling over his shoulder, and a cutlass. Until his death he went into battle also wearing a scarlet damask waistcoat and breeches, a crimson plumed hat and the massive chain with the King of Portugal's jewelled cross on it. This red silk outfit, with the huge diamond cross, gave him the epithet by French merchants and pirates of *Le Joli Rouge* (the pretty red), probably the origin of *The Jolly Roger*. About this time he started to be known as Bartholomew Roberts, or *Black Bart*. (Bartholomew Sharp was another famous pirate of the day, so perhaps Roberts was aping him. The other explanation is that he was trying to escape the identity of John Robert, in case he ever returned to Wales).

DEVIL'S ISLAND AND THE SIXTH PRIZE

Roberts now sailed north and north-west, past the Amazon estuary to the Iles du Salut off Surinam. The pirates anchored at Ile du Diable, Devil's Island and Cayenne Island off Guyana, and had a debauched time for two weeks. Now the former is renowned as the former French prison colony and the *Dreyfus Affair*, but then it was a Spanish possession. The Spanish Governor of Guiana apparently welcomed this sudden influx of wealth into his territories. Surgeon Murray tended to the injured from the *Sagrada* battle, while the Portuguese prisoners rotted in the hold. The pirates had now acquired huge wealth to add to their previous acquisitions under Davis, and Roberts had his fiddler and trumpeter play through the days to celebrate.

In October 1719, Roberts moved to the mouth of the river Surinam, and easily took a small Rhode Island sloop under Captain Cane. Cane told them that there was a far larger Rhode Island brig, with a much better cargo sailing towards Surinam. Back on the island, Roberts sent the *Royal Rover* to a nearby islet to be careened, while he checked the stores with his boatswain. He next wished to sail north to the West Indies, and provisions were needed. However, 30 crew members, under Eastwell, Rogers and Hews, deserted in a longboat which was soon recaptured. Ashplant wished to maroon them - the standard punishment - but Roberts desperately needed to keep his crew, and Kennedy relished whipping the deserters, paying particular attention to the ringleaders, whom he left half-dead. They were locked up in the hold, to reflect upon their misdemeanours. A mast-head was now sighted on the horizon, and thinking it to be the ship that Cane had promised, Roberts took forty of his best men in the sloop and raced after it. The *Royal Rover* was still laden with cargo and much of the treasures of the *Sagrada Familia*, so was neither fast nor worth the risk of losing. There were no provisions on the sloop, which he had renamed the *Fortune*, as they had been transferred to the *Royal Rover*. Black Bart lost sight of the quarry, and was becalmed for eight days, ending up ninety miles offshore. The *Royal Rover* had returned to Devil's Island, and the carousing pirates were blissfully unaware that a naval man-of-war, the *Seaford*, was now patrolling the West Indies. Two more naval sloops, the *Rose*, and the *Shark*, were also on their way from England.

DESERTION

Roberts was in a dilemma - he was becalmed, with no provisions in his haste to chase the merchantman. There were no creeks or inlets for mooring for his stricken ship. The *Fortune's* only boat was rowed back to order the *Royal Rover* to come and assist. The crew were near death's door from lack of water, and despite rationing of food and water Roberts had to rip up some planking to make a raft to go ashore and bring in water. Roberts had sent Moody and five others for assistance, but they returned a few days later with bad news. Lieutenant Walter Kennedy had vanished, taking the *Royal Rover* and the *Sagrada Familia* with him. Back on the coast of Guiana, Black Bart decided that Ship's Articles must be drawn up, and signed by all the crew. Many of the crew had been with Howell Davis. They had had a good run under these two Welsh captains,

Bart Roberts

and it was only because of Portuguese and Irish treachery that events had ever misfired. The hardened cadre of Howell Davis's '*Lords*' (Valentine Ashplant, Henry Dennis, William Magness, Christopher Moody, Richard Hardy, Thomas Sutton and Thomas Anstis) were still with Roberts. They unanimously decided to ban all Irishmen from ever sailing with them, and Bart became an implacable enemy of everyone and everything Irish.

However, it seems with hindsight that Kennedy had not deserted. Moody had reached Devil's Island to find that Kennedy had vanished, leaving no message. However, the 24 year-old Kennedy had seen his captain and the *House of Lords* vanish over the horizon, and had expected them back within 24 hours at the most. He had two ships stacked with treasure trove from half-a-dozen captures, and dozens of Portuguese prisoners. The 30 men who had tried to desert and whom he had badly beaten were also chained in the hold, and many forced men who were looking for any opportunity to escape. The pirates wanted to leave the island, and after 11 days Kennedy sailed for the West Indies. Although he was young and no navigator, it seems that the crew elected him captain because of his strength of character. Because of the crew shortage, Kennedy transferred all the loot to the *Royal Rover*, and gave the *Sagrada Familia* to Captain Cain. Kennedy believed that the *Fortune* must have been captured or sunk. Cain took the *Sagrada Familia* and the Portuguese prisoners to British Antigua and gave it to Governor Hamilton of the Leeward Islands. After Kennedy's 'desertion', the despondent Black Captain drew up his famous '*articles*' to be kept by the crew, and signed by all new members. Each pirate signed the articles, as

Black Bart commented *'for the greatest security it is in everyone's interest to observe these articles if he is minded to keep up so abominable a combination (profession)'*

THE ARTICLES OF CAPTAIN ROBERTS

According to Charles Johnston (Daniel Defoe), writing just four years later, in 1724, *'The following, is the Substance of the Articles, as taken from the Pyrates' own Informations.*

I

Every Man has a Vote in Affairs of Moment; has equal Title to the fresh Provisions, or strong Liquors, at any Time seized, and may use them at Pleasure, unless a Scarcity make it necessary, for the Good of all, to vote a Retrenchment.

II

Every Man to be called fairly in Turn, by List, on board of Prizes, because, (over and above their proper Share) they were on these occasions allowed a shift of Cloathes (change of clothes): But if the defrauded the Company to the Value of a Dollar, in Plate, Jewels or Money, MAROONING was their punishment. This was a barbarous Custom of putting the Offender on Shore, on some desolate or uninhabited Cape or Island, with a Gun, a few Shot, a Bottle of Water, and a Bottle of Powder, to subsist with, or starve. *If the Robbery was only betwixt one another, they contented themselves with slitting the Ears and Nose of Him that was Guilty, and set him on Shore, not in an uninhabited Place, but somewhere, where he was sure to encounter Hardships.'*

III

No Person to Game at Cards or Dice for Money

IV

The Lights and Candles to be put out at eight a-Clock at Night: If any of the Crew, after that Hour, still remained inclined for Drinking, they were to do it on the open Deck; which Roberts believed would give a Check to their Debauches, for he was a sober Man himself, but found at length, that all his Endeavours to put an End to this Debauch, proved ineffectual.

V

To keep their Piece (firearm), Pistols, and Cutlass clean, and fit for Service: In this they were extravagantly nice, endeavouring to outdo one another, in the Beauty and Richness of their Arms, giving sometimes at an Auction (at the Mast) 30 or 40 pounds a pair, for Pistols. These were slung in Time of Service, with different coloured Ribbands, over their Shoulders, in a Way peculiar to these Fellows, in which they took great Delight.

VI

VI No Boy or Woman to be allowed amongst them. If any Man were found seducing any of the latter Sex, and carried her to Sea, disguised, he was to suffer Death; so that when any fell into their Hands, as it chanced in the *Onslow,* they put a Sentinel immediately over her to prevent ill Consequences from so dangerous an Instrument of Division and Quarrel; but here lyes the Roguery; they contend who shall be Sentinel, which happens generally to be one of the greatest Bullies, who, to secure the Lady's Virtue, will let none lie with her but himself.

VII

To Desert the Ship, or their Quarters in Battle, was punished with Death or Marooning

VIII

No striking one another on board, but every Man's Quarrels to be ended on Shore, at Sword and Pistol, thus: The Quarter-Master of the Ship, when the Parties will not come to any Reconciliation, accompanies them to Shore with what Assistance he thinks proper, and turns the Disputants Back to back, at so many Paces Distant: At the Word of Command they turn and fire immediately, (or else the Piece is knocked out of their Hands:) If both miss, they come to their Cutlashes (cutlasses), and then he is declared Victor who draws the first Blood.

IX

No man to talk of breaking up their Way of Living, till each had shares a 1000 pounds. If in order to this, any Man should lose a Limb, or become a Cripple in their Service, he was to have 800 Dollars, out of the publick Stock, and for lesser Hurts, proportionately.

X

The Captain and Quarter-Master to receive two Shares of a Prize; the Master, Boatswain, and Gunner, one Share and a half, and other Officers one and a Quarter.

XI

The Musicians to have Rest on the Sabbath Day, but the other six Days and Nights, none without special Favour.

These, we are assured, were some of Roberts' Articles, but as they had taken Care to throw over-board the Original they had signed and sworn to, there is a great deal of Room to suspect, the Remainder contained something too horrid to be disclosed to any, except such as were willing to be Sharers in the Iniquity of them; let them be what they will, they were together the Test of all new Comers, who were initiated by an oath taken on a Bible, reserved for that Purpose only, and were subscribed to in the Presence of the worshipful Mr Roberts.'

Roberts was the only known teetotaller amongst pirate captains – his *'House of Lords'* were known from their Howell Davis days as hardened drinkers (related in Captain Snelgrave's account that they took his ship off Guinea, drank the claret and brandy, threw alcohol at each other and ended up swabbing the deck with what was left) – so control was difficult for him. He also observed the Sabbath, again marking him out as a very different kind of leader.

CHAPTER IV

1720 - TO THE WEST INDIES
AND MORE PRIZES

Roberts seems to have been a changed man after what he saw as Kennedy's desertion. He did not seek counsel as much as previously from the Lords. He withdrew even more from his men. 'Lord' Christopher Moody, who had previously captained pirate ships, was voted sailing master until a more experienced man could be taken. 'Lord' Thomas Anstis was voted quartermaster to replace Kennedy. Jones and Dennis were re-elected boatswain and gunner. Roberts' little sloop was repaired where he had broken up the decking to make a raft. Black Bart had christened the his little sloop *Fortune*, and the Council decided to sail, as agreed previously, to the West Indies. There was a better chance of gaining provisions, and thousands of hiding places around the cays. Roberts also knew the area from his days as mate on the Barbados sloop.

The pirates desperately needed success after the loss of their huge treasure. Sailing past Trinidad, they spied the sloop *Philippa* anchored of Laquary Roads. Roberts held his distance during the night. Captain Daniel Greaves was below decks suffering from gout, but his mate John Wransford noticed a canoe approaching from the *Fortune*, just after dawn on January 10th, 1720. Greaves shouted at Wransford and the crew to fire their pistols at the canoe, and stop its occupants getting near the *Philippa*. Anstis swore at the sailors that if there was any more firing they would all be killed, and the guns fell silent. On board, Anstis announced to Captain Greaves that he was *'impounding'* his boat, and the sloop was sailed to join the *Fortune* at Sandy Point. Roberts saw no benefit in exchanging ships - although he desperately needed a better ship like the mighty *Royal Rover* - and contented himself with transferring the cargo.

They took two guns, a 60-gallon cask of rum, 300 pounds of sugar, firearms, food and some slaves for menial tasks. Three of Greaves' men also wished to join, including a large man known as *'Little David'* Sympson, who was to become one of the leading *Lords*. Luckily at this time for Roberts, the Royal Navy was preoccupied with the war with

Spain, from the West Indies to the American Colonies. Near Deseada Island, close to Guadeloupe, another two merchant vessels were taken and stripped of provisions. Because of merchant distress on Jamaica and Barbados, the Leeward Isles Governor Hamilton asked Captain Rose in the *Seaford* to turn from anti-Spanish duties, and search for Roberts, but he could not find him. There were five Royal Navy ships stationed on and around Jamaica, with 148 guns between them, and another nine stationed at Barbados, the Leeward isles, Virginia and New York. However, because of logistical problems, there were only ever around 6 naval ships at sea, covering the open sea from Newfoundland to the Tropics, with the thousands of islets and creeks and inlets where pirates could be hidden.

Off Barbados, an inwards-bound Bristol trader was taken, although it had ten guns. Apart from clothes, gunpowder, oatmeal and beef, Black Bart gained five seamen who decided to join '*on the account*'. The prize and its remaining crew was ordered not to sail for three days, and when it eventually reached Barbados, the Governor was informed that Black Bart was active nearby in the Caribbean. More ships were taken by Roberts by February 12th, 1720, including the *Benjamin* from Liverpool, and on the 18th the Sloop *Joseph*, commanded by Bonaventure Jelfes. However, these were little prizes to the conqueror of the Portuguese treasure-ship, and other pirates such as '*Jolly Jack*' Rackham were also scouring the nearby seas. The day after taking the *Joseph*, Roberts spied a small sloop, the *Sea King*, and chased it. Roberts hoisted the black flag, expecting the boat to make a run for it, but it turned towards him and hoisted its own black flag. Its pirate captain was Montigny la Palisse. Roberts' *Fortune* needed to be replaced desperately by a bigger, faster boat, and he took la Palisse as a partner to cover his weakness until he could acquire a better ship.

THE BARBADIAN EPISODE
Because of the losses to trade, Captain Witney was now ordered to take the naval ships *Rose* and *Shark* to the Leeward Isles and help Captain Rose search for Roberts, and Whitney sailed to Antigua after an 8-day delay because of sickness in his crews. Captains Roberts, La Palisse and Rackham took a few more prizes off Barbados, and the traders of Barbados decided something had to be done, as Governor Lowther had no wish to help them. (It was rumoured that he had dealt with pirates in the past, and had been recalled to London in 1714 on corruption charges,

and in 1720 to be accused of taking bribes. In October 1720, he was found guilty in London on several accounts. Lowther was charged with imprisoning naval captains to prevent their chasing pirates, and found guilty of allowing trade with a Spanish ship despite the Navigation Act, and of misappropriating £28,000 of Barbadian funds.)

The merchants petitioned Lowther on February 19th, 1720 that they had to take steps to avoid certain ruin and defend themselves; as '*a certain pyrate sloop carrying 12 guns and manned with 70 men hath lately taken several vessels to windward of this island and still lyeth there to intercept their trade.*' Barbados and Jamaica were the only real British colonies in the West Indies. Lowther decided that he had to allow the petition, such was the resentment of men losing their livelihood. Governor Lowther had no men-of-war close to call to his aid, so he allowed the traders to fit out a Bristol galley, the *Summersett*, captained by the Bristolian Owen Rogers with 16 guns and 130 men (other sources give 20 guns and 80 men); and a sloop the *Philippa* commanded by Daniel Greaves, with 6 guns and 60 men (another source gives 10 guns and 60 men). The Governor gave a Letter of Marque (commission) to Captain Rogers of Bristol for the expedition against Roberts. Rogers on the galley was made Commodore, and Captain Greaves took command of the sloop. The two privateers made all speed to find Black Bart and the *Fortune*.

Rogers and Greaves left the harbour on February 22nd, and 2 days later caught up with a small French pink off Barbados. Its mizzen mast and part of its main mast had been cut down by Roberts, and its captain told Rogers that Roberts now had a smaller consort sloop, formerly from Virginia. Rogers now prepared the *Summerset* for action, bringing portable bulwarks up to the quarterdeck to minimise cannon damage, stringing netting up to impede boarding parties, and setting hammocks around the masts to disguise marksmen from the pirates. However, Greaves had fallen sullenly silent since realising that there were now two pirate ships, and refused to prepare for action. On February 26th, the two sloops were sighted, charting a course towards their two 'merchantmen'.

Rogers and Greaves now sailed on slowly alongside each other, pretending to be normal merchantmen, then suddenly piled on full sail, as if to flee the pirates. Greaves steered his ship into the protection of Rogers' port side, as Roberts approached its starboard, and Rogers fired at the *Fortune*. Now Rogers sailed past the *Fortune*, exposing the *Summersett's* starboard to a broadside, knowing that the *Fortune* would then itself be exposed to a broadside from Greaves' *Philippa*. The *Fortune's* broadside, from point-blank range, tore into the *Summersett*, killing men. Musket fire was exchanged. Black Bart's band played. Another cannon ball hit the *Summersett*, from la Palisse's *Sea King*, which promptly fled the action. However, Greaves did not fire at Roberts, and Black Bart took advantage of his luck to circle around to approach the stern of the *Summersett*. This was the easiest way to take a ship, throwing bombs of sulphur and tar onto the merchantman's deck, which would suffocate and blind its crew and its marksmen in the rigging. Swivel guns would spew glass and nails across its decks. Few guns could be brought to bear on the *Fortune*. The *Fortune* was towing a small boat full of pirates armed to the teeth, which would swarm up the sides of the *Summersett* to aid the direct attack from the boarding party. The *Philippa*, under the cowardly Greaves, moved further away from the impending action, and Roberts changed course slightly to deliver another broadside to the merchantman. However, as Roberts approached the stern, he veered away. It may have been that Black Bart thought that the *Summersett* had been damaged and could be taken by easier methods than a boarding party, or that he had spotted the hammocks, nets, barricades and numbers of men that were on this 'innocent' trading ship. Obviously she was no mere merchantman - was she a naval ship in disguise? Would the *Philippa* rejoin the fray when he had boarded and the *Fortune* was defenceless? Was it a trap? After la Palisse had fled, he had to make sure of his course of action.

The two gun decks of the *Summersett* fired into the *Fortune*. Its drummer was hit and fell off the roundhouse. Musket and pistol fire was exchanged, with pirates in the unprotected towed boat also being hit. Rogers now realised that Greaves in the other ship would not join him in the action, and altered course to yet again hit Roberts with a broadside. The lightly armed *Fortune* was hit below the waterline and now in great trouble. Some of its depleted crew were sent down to effect running repairs, and at least two of them were drowned as they lost their footing, as Roberts desperately tacked the *Fortune* to try and get away from the withering fire. The *Summersett* positioned itself for one last broadside to finish off the limping *Fortune*, and amazingly, the *Philippa* returned to the action, stationing itself between the *Summersett* and the *Fortune*, so that Rogers could not fire without hitting Greaves's sloop. Rogers believed that either Greaves would fire a last broadside into the *Fortune*, or board the severely damaged ship.

However, Greaves did nothing. Roberts took advantage, hauling up full sail. The *Fortune* came up alongside, fired a shot across the *Phillipa's* bows and hoisted Roberts' *Black Flag*. It seems that the raising of the flag was a decoy to pretend that the pirates intended to stay and fight to the death. However, Black Bart had no choice against crews that were on commission to kill him, and *cut and run*. Greaves' *Philppa* did not give chase. The *Summersett* galley gradually closed on the *Fortune*, and kept up fire from its bow chaser, killing more of Bart's crew. The pirates had to throw precious guns and heavy cargo overboard to eventually outstrip the privateers. Rogers fumed at losing his prize. By dusk Roberts had lost Rogers, but had to effect urgent repairs to his bloody ship and to tend to his wounded and dying. Almost half the crew had died or were wounded, and since Archibald Murray had left, there was no surgeon to amputate or prevent gangrene. Men were anaesthetised with rum, until they died. From henceforth Bristolians and Barbadians were added to Black Bart's pet hate of Irishmen, formerly incurred by what he thought was Kennedy's treachery. All were singled out for special treatment if captured.

The '*Weekly Journal*', June 25th, 1720, noted the action as follows: *From Portsmouth in New Hampshire they tell us that a brig arrived there from Barbados in 22 days and reported that a Bristol galley and a sloop were fitted out to take a pirate ship of 12 guns that lay to windward of the island; they came up and engaged her but the pirate having a great number of men on board gave them such a warm reception that they were obliged to go back to Barbados without her. In this engagement many men were lost on both sides.'*

THE MARTINIQUE GOVERNOR

The *Fortune* sailed for 200 miles, not daring to land on St Lucia or Martinique, losing 20 men on the way. The *Fortune* landed at Dominica to make repairs, and more men died. Over half of Roberts' 70 men had perished because of the sea fight. He dared not stay long, because if their presence was reported, the French governor of nearby Martinique would send a force to destroy them. For two days they bartered with natives, took on water and provisions and cut timber to repair the *Fortune*, desperately trying to conceal their presence. Then their lookouts sighted a group of 13 naked, unarmed men. Robert Butson explained that they had been landed by the sloop *Revenge*, out of Antigua, and that this costagarda had marooned them there without clothes, food, or equipment, 3 weeks earlier. A '*garde de la coste*', the French sloop *Revenge*, had put down thirteen Englishmen from two New England trading ships there. They included Joe Mansfield (a deserter from the *Rose*), James

Black Bart's personal flags

Phillips and Robert Butson, all later hanged at Cape Corso. Anstis had badly wanted them to join the depleted pirate force, but Roberts had told the unfortunate men that he would not *force* any of them to become pirates. The sailors eagerly signed Roberts' Articles - they desperately needed to escape the island. Within an hour, the *Fortune* made heavy way towards the relative safety of the Grenadine Islands.

However, the French Governor of Martinique had discovered that the pirates were on Dominica. Just 12 hours after the *Fortune* limped away, two armed sloops from Martinique landed and discovered from the natives that Roberts had just eluded them. Roberts and his men sailed in the unseaworthy *Fortune* to Carriacou, just 20 miles north of Grenada in the Windward Isles. He knew that the ship would be hidden on all sides by high land, while he quickly careened it and the carpenters made repairs. Roberts knew that time was of the essence - his sloop had too few guns (after jettisoning some to escape the *Summersett*), to fight properly at sea in these hostile waters. Some men were still wounded, and were fortified by a diet of land-tortoise.

Roberts now called his *Lords* to Pirate Council. He had decided that attacking ships at sea was pointless. It was a lottery as to what they would be carrying, and the fact that the merchantmen *Summersett* and *Philippa* were in fact heavily armed privateers, meant that appearances could now be deceptive. A far better plan of action would be to attack ships at anchor, and to loot the riches of the ports which supplied them. The *Lords* agreed, and the new strategy was to be followed. During this week, spirits rose, despite the lack of taverns and women, but lookouts noted that the two sloops from Martinique were combing the surrounding islands, and that they had to move quickly before they were penned in. The *Fortune* left in early March, just a half-day before the French chasers sailed into the bay. This event added Martinicans to Bart's hate-list. Around this time he had his famous flag made. Designed by himself, his personal jack-flag always now flew in action – it portrayed Black Bart holding a sand-glass and a flaming sword in each hand, with each foot resting on a skull marked *ABH* and *AMH* – 'A Barbadian's head' and 'A Martinican's Head'. His intention was to hang the governors of both islands. His personal ensign, or Jolly Roger, showed Roberts holding an hour-glass with a skeleton. The skeleton also holds a flaming lance, or arrow, and there is a heart dripping three drops of blood under the hour-glass.

THE NEWFOUNDLAND BANKS
Roberts took the *Fortune* north, through the West Indies, past the American colonies, and up towards an area which had not suffered from much piracy in these times. Newfoundland was the centre of the fishing industry, with many small vessels, and no men-of-war patrolling. It would be easy pickings after the problems of the African coast and the West Indies. Also, his old *Fortune* would be at huge risk during the worst of the hurricane season, towards August and September if he stayed in the West Indies. Indeed, he just escaped an early hurricane. On June 15th of that year, the man-of-War *Milford* was lost off Cuba escorting a Jamaican fleet to England, with another 14 ships it was escorting. In summer, the northern traffic across the Atlantic increased. The King's ships stayed at

their stations, and the majority were in the West Indies. In June 1720, naval ships were clustered at the West Indies. Jamaica had the fourth rate man of war *Mary* (320 men, 60 guns); the fifth rate *Adventure* (190,40); *Mermaid* (135,30); and the sloop *Happy* (80,14). Barbados had the 5th rate *Milford* (155,30). The Leeward Islands had the 6th rate *Rose* (115,20) and the sloop *Shark* (80,14). Off Guinea, the 5th rate *Royal Anne* Galley (190,40) and the *Lynn* (190,40) were stationed. The American mainland was protected by the following sixth raters: *Rye* off Virginia (115,20); *Flamborough* off Carolina (115,20); *Phoenix* off New York (100, 20) and *Squirrel* off New England (100, 20). The 5th rate *Kinsale* (135,30) was being used to take despatches to and from North America.

With the French and Spanish sloops and '*coastguards*' (revenue cutters) also posing a threat, the West Indies had been a dangerous place for Black Bart. Off the English colony of North America, he could acquire a better ship, at the very least. It seems that he sold his slaves and some goods in New England on the way up to Newfoundland, where he captured and looted around a dozen vessels including a pink, by mid-June 1720. There were too many captives now, so he sent all those unwilling to join him on a captured brigantine to Newfoundland. They obviously raised the alarm. In June he raided the small harbour of Ferryland, and burned the largest ship, the Admiral's, as a warning to the townspeople not to become involved. Another ship was looted. There was no resistance to this unexpected threat from any ship or the port.

Roberts plundered some more shipping, as he headed south, and sent a message to the major port of Trepassey that he was about to visit them. Now that the coastal towns knew that a pirate ship was in the area, it was pointless trying to nose into any harbours by stealth, as when he took the *Sagrada Familia*. He also knew that crews and their masters would tend to stay ashore, rather than risk their lives. On June 21st, Roberts unfurled his black flag of skull and cutlass, set his musicians playing, fired a broadside and roared into Trepassey harbour, Newfoundland. There were 1200 men from 22 sloops in the harbour, but few were aboard their ships. With just 70 men and ten guns, Roberts had made directly for the *Bideford Merchant*, under Admiral Babidge, one of the richest men in Newfoundland. Babidge scrambled onto a dinghy to escape, and Thomas Anstis led the boarding party aboard the biggest ship in the port. The *Fortune* fired a broadside into the wooden houses along the harbour-side, but there was no reaction.

Roberts sent a message that all the captains were to come to the *Fortune*, and berated them that they had not defended their ships, nor welcomed him as a distinguished guest. It seems that the recent deaths in battle had affected Black Bart's state of mind. As an example, he tied Babidge to the mast and had him flogged. He told them that at the sound of his morning gun, they must come to the *Fortune* every morning, to help him oversee the looting of their ships, otherwise the boats would be burned. Roberts disabled every boat to stop any escapes, except for a two-masted, square-rigged *Bristol* 16-gun brig under Captain Coplestone. It was the ideal replacement for the *Fortune*. Batches of up to 50 pirates were allowed ashore at night to enjoy the local taverns and prostitutes, but Roberts stayed aboard, supervising the conversion of the brig to his liking. By late-June, Black Bart was ready to leave. He told the captains that he intended to sail to St Mary's, where he could commandeer a good ship belonging to a Mr Hall. As he prepared to depart, he reneged on his promise, and burned all the boats in the harbour.

The *Weekly Journal* reported the event as follows: '*A pyrate in a small sloop of 12 guns and 160 men entered Trepassy on Tuesday the 21st inst., and made himself master of the said harbour and of all the ships there, being 22 sails and 250 shallops. He made the masters all prisoners and beat some of them heartily for their cowardice for not making any resistance. The Admiral, one Babidge, in the Bideford Merchant, suffered most because he and all his hands left their ship with jack, ensign and pendant flying, his guns all loaden, in order to defend themselves but the pyrate was close alongside him, struck his colours, hoisted their own, and fired all his guns. They cut his masts and several others close by the deck. He cut all the other ships' cables in junks and their shrouds. He seized one Copleston's ship for himself, and set all the ship's carpenters to work to fit her for this purpose. They threatened to burn all the rest and to hang one of the masters at least for their incivility in not waiting upon him to make him welcome at his entrance. He destroyed about 30 sail, French and English, on the Banks.*'

Black Bart now repeated the act in St Mary's harbour, and a letter from the small port of Placentia near Trepassy stated: '*There are many ships drove in here by the pirates who infest our coast and in one of our next ports they have burnt and destroyed 26 ships and a great number of fishing craft. Those pirates have now destroyed near 150 boats and 26 ships at Trepassy and St Mary's which, if a communication had been cut overland (roads through the thick forests), it had not been a two-days march to have rescued these harbours where the pirates have been repairing their ships for 14 days past, nor could any vessel sail from hence to reprieve them if we had any ships of force.*' Even the

Governor of New England was moved to report of *'The Black Captain'*, *'one cannot withhold admiration for his bravery and cunning.'*

Roberts returned to Trepassey immediately. He also recruited some cod-splitters, who were only too happy to leave their terrible jobs. Many men joined Roberts' crew from his Newfoundland ravages. West Country fishing vessels brought over every year many poor labourers who were paid low wages, and who by contract had to pay for their voyage back to England. By day they fished, split and dried fish and warded off the bitter winter evenings by drinking *'black strap'* (a vicious combination of rum, molasses and chowder beer). The cost of the *'black strap'* meant that many could not afford their way back home, and were compelled to agree articles of servitude that kept them on the island over the winter. Their new masters now charged them exorbitant prices for food and clothing, so that they were *'bound'* to them for the next season's hard labour, and so on and so on. It is no wonder that these poor men readily joined the pirates or sometimes seized a small boat or shallop and traded *'on their own account'*.

A pirate was flogged by Anstis for trying to conceal a bolt of cloth for himself. Now Black Bart feared no-one. He came across a French flotilla of six sail near the Newfoundland Banks and captured them all. He chose the best of the French ships, a square-rigged brigantine and transferred all the guns from his new flagship to the new ship, which he called the *Good Fortune*. With 28 guns, it was a powerful ship, and he set his *Fortune* galley adrift. The next day he came across the *Fortune* again, and put his French prisoners on it. He said he would only *'force'* English sailors to go on the account with him. Although it did not handle as well as the *Fortune*, the *Good Fortune* was a powerful ship, in which they could enter action stations with far more confidence. More boats were taken, including another four French vessels, during which time Montigny la Palisse unexpectedly rejoined him, apologising for his actions off Barbados.

After the hard work in the Gulf of Guinea and the West Indies, taking ten ships, Bart had now taken another sixty merchant ships and one-hundred and fifty fishing vessels, in just a few weeks. Among the vessels recorded taken in June and July were the *Expectation* of Topsham, and a brigantine from Teignmouth. Joseph Nossiter joined from the *Expectation*. Among those captured and sunk in July were the brigantine *Thomas* of Bristol, the pink *Richard* of Bideford, the *Willing Mind* of Poole, the *Blessing* of Lymington, and the *Happy Return*. James Harris joined from the *Richard*. The boatswain Thomas Wills, who loved reading, also joined Roberts from the *Richard*. John Parker and Hugh Harris joined from the *Willing Mind* and Robert Crow from the *Happy Return*. John Walden of the *Blessing* joined, who would feature strongly in Black Bart's later career. A Dutch ship was taken after resistance off Cape Broyle, and its crew pleaded successfully to Roberts not to burn their ship.

MORE NEWFOUNDLAND PRIZES

On July 13th Captain Thomas Cary (Curry) on the sloop *Samuel* was bound for Boston from England. Seeing two ships approaching, he did not expect pirates this far north, and surrendered immediately upon the hoisting of the black flags, the musicians playing and the firing of warning shots. Roberts and la Palisse took over £10,000 worth of goods and threatened the passengers to make them tell where their valuables were hidden. Charles Johnson wrote in 1724: '*The Samuel was a rich ship, and had several Passengers on board who were used very roughly, in order to make them discover their Money, threatening them every Moment with Death, if they did not resign every Thing up to them. They tore up the Hatches and entered the Hold like a Parcel of Furies, and with Axes and Cutlashes, cut and broke open all the Bales, Cases and Boxes, they could lay their Hands on; and when any Goods came on Deck, that they did not like to carry aboard, instead of tossing them into the Hold again, threw them over-board into the Sea; all this was done with incessant Cursing and Swearing, more like Fiends than Men. They carried with them Sails, Guns, Powder, Cordage, and £8,000, or £9,000 worth of the choicest Goods; and told Captain Cary that they should accept no Act of Grace; that the King and Parliament might be damned with their Acts of Grace for them; neither would they go to Hope Point (London) to be hanged a-sun-drying as Kidd's and Bradish's crews were, but if we are captured we will set fire to the powder with a pistol, and all go merrily to Hell together.*' 'The Boston News Letter' also commented that the pirates behaved '*like a parcel of furies, breaking open every bale and packing-case aboard the Samuel in search for plunder.*' The pirates took their time, fearing no-one, to ensure that they properly stripped the ship. Captain Cary noted that they took 48 hours to despoil the *Samuel*.

His men took two heavy cannon, sails, powder, rope, and forty barrels of gunpowder, before a bejewelled, crimson-frocked Roberts stepped aboard the *Samuel*, asking for men to join him. Since taking up a pirating career, the *Black Captain* had totally transformed from a dour ship's mate to a dandy. Several joined Roberts, including Hugh Menzies, pleading to

Newfoundland Fish-splitters

Captain Cary would he would state that they had been *'forced'*. Anstis found the *Samuel's* mate, Harry Glasby, hiding in the hold, and he was thrown into the sea, and then made to join Roberts' crew for his deception. This was extremely rare for Roberts, who had boasted that, like Howell Davis, he never took a man against his will. He must have been in dire need of another experienced sailing-master to take the weight off his shoulders. Roberts would only allow experienced seamen to join his ships. One of the House of Lords commented to Captain Cary at this time that *'if we are captured, we will set fire to the powder with a pistol, and all go merrily to Hell together.'*

Bart was discussing whether to burn the ship on July 15th, when a new sail was spotted on the horizon, and the *Samuel* was left with Captain Cary, while the *Sea King* and *Good Fortune* gave chase to take a merchant snow from Bristol under Captain Bowles. On July 16th, the *Little York*, out of Virginia was taken, on the same day as the Bristol sloop *Sidbury*. From the *Sidbury*, two men named William Williams, Roger Scott and a William Fernow gladly joined Roberts' crew. The day after, the Bristol snow *Phoenix* was taken, making six merchantmen in five days. Richard Harries and David Littlejohn joined from the *Phoenix*. Roberts now had a crew of *'sea-artists'*, skilled seamen who left miserable lives to join a successful ship. All were *'forced'*, but this was a voluntary farce as some sort of defence in the event of their capture. On July 18th, Roberts took Captain James Phillips' *Little York*, out of Bristol, off Virginia when William Taylor, Thomas Owen and James Greenham joined. On the same day Captain Thomas's *Love* of Lancaster was also captured off Virginia, when John Jaynson joined. Thus Roberts had taken 8 ships in 7 days. Also in July he took a ship of 26 guns and its consort sloop, with 200 men on both ships, back on the Newfoundland Banks

In October, *Appleby's Original Weekly Journal* reported that '*two light men-of-war are ordered for Newfoundland in quest of Roberts and other pirates who continue to commit great depredations on our merchant ships that way.*' It was too late for the *Rose* and the *Shark*, which sailed from the West Indies up to Newfoundland to eradicate '*the pyrates that infest there.*' '*That Great Pyrate*' had disappeared.

BACK TO THE CARIBBEAN

Black Bart was now famed from Britain to America, from the West Indies to the coast of Africa. He had sensed that it was time to move. It was thought that he had gone to Africa or Madagascar, or had been lost at sea. The Governor of New England had noted that '*one cannot with-hold admiration for his bravery and courage*', while the Governor of Virginia fulminated against him. The Royal Africa Company and the Admiralty changed their policies towards piracy, under pressure from London merchants. *The American colonies started to wonder if they were better off as an independent country instead of paying taxes for a non-existent defence.* The Royal Navy made the case that it needed more investment from the Government to help trade and retain the colonies. Forces were gathering that would spell the end of the '*Golden Age of Piracy*'.

In fact, Roberts had unfinished business with the governors of Martinique and Barbados. Booty had dried up as transatlantic shipping almost halted, as did shipping along the North American coast. With the winter approaching, his men wanted to return to the sunny climes of the Caribbean, now that the hurricane season had ended there, where there were hundreds of hidden bays to drink and while away their hours. Harry Glasby (Gillespie) was appointed sailing-master, and had invaluable knowledge of these coastal waters. He also altered the rigging of the *Good Fortune* to make it almost as fast and manoeuvrable as la Palisse's sloop. The dour Northerner Glasby, bemoaning his lot, was curt with Roberts and Anstis, but friendly with the coarse Londoner Lord Valentine Ashplant. One day a pirate hit Glasby to the deck, being tired of his stubborn, unfriendly attitude. Ashplant leaped on the offender and half-strangled him before being pulled off. After that day, no-one harmed Harry Glasby.

Roberts now had Anstis to run the ship and Glasby to sail it. He dressed up in his lace and crimson finery and freshly powdered wigs every day, rested in his Great Cabin, or walked the quarter-deck, incessantly drinking tea. He had taken over 100 ships, the most successful pirate in history, and he promised his drink-sodden crew a thousand captures. It is difficult to know what forces drove Roberts - he was still a teetotaller, an outsider who did not consort with tavern harlots, a thoughtful, brooding tall man who had the crew's respect as being 'pistol-proof'. Roberts was in no hurry to reach the West Indies. In August, Captain Wallace Fensilon's sloop was taken off South Carolina, with supplies of fresh water and 8 hogsheads of rum. James Clements joined Roberts' crew, along with Fensilon's mate and carpenter. Before Fensilon reached Virigina, Captain Jack Rackham also boarded him and stripped the ship of its few remaining provisions.

Roberts made for the island of Deseada (Desirade, off Guadeloupe in the Lesser Antilles) to get fresh provisions, and to barter his booty ashore with smugglers. A hurricane hit them before they reached its shelter. The top-sails were furled hastily. In the storm La Palisse's *Sea King* vanished. A cannon broke loose on the *Good Fortune* and smashed into the gunwhales. Sailing the gale out, Roberts reached the tiny island to find it deserted. There were traces of camp fires and of boats being drawn up in the sand, but no smugglers. Roberts decided to make for Carriacou again to careen the *Good Fortune*. Incredibly, on the journey, la Palisse linked up with him again. On September 4th, the pirates sailed into the lagoon to find a merchant captain, Robert Dunn of the sloop *Relief*, catching turtles there. Friendly negotiations were held with the merchant captain, while the three crews feasted on turtle stew. Dunn later reported that the pirates had kept him prisoner for 3 weeks, supplying fresh turtles to them, and that their ships had 28 and 6 guns. Valentine Ashplant concocted his favourite variation of rumfustian for a party. He mixed eggs, beer, sherry and gin, added brown sugar, cinnamon and nutmeg and heated the brew until it was ready to drink.

Over the days, Dunn's sloop was loaded with goods that the pirates wished to sell, which he would take to sell at Basseterre on St Christopher (St Kitts). The *Good Fortune* was careened and repaired, and Roberts agreed to meet Dunn off St Kitts on September 26th. The deal was that the pirates should take half of the revenue, otherwise they would burn the settlements on St Kitts. Black Bart renamed the *Good Fortune* as the *Royal Fortune*, and renamed the *Sea King* the new *Good Fortune*. While the pirates lazed and drank on the beach, three forced men tried to escape on the 17th, but were quickly caught on the 18th, on the small island. On September 19th the pirates took a French sloop carrying brandy and wine. On here was held the trial of the three deserters. After being flogged, two were pardoned by the Pirate Council, but the third was condemned to marooning as an example. Towards the end of September he was stripped naked and put ashore on a half-mile islet, with just a few trees for cover. Anstis threw him a flask of water, a musket, one lead ball and a small amount of powder so that he could shoot himself. It appears that this man was the luckless Richard Luntly, a carpenter captured by Howell Davis on the Guinea Coast. Now in Roberts' crew, he had been heard conspiring with other forced men to take the ship and sail her to the West Indies and freedom. Reported to Roberts and the quartermaster, '*immediately all hands were called up to know what they should do with us, some of them was for shooting us, others not, and so they consented to put us on a desert island.*' Rescued by an English ship, the unlucky Luntley was tried for consorting with the '*great Pyrate Roberts*' at an Admiralty Court in Scotland. He complained '*we were forced men, compelled by force of arms to do things that our conscience thought to be unlawful*', but he was condemned and hung at Leith on January 11th, 1721.

It appears that the luckless Captain Cane was again captured around this time, and rum and sugar taken from him. The *Royal Fortune* sailed on to reach the waters off St Kitts at dusk on September 25th. Roberts waited all day in Basseterre Roads upon the 26th, but suspected Dunn of betraying him when he saw the cannon in the forts covering Basseterre harbour being moved. Fort Smith, overlooking one side of Basseterre, had better fortifications and firepower than another fort at Bluff Point, on the other side of the harbour, so Black Bart decided to attack on the Bluff Point side. Militiamen were despatched to all four forts on the island by its governor, Lieutenant-General Christopher William Mathew, who was suspicious of the strange ship lying outside the harbour. While Mathew was preparing the defences, Roberts hoisted his new pennant with the Barbadian and Martinique skulls, and early in the morning sailed swiftly into the harbour. All the ships anchored in the Road immediately struck their flags at the sound of Roberts' musicians and the sight of his ships. A ship's boat rowed towards them, and asked what they wanted. The two *sea-artists* upon it, the Mary and Martha's mate Bridstock Weaver, and its boatswain George Smith, were swiftly made to sign Roberts' Articles, as five ships were quickly looted. In the harbour, one ship under Captain Fowles was grappled as she briefly fought back.

Captain Wilcox of the *Mary and Martha* argued with the boarding party, and for his impertinence, his ship was burnt. Captain Cox's *Greyhound* was also burnt, because Owen Rogers had a hatred for ships from the port where he had been press-ganged. The *Greyhound's* Welsh mate, James Skyrme, became an important member of Black Bart's crew, and willingly signed articles for *Barti Ddu*. Another of the five ships, Monsieur Pomier's French sloop, was towed out to sea, as Roberts considered using it for his own purposes. Roberts wanted to take Captain Hingstone's new ship, as it had a steering-wheel instead of the traditional whipstaff, but Hingstone had taken the wheel ashore with him. Captain Henry Fowles of the fifth vessel discovered that Roberts needed fresh meat, and offered to send a letter asking for sheep and goats to be brought to the harbour-side. The letter was dated September 27th, 1720. Fowles informed Roberts that Dunn had not been treacherous. He had been caught unloading his smuggled goods two days before, and was threatened with hanging. He told the governor that if he was hung, the island would be attacked. Thus Mathew began his preparations at about the same time as the pirates hove into view. Roberts was now in control of the town, and wanted to provision his ship for a quick getaway, before he allowed his men ashore to get roaring drunk. As evening approached, he moved *the Royal Fortune*, the *Good Fortune* and Pomier's and Hingstone's ships out to sea, out of the range of the forts' gunnery.

Carcasses were shipped to the pirates, but Hingstone refused to send his precious steering wheel, so his ship was set alight. Some of Hingstone's seamen were sent with messages from Roberts. One was to the Governor of nearby Nevis, stating that Roberts intended to visit him next and burn the settlement, because he had hanged some men from the *Royal Rover* some months before. The other letter was for Governor Mathew of the Leeward Islands. Captain Hingston gave this letter from Roberts to Lieutenant-Governor Mathew, which reads:

Royal Fortune, September 27th, 1720

'This comes expressly from me to let you know that had you come off as you ought to a done and drank a glass of wine with me and my company I should

not harmed the least vessel in your harbour. Farther it is not your guns you fired that affrighted me or hindered our coming on shore but the wind not proving to our expectation that hindered it. The Royal Rover you have already burnt and used barbarously some of our men, but we now have a ship as good as her, and for revenge you may assure yourselves here and hereafter not to expect anything from our hands but what belongs to a pirate. As farther, Gentlemen, that poor fellow you have in prison at Sandy Point is entirely ignorant and what he hath was gave him and so prey make conscience for once let me beg you and use that man as an honest man and not as a C. (Criminal) If we hear any otherwise you may expect not to have any quarters to any of your island.

Yours,

(signed) *Bartholomew Roberts'*

It seems that the *'criminal'* referred to was one of his old crew from the *Rover*, left behind by Kennedy.

Mathew had worked through the night bringing 13 new cannon in from the other forts and repositioning them to defend the bay much better. The next morning the *Royal Fortune* re-entered Basseterre to take back Captain Fowles and two of his men, but were hit by seven cannon balls from the fort. His 13 guns, including the 24-pounder, fired two rounds before Roberts escaped, his sails ripped. He gave Wilcox Pomier's sloop, left Fowles' boat at anchor and headed towards Nevis for his next assignment, knowing that Basseterre was now a lost cause. However, prevailing winds forced him to change his mind. The crew needed money, after Captain Dunn's unfortunate capture, and Roberts decided to fix up the *Royal Fortune* and reprovision at St Bartholomew's, the 8-mile square French possession of St Barthelemy. Its governor has precious few resources, and little fresh water, and the rocky scrub yielded little food. He therefore was known to be susceptible to giving leniency to pirates, in return for trade. The grateful inhabitants of the island took all the treasure from Newfoundland to St Christopher's, into a warehouse, and the pirates gave them generous terms. The governor was presented with a gold chain worth more than a year's salary by Roberts. The pirates accepted not just coin, but payment in kind at the two small taverns and with the women of the island. For three weeks the pirates roistered happily ashore, but Bart kept a heavily-armed night-watch on each of his ships, to prevent desertion by the forced men, or a *soft farewell* by some disaffected pirates.

Roberts next took his ships to Tortola in the Virgin Islands, and took a 22-gun brig there. He converted it to the new *Royal Fortune*, and gave the furious captain his rotting hulk in exchange. On October 25th the new *Royal Fortune* was at St Lucia, near Martinique, and looted an English brig lying there. He also took Monsieur Courtel's sloop to act as a storeship, and prevent the *Royal Fortune* and *Good Fortune* being weighed down when chasing merchantmen. In total, fourteen English and French ships were taken between October 23 and 26, 1720. A hundred miles north of St Lucia, Roberts' small fleet came across a Dutch ship. The Dutch interloper had 30 guns and 90 men and lay in harbour of St Lucia. Suddenly there was cacophony of noise and banging as the 32-gun *Royal Fortune* and 18-gun *Sea King* sailed into the harbour under the black flag.

However, the Dutchman, faced with 350 pirates, still did not strike its colours, and prevented grappling by using booms and fenders. There followed a 4-hour gun battle – with many lost on both sides, but the beleaguered Dutch ship had no room to manoeuvre. Roberts knew that the larger 'interloper' would definitely resist vigorously even against 350 pirates, and carried on a broadside battle, while Courtel's storeship/sloop and the *Good Fortune* tried to attack its poorly defended stern. (Dutch 'interlopers' were forbidden to trade with the British, under the Navigation Acts, but were known to carry large amounts of gold and coin). After a horrendous, bloody encounter, the Dutchman was boarded, and her crew all killed. La Palisse went on to loot 15 vessels in the nearby harbour, and Roberts' bloodthirsty crews went on an orgy of vengeance for their recent losses, slaughtering every Dutchman they found aboard the ships.

The great Dutch ship was taken by Black Bart to be his new flagship, again called the *Royal Fortune*. A deserter from the Royal Navy's *Rose*, John Mansfield, volunteered to join Roberts, but proved to be a terrible drunk. Roberts' fleet now comprised the 48-gun *Royal Fortune*, the large Tortola brig, the St Lucia sloop and la Palisse's *Good Fortune*. He was at the zenith of his powers. The *Royal Fortune* held 180 hardened pirates and *sea-artists*. It had seven 2-pound and 3-pound guns in its bows; four 4-pound minions on each side; six falconers on each side, each firing 6 pounds of shot, twelve half-ton demi-culverins, each firing 8-pound cannon balls, and four massive 12-pound cannon - 44 guns in total, with a vast assortment of types of shot with different uses from disembowelling men to bringing down rigging. The French Leeward Isles Governor reported that in 4 days at the end of October 1720, Black Bart had '*seized, burned or sunk 15 French and English vessels and one Dutch interloper of 42 guns at Dominica'.*

The *Mary and Martha* of St Christophers was now taken again, under a different captain, Wilson in December 1720, when George Smith of Wales joined the pirate crew. Martinique's governor had heard of Roberts' new pennant featuring his head, and wrote anxiously several times to the Governor of Nevis, asking that Captain Whitney's *Rose* be sent to protect them. The London Journal reported in January 1721, *'we are in expectations of hearing of a bloody action with the pyrates in the West Indies, three of His Majesty's ships well-manned being gone from Barbadoes in quest of them upon information of the place of their rendezvous.* Roberts was again becoming nervous - he sensed that forces were moving against him. In Dominica he had let it be known that his next target was St Eustatia, and stayed near, but out of sight of Dominica, wondering where to go. Back north was unattractive - the weather was bad. Africa beckoned once again, from where he could explore the Red Sea and the Indian Oceans. Preparing for Council, the ships sheltered in a hidden Dominica Bay. After a couple of days, Harry Glasby and two other men tried to escape but were hunted down as they climbed the hills to reach the townships on the other side of the island.

The jury was all for hanging, shooting or marooning them for desertion until Lord Valentine Ashplant stood up and stated *'By God, Glasby shall not die, damn me if he shall'*. He sat down and smoked his pipe, ignoring his fellow *'Lords'* on the jury. The other pirates had unanimously agreed, and shouted that they must die, whereupon Ashplant again removed his pipe to stand up, and argued *'God damn ye gentlemen, I am as good as the best of you, damn my soul if I ever turned my back to any man in my life, or ever will, by God; Glasby is an honest fellow notwithstanding this misfortune, and I love him, Devil damn me, if I don't. I hope he'll live and repent of what he has done; but damn me, if he must die, I'll die alongside with him.'* He then pulled out his brace of pistols and pointed them at the judges, who agreed that Glasby should be acquitted. The other two unfortunates were tied to the mast and shot dead, however, not having as effective a defence counsel to support them. Glasby was never to be allowed ashore again. Ashplant seems to have been listened to, as he was the chief brewer or distiller on ship - he had a genius for making something alcoholic and potable out of anything that was available, and thus a man of some importance.

In mid-November, Roberts sailed north towards the Bermudas, to pick up the currents and winds for Sierra Leone and Africa. Again, he was one step ahead of his pursuers. The brig was leaking, and with the sloop was left to drift away. *Appleby's Original Weekly Journal* commented in March 1721 '*A pirate of 40 guns and 2 smaller ships caused havoc on the coast of Carthagena and St Martha (in the West Indies). They have taken several rich French ships from Petit-Guaves and 2 Dutch and about 5 English ships and sloops. But we hear since that the pirates have left for Cuba and design to go from there to Martinique. They take any nation's ships. What exploits our men-of-war have done against them we hear but little.*'

Near the Bermudas, the pirates bore down upon Captain Thomas Bennett's *Thomas Emanuel*, which immediately surrendered. After looting, it was towed as a storeship, but its captain reported that its lightened weight put it in danger of sinking, in heavy and worsening seas. A boat was sent to rescue Bennett and his men, and the towrope was cut. Heading towards Africa, Roberts was going to land and reprovision on the Cape Verde Islands, when he saw two merchantmen off the coast and headed to intercept them. However, they were escorted by two Portuguese men-of-war, one with 40 guns and the other 80. La Palisse veered off again, repeating his previous cowardly departure, while Roberts attacked, remembering the glory of Bahia. The Portuguese naval ships piled on full sail and fled. Roberts chased the merchantmen but found that he was being pushed by the winds away from the islands and their precious water supply. Desperately he and Jones calculated that they could just reach the most southerly island, Brava. However, constantly adverse great winds meant that they missed it. Gillespie (Glasby) now tried to bring the *Royal Fortune* around again, and failed, leaving them heading back towards the Americas. The contrary winds meant that they could no longer find a safe nearby landfall, so there was no choice but to return to the Caribbean and wait for more favourable winds to take them again to Africa. Roberts calculated their quickest landfall to be Surinam, 700 leagues (2100 miles) away, using the favourable north-easterly Trade Winds. They had one hogshead (63 gallons) of water, rationed to one cupful a day for the 124 men. After a few days the ration was a mouthful a day. Men drank their own urine over and over until it was almost black. They wetted their lips with sea-water so that they could open their mouths to speak. Those that ate too much died horrible deaths. The wiser and older pirates, the *Lords*, rationed themselves to one mouthful of bread a day, and just rested in whatever shade they could find. Those who drank sea-water died in agony. Sails were rigged to catch and trap sea-mists at night as precious water. Fever and dysentery racked the ships. Water rations dropped to a swallow a day.

Anstis guarded the near empty water barrel, while the men died agonising deaths.

At last la Palisse and Roberts reached the mouth of the River Maroni in Surinam, a remarkable navigational feat for men who were close to death. They had no water at all for the last two days of sailing. They headed north. In December 1720, they landed on Tobago to reprovision. With the latest acquisition, Roberts felt strong enough to try and capture his hated enemy, the governor of Martinique, who had tried to capture him in Carriacou. Despite the pull of 'hiraeth', he could never return to Pembrokeshire - he was now too famous. (Hiraeth is a Welsh word, difficult to describe, which is the longing for home felt by Welshmen outside their country. Many expatriates return to Wales, thus there are not the huge colonies of Irish and Scots in former English colonies. There are 40,000,000 people in the USA who declare Irish ancestry, against 2,000,000 Welsh. The Welsh are the salmon of the world). A pardon may be extended to other, lesser, pirates, but not to Roberts. The English, French, Spanish and Dutch - the day's great international powers - all wanted his blood. The Americas offered no outlet. As he drank his tea, he knew that his position was only as secure as the next successful capture. After filling up with loot, the pirates then wanted to spend it in an orgy of onshore drunkenness and whoring. Then it was off to sea again, avoiding men-of-war and increasing anti-pirate activity, looking for increasingly heavily-armed merchantmen, and the cycle repeated itself. He was forever trapped as a pirate. Roberts seemed to celebrate his safe arrival back in the New World by going on a terrific rampage. His original plan to try to make for Africa was forgotten. He wanted to go out in a blaze of glory.

CHAPTER V

1721 - BACK TO AFRICA

In early January, Bart sailed quickly (and presciently) to avoid Barbados and headed for Pigeon Island, just a mile off St Lucia, and on the 13th he found a sloop and a brig anchored in a small bay. Captain Benjamin Norton's Rhode Island brig, the *Sea King*, was stripped of its guns, and used to replace la Palisse's clapped-out sloop. Captain Richard Simes' Barbados sloop, the *Fisher*, was chased, ran aground and unfortunately caught fire. Captain Norton offered, like Captain Dunn, to trade some of their plunder at Rhode Island. The old *Good Fortune* was burnt, and the *Royal Fortune* and new *Good Fortune* for the next two weeks took some more trading ships off St Lucia, forcing some more men to join them to replace those they had lost on the dreadful Atlantic crossing. He took a much-needed surgeon off one boat, possibly from Captain John Rogers' sloop the *Saint Anthony*. He allowed Captain Simes and some prisoners to sail off on one captured sloop, along with Captain Bennett, who was lucky to have survived the crossing from Cape Verde to Surinam.

While there, two sloops, one under Captain Porter, and the *Adventure* under Captain Tuckerman came onto the island. According to Defoe, they greeted the great Pirate Roberts with the following message: '*We have heard of your fame and achievements, and we have put in to learn your art and wisdom in the business of pirating, since we are of the same honourable design as yourself. We hope, that with the communication of your knowledge, we shall also receive your charity as we are in want of necessities for such adventures.*' Not averse to such flattery, Barti gave them powder, guns and provisions, and swapped eighteen of his captured negroes for four white pirates, including the Welshman John Coleman who wanted to join his crew. Off Dominica, a Dutch interloper was taken after a brief fight. *El Puerto del Principe* from Flushing was now towed behind Roberts' ship while it was decided what to do with her.

The fleet of two great brigantines (the *Royal Fortune* and *El Puerto del Principe*), another brig (the *Good Fortune*) and two small pirate sloops, now sailed towards Guadeloupe, and approached Basseterre with no colours flying. The *Royal Fortune* hoisted French colours, sailed into the harbour and fired across a French flyboat which was anchored out of reach of the fort's guns. As its crew fled in boats, a tow-line was attached, and the prize was taken out to the open seas. Roberts now took his crews for *'rest and recreation'* in Hispaniola, and *'boot-topped'* the *Royal Fortune* and the *Good Fortune*, one after the other. He seems to have suspected that the seas were too quiet for comfort. While Captain Whitney, in the *Rose* was not particularly interested in battling with pirates, more in lucrative dealing with them, Captain Durrel in the *Seahorse* was a far different *'kettle of fish'*. At Boston the Council had suggested that he went down to protect the West Indian colonies, and he had just missed Roberts off Barbados in early-January. Roberts had seemed to have sensed there was a problem at this time, and had piled on sail to keep away from the Barbadian shipping lanes. Durrell could not reach Roberts off Martinique because of prevailing winds, and while he waited at Barbados, he sent for 90 more men and more munitions from Massachusetts. While waiting, Durrell had press-ganged 86 Barbadians by early February. At this time, the Admiralty had sent the *Swallow* and *Weymouth* to Africa to protect the slave-trade from piracy.

While Durrell was frustrated in his attempts to reach Martinique, Black Bart moved his fleet to careen properly on Mona, just off Puerto Rico, but sea conditions meant that he landed a hundred miles away, at Bennet's Cay, in Bahia de Samana, Eastern Hispaniola. Porter and Tuckerman left for Jamaica, where they were thought of as honest merchantmen. For a week the pirates lazed, sang, gambled and drank Valentine's Ashplant's potent *'rumbullion'*, while the brigs were careened properly, finishing off the earlier *'boot-topping'*. Dan Harding joined from the *El Puerto del Principe*. The pirates revelled the nights away. Although Roberts did not drink, and hated his crew drinking at sea, he did not mind them carousing in secret places such as Bennet's Cay. While the mayhem was going on, Harry Glasby and nine other forced men tried to escape, but became lost in the dense forests. They returned after three days, professing that they had got lost chasing pigs. Luckily they were believed, and lived to tell the tale. Roberts now trusted Captain Norton a little more, and asked him to examine the cargo of the *El Puerto del Principe* with him, with the intention of fencing it in Rhode Island. Porter and Tuckerman rejoined Roberts. Their *'front'* as merchantmen in Port Royal, Jamaica, was crumbling. Local people had discovered that Porter and his brother had been in New Providence to accept Woodes Rogers' Pardon to all pirates, and Tuckerman had been previously imprisoned for assisting in the escape of the pirate Stede Bonnet. (Bonnet was an unusual man, a gentleman estate-owner who had turned to piracy as an optional career to escape his nagging wife). Tuckerman was later taken to London on piracy charges, but his fate is unknown.

Norton was given the *El Puerto del Principe* and a skeleton crew of his own trusted men who would not talk to the authorities, to sail to Rhode Island, full of '*normal*' trading goods like food, cocoa, ironmongery, cloth and flour which were not needed by the pirates. All '*incriminating*' goods such as gold and jewellery were left with Roberts. An agreement was made that they would return with cash for Roberts in 6 weeks, meeting off South Carolina, where Roberts would refill the brig's hold with more captured goods. It seems that Roberts now had a trusted, and far less risky, channel of distribution for his gains. Captain Norton now sailed his great ship to Tarpaulin Cove, New England, but his protestations that Black Bart had '*given*' him the ship were unfortunately not believed.

In February Roberts took the sloop *Mayflower*, and Joseph Moore joined his crew, and soon after Black Bart took a ship off Guadeloupe, with 600 hogsheads of sugar, and set fire to her. On February 18th, Roberts moved in on the harbour of St Lucia yet again, seeing another large Dutch interloper, with 75 men and 22 guns, lying in the roads. The settlement's inhabitants witnessed a fierce battle which lasted for hours, with the Dutchman putting out fenders and booms to prevent the *Royal Fortune* boarding. Gunner Dennis fired a close broadside, and the *Good Fortune* attacked its stern with swivel guns, ensuring that the decks were clear of crewmen to defend against the inevitable boarding party. Resistance was futile, and Anstis, wearing a bright yellow bandana, was seen to be attaching tow-ropes to the ship. The few survivors were killed, and the capture was repaired by Roberts' carpenters. Anstis, Richard Jones and the seasoned members of the *House of Lords* now took over the ship, while the *Royal Fortune* and *Good Fortune* were sent southwards for a later rendezvous. Roberts had a debt to repay in Martinique.

Roberts cheekily took the 22-gun Dutch interloper as a decoy, under Dutch colours, alongside the harbours of Martinique. He slowly sailed past Vauclin, Sainte Marie, Morrain and St Pierre, Schoelcher and the Fort de France. This was a sign for the islanders that there were cheap Guinea slaves available from this unlicensed trader, a chance to make some quick profits. Bart then went to St Luce, an isolated bay in the south of Martinique, where the Martinican vessels always came to make their illicit trades. Sloops were fitted out to go and fetch the slaves, and one by one they approached Roberts' ship over a few days. 14 boats, laden with gold and coin for barter were captured in this way, and were also filled with tradable goods. Roberts threw each captain and crew into the hold. These islanders were now badly abused by Roberts' crew, some being suspended from the yard-arms for target practice. His feelings towards Martinique had festered, and Roberts did not attempt to stop the cruelty. Every sailor was whipped or killed. Thirteen of the sloops were burned, and the remaining captives put on the fourteenth sloop, and told to tell the governor that Roberts 'hoped we should always meet with such a Dutch trade as this was'.

Around this time Christian Tranquebar was on a Danish ship attacked by Roberts in two vessels, and reported that Roberts' ship was manned by 180 white men and 48 French Creole blacks, and that his consort brig was crewed by 100 white men and 40 French blacks. On the *Royal Fortune*, Roberts had mounted 42 cannon, from 4-pounders to 12-pounders, plus another 7 guns. The Governor of Martinique now implored Governor Hamilton of Antigua for aid. Hamilton thus wrote to the Lords Commissioners for Trade and Plantations that 'The Great Pyrate Roberts' was wreaking havoc around the islands, and that the French Governor-General in the Caribbean wished to act jointly to dispel the pirates. The HMS *Rose* was in the area under Captain Witney, after moving down from guarding the New England coast, but showed little interest in facing up to the *Royal Fortune* and *Good Fortune*. Witney wrote to Hamilton saying that that Roberts was off Deseada and that he was waiting for the snow *Shark* to join him before attacking the *Great Pirate* Roberts. Hamilton responded requiring Witney to protect the islands, but Captain Witney sailed away from any possible point of contact with Roberts. Witney's men were probably in a state of near-mutiny, like most naval ships of this time, and he was almost certainly engaged in illicit trades to pay them. Naval crews, because of shortage of funds, were often paid in credit notes, which were worth less than half their value when eventually exchanged for cash. The majority of the men were pressed into service, half-starved, beaten, living in filthy cramped conditions, over-worked, disease-ridden, and not allowed to ever leave the ship for fear of desertion. Some of the more 'enlightened' captains ferried a boatload of prostitutes to the ship when it arrived at port, to alleviate the boredom. Most naval and merchant captains hated and brutalised their crews. When a ship was taken, its crew were always asked about their treatment by its officers. A tyrannical captain was usually killed by the pirates in their empathy for their former lives.

Black Bart and his crews now spent a month on St Barthelemy, during which time he took Captain Andrew Kingston's galley *Lloyd*, with 12 guns and 18 men off Antigua on March 26th. Poor Kingston was then taken again on March 27th by a rare Spanish pirate ship, and marooned when they found his boat had already been ransacked. Fortunately he and his men were seen by a passing trader and taken to St Christopher's, where the reluctant Captain Whitney was persuaded to take the *Rose* out to look for Roberts. Captain Kingston recounted his travails in a letter sent on April 24th from St Christopher's (St Kitts) to his London employers: '*I am sorry to give you this account of my great misfortune with this voyage. On 26th of March I made the island of Desirade about 11 o'clock of noon and soon after saw two sail standing the same course as I did. I made the best of my way from them, but about 8 at night they came alongside me. I was then about 4 leagues (12 miles) off Antigua. They fired at me, being pyrates, one a ship of 36 guns and 250 men and 50 negroes; the other a brig of 18 guns, 46 men and 20 negroes; these I could not withstand. They had been but 2 days upon that station before they saw me, and are both under the command of Captain John Roberts. They carried me into Bermuda* (actually, it was Barbuda, just north of Antigua), *there kept me 5 days, and what of the cargo was not fit for their purpose, they threw overboard. They took away most of my rigging and sails, all my anchors, blocks, provisions, powder, small arms etc., and 12 of my men, and then carried me to the northward that I might not come into these islands to give an account of them; and the 1st of this instant (April 1st) they left me in latitude 30 degrees North in a very sad condition. I hope the ships bound from London to Jamaica after me may escape the said Roberts: for he designed to keep the station and destroy all ships that come to these islands which may fall into his hands. They left me without any manner of clothing; and Roberts brought my brother (the chief mate) to the gears and whipped him within an inch of his life by reason he had concealed 2 gold rings in his pocket. This is the dismal account I am to give of this voyage. A. Kingston*'

The pirates now left St Barthelemy to rendezvous with Norton off the Carolinas, chasing a ship into New Providence harbour on the way. However, a British man-of-war was stationed there, and three pirate longboats creeping up on the merchantmen were spotted, and the chased trader moved closer to the naval ship. The pirates returned to the *Royal Fortune*. At this point, a forced man, Joseph Slinger, jumped from the *Royal Fortune* as she started to move off, and swam for hours until he drifted ashore with the tide to safety. Roberts now stationed himself off Charleston, South Carolina, but Captain Norton did not appear with the expected returns from his trading. La Palisse, in frustration with waiting, returned to the West Indies in a captured sloop. Roberts was not sorry to see him go. Twice in battle he had vanished from the scene *'at a rate of knots'*. *Lord* Thomas Anstis was given the *Good Fortune* after la Palisse's defection, but he complained that it was difficult to sail, because it was carrying Norton's second cargo, ready for another round of trading..

Norton was not to come, and Roberts was fuming with waiting for someone he had trusted. Norton had left the laden *El Puerto del Principe* at Naushon in the Elizabeth Isles, then gone on to Rhode Island to let his trader friends know, so they could bring their empty sloops out to Naushon to do (illegal) business. The excitement was so great at the prospect of being able to *'fence'* the proceeds of the *Great Pyrate* for the foreseeable future, that too many people in the tiny colony became involved, and Governor Cranstone of Rhode Island soon found out the truth of the matter. The Royal Navy's Lieutenant Hamilton was sent to Tarpaulin Bay, to find Norton's friends loading up their sloops with cocoa, sugar and bolts of cloth. Norton would not allow Hamilton on his ship, and Hamilton returned to the Governor for fresh instructions. The traders sailed off to their separate landing places. Then the sheriff of Bristol County, Massachusetts appeared and impounded the *El Puerto del Principe* and another trader's sloop, and took them to Rhode Island. Benjamin Norton had managed to escape on the arrival of the sheriff.

The pirates became restless. La Palisse had left. Anstis did not like the *Good Fortune*. He had been a popular quartermaster on the *Royal Fortune*, but had been replaced by the pugnacious and disliked bully, David Sympson. The *Lords* had been increasingly annoyed by Roberts' growing autocratic manner - he listened to Council less and less, in line with his growing success as a pirate captain. The crews were bored. The food and drink were bad. They wanted to go ashore, or return to the warm climes of the West Indies. The money they had been reliant upon from Norton seemed to have disappeared. Tempers frayed with the waiting. Roberts responded to the growing tension by offering to fight a duel with anyone, with sword or pistol, *'for he neither valued or feared any of them.'*

At this time Roberts finally lost his temper badly, with a crewman who insulted him. The man had been helping load fresh water onto the *Royal Fortune*, but drunkenly mishandled a cask, which had fallen back into the longboat and hurt one of the landing-party. Roberts swore at the culprit, and he swore back and spat at Roberts. Incensed, Black Bart shot the drunk on the spot. The Welshman Thomas Jones, one of Howell Davis's original crew, was also bringing in water when it happened, and he cursed Roberts for killing his friend. As Roberts had fired his pistols, he ran Jones through with his sword, but Jones furiously lashed out with his knife, and as Bart ducked away, he fell over a gun-barrel. Thomas Jones fell on him and repeatedly thrashed Roberts over the gun barrel, before he could be dragged off. The crew was divided upon which action to take, but most sided with the honour of the captaincy, and the quartermaster Sympson decided that the punishment for Thomas Jones was to be two lashes from each member of the crew when his sword-wound healed.

Roberts' position was becoming precarious, and he needed success. On April 9th the *Jeremiah and Ann* was taken, and Robert Johnson and William Shurin joined Roberts. In his defence at his trial, Johnson was later to call witnesses to claim that he was so drunk that he had to be hoisted out of his own ship *'in tackles'* to join the pirates. In April 1721 Roberts took a French man-of-war of 32 guns and 9 swivel guns with 140 crew off the Leeward Islands. It seems that it had not been keeping an adequate watch, because it was taken very quickly by the *Royal Fortune* and *Good Fortune*. Roberts was extremely pleased with the prize, for it was carrying the Governor of Martinique. True to his word, Roberts had him promptly hanged from the yard-arm of the French ship. Walter Kennedy at his trial in 1721 stated that *'Roberts could have no peace of mind if only for murdering the French governor.'* Roberts kept the ship, and called it the *Sea King*, marooning its crew. He could now look for the head of the Governor of Barbados, and make his personal pennant a statement of fact, with both governors' skulls displayed on it. A few days later a Virginia merchantman was taken, and the *Royal Fortune, Good Fortune* and *Sea King* set course for Africa, as had been decided in the West Indies. Prevailing winds and currents made the passage from New England and Newfoundland to Africa or Europe easy.

By Spring 1721 there was little left to plunder in the Americas. The *Royal Fortune, Sea King* and *Good Fortune* were *'filled to the gunnels'* with gold and booty, and Roberts knew that there was trouble brewing for him along the coastlines of the Americas if he tried to trade his loot. The Governor of the Leeward Islands was lobbying for more men-of-war to be sent to protect shipping against Roberts. Governor Spotswood of Virginia had erected 54-gun batteries along his coast specifically to prevent Roberts attacking. He had discussed matters with the *House of Lords*, who had wanted to return south, but had his way and at the beginning of April set sail for Africa. He was not driven away - most merchant shipping would not approach the area, and prizes were becoming harder to take. His crew was getting restless. Roberts knew that his crews needed a fresh challenge, and knew that the Royal Navy was becoming more active in the West Indies and along the American colonies coastline, so he decided to make for Brava island in the Cape Verde Islands, and maraud the Guinea coast.

THE DESERTION OF ANSTIS

However, the aggrieved Thomas Jones went with some other pirates to the *Good Fortune*, captained by Thomas Anstis, one of Howell Davis' old *House of Lords*. Anstis was disaffected because Roberts was becoming prouder and less approachable, probably becoming mentally unstable with the problems of holding together a bunch of psychopathic alcoholics over three years. The brig *Good Fortune* was just being treated like a supply ship, and a tender for loot. On April 18th the disaffected Anstis, Jones and a hundred crewmen and forty French negroes stole away into the night, away from Roberts forever, with most of his bulkier loot.

The 180 men (and 48 Creole negroes) on the *Royal Fortune* were not overly worried, as their ship was fully provisioned and by far the better fighting ship. Roberts on April 17 in the mid-Atlantic had taken the Dutch *Prince Eugene* under Captain Bastian Meake, and then a small snow was also captured. In the mid-Atlantic in May the Dutch snow *Christopher*, captained by Nicholas Hendrich was seized. Off Cape Verde the galley *Norman* was then taken in May 1721, when Benjamin Jeffries and John Little joined Black Bart. One account is that poor Jeffries did not wish to go on the account, saying '*None who could get their bread in an honest way would be in such an account*', and for his impudence was whipped six times by each member of the crew. However, it was Roberts' proud claim that he never 'forced' anyone to join him. Gosse's account is as follows: '*Roberts allowed those of the crew who did not wish to join the pirates to return to the Norman, but Jefferys had made such friends on the pirate ship that he was too drunk to go, and also was abusive in his cups, telling his hosts that there was not one man amongst them. For this he received six lashes from every member of the crew, "which disordered him for some weeks." But Jefferys eventually proved himself a brisk and willing lad, and eventually was made bosun's mate.*' The Dutch *Royal Fortune* was left at Cape Verde because of leaks, and its guns and booty taken on the French *Sea King*, which became the new *Royal Fortune*.

Deciding to trade their booty for Guinea gold, Roberts moved on towards the Sierra Leone coast of Africa. He did not yet know that the men-of -war *Swallow* and *Weymouth* had escorted a fleet of East Africa Company ships to Africa and that both were off Sierra Leone. However, as they cruised east 700 miles from Cape Three Points to the island of Principe, Black Bart had moved to Sierra Leone, 800 miles north-west of Cape Three Points. His luck had held out. In June, 1721, two French ships guarded the gum trade at Senegal. One had 10 guns and 65 men, and the *St Agnes* had 16 guns and 75 men. They chased Roberts, thinking he was a Dutch interloper, an unlicensed trader. As soon as Roberts raised his Black Flag, and ran out his 40 cannon, they surrendered. The *Comte de Toulouse* was renamed the *Ranger*, and the smaller ship *St Agnes* named the *Little Ranger* and used as a storeship. There was now a pirate council for officers of the new prizes. *Lord* David Sympson was dismissed as quartermaster because the pirates thought him too much of a bully. On the *Royal Fortune*, under Black Bart were 'Lord' William Magnes as quartermaster, the Welshman James Philips was boatswain, 'Lord' Henry Dennis (as always) was gunner, and the forced Harry Glasby (Gillespie) was nominated and elected as sailing-master. Thomas Sutton became captain of the *Ranger* for a short time before he was deposed by a vote, with William Main as boatswain. The Welshman James Skyrme was then elected captain of the *Little Ranger*. Black Bart, as overall commander of the flotilla, reminded his crews that they had no surgeon, and one was desperately needed.

Roberts had sailed into the mouth of the Senegal River on June 12th - the *Swallow* had left just six weeks previously, and the government agent Plunkett could do nothing from his rebuilt Brent (Bence) island fort. Black Bart's crew was welcomed with a celebratory fusillade from the brass cannon of *Old Crackers*, the private trader in anticipation of doing some lucrative business. On that June day in 1721, Roberts took a merchant ship in Frenchman's Bay. He anchored in a long narrow inlet near the Cape, which is now known as Pirates' Bay and then careened the fleet of the *Royal Fortune* and the three new prizes. The Sierra Leone river has a large mouth with small hidden bays on either side, excellent for cleaning and watering vessels. Many outward-bound ships also used the mouth of the river for taking on water, so there were plenty of ships to be taken in the area. Local traders bartered with the pirates, the local tribes were friendly and some of Howell Davis' old crew from 1719 knew the best places for local women. 'Old Crackers' (John Leadstone), a former pirate, had been a friend of Davis, and not only traded but ran the best brothel in the area. There were thirty traders on the mainland, and in Rio Pungo Benjamin Gunn lived a hermit-like existence (he was later

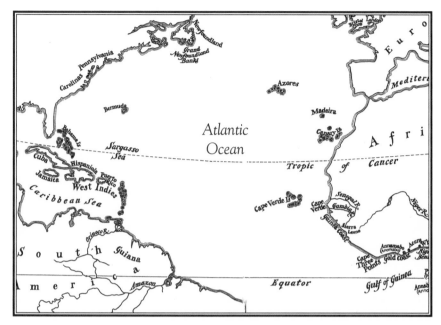

The Pirate Seas

to become famous as the character Benn Gunn in Treasure Island). These ruffians exchanged slaves, dye-woods and *elephants' teeth* (ivory) for alcohol, guns and the like. Over the next two months, Roberts did lucrative business with local traders.

The Royal Africa Company had a very weakly defended fort on Brent Island, so it seems the coast was made for Black Bart's company. Roberts was now told that the Royal Africa Company had asked for men-of-war to come to the area, after the depredations of Captains Davis, England, Cocklyn and La Bouche. The two third-raters, the *Swallow* under Captain Challoner Ogle and the *Weymouth* under Captain Mungo Herdman had left the area in April and were not expected back until Christmas, so Roberts felt doubly safe – friendly natives, plenty of places for his men to expend their energy and money, and no Royal Navy vessels for at least six months.

There was a rumour that Bart buried his personal treasure from the Caribbean on the Isles of Idols off Sierra Leone, known as Los Islands at this time. In July, Roberts sent a boat to the fort on Brent Island asking for gold dust, powder and ball-shot. Governor Plunkett informed the pirates that he had no gold, but plenty of powder and ball if Roberts would come for it. (The same story occurred when Howell Davis met Plunkett). Plunkett had been captured by Howell Davis and some of the *House of Lords* two years previously. Roberts took three ships and bombarded the fort for a few hours. When the fort ran out of ammunition to return the cannonade, Plunkett rowed to hide on the nearby small island of Tombo, but was soon captured and brought before Roberts at the fort. With his natural hatred for the Irish after the Kennedy desertion, Black Bart berated the old man harshly for having foolishly resisted. Plunkett, an old Africa hand, exploded with such a tirade of oaths and curses that the House of Lords roared with appreciative laughter. Most of the watching pirates were doubled up in laughter, seeing their feared captain being outsworn by the fearless Governor. Even Roberts eventually saw the funny side of things, and after exhausting his vocabulary allowed Plunkett to have his fort back, after the warehouses had been ransacked. (Plunkett had previously been under attack by Howell Davis in Gambia in 1719, and this same story is related with regard to Thomas Cocklyn and Plunkett). Plunkett had nowhere to go. All boats were guarded, and some slave ships burnt.

Two men joined Roberts' company from the fort. William Watts was one, employed by Captain Glynn, a trader who was a former pirate and knew Cocklyn, La Bouche and especially Howell Davis. Roberts spent several days in the company of his fellow-Welshman Glynn, recounting their anecdotes of Howell Davis. The other man taken aboard is notable in that he was too much of a drunken thug for even Robert's crew of reprobates. William Davies had beaten up the second mate on the galley *Ann* at Sierra Leone, in a drunken rage, and deserted to join the negroes in the shanty town. They gave him a wife, who he immediately sold in order to buy punch. After spending his money he sought protection from Governor Plunkett, but his wife's relatives soon came for compensation. Plunkett surrendered Davies to them, stating that they could cut his head off as far as he was concerned. Plunkett was obviously a wise judge of character. The negroes then sold him to Senor Joseph, a negro trader and landowner, who indentured him for two years. Soon after joining Roberts' ship, the *House of Lords* and *House of Commons* decided unanimously to get rid of Davies. However, it appears that he managed to hang on in service, as he was later tried and hung at Cape Corso Castle. William Williams tried to escape with two other forced men into the jungle, but was recaptured and whipped. The other two men probably died in the jungle, killed by natives or wild animals.

During June and July, the pirates drank, caroused, gambled and fornicated while their musicians played. The musicians looked forward to Sunday, the day that Roberts had decreed was free of music. Otherwise, they were at the inebriated pirates' beck and call at any hour of the night or day. Any ship that came into port was taken, so that the news of their whereabouts could not reach the *Swallow* or *Weymouth*. Sensing that the Royal Navy might visit, Roberts now took the Royal *Fortune* and the *Ranger* away from Sierra Leone at the end of July, with Lord Sutton commanding of the *Ranger*. Plunkett despatched messages to the captain of the *Providence*, noting the traders who had dealt with Roberts: Glynn, 'Old Crackers' , Lamb, England, the Presgrove brothers, Bonnerman, Warren, and another Welshman, Pierce. Roberts was not to know that the *Weymouth's* crew was anchored off Principe, with its crew suffering terribly, many dying from yellow fever from mid-July to the beginning of September. At the end of July, the Dutch galley *Semm* was taken at Axim, with little booty except some cloth, but several men were forced, including Charles Bunce and Robert Armstrong. Armstrong had deserted from the HMS *Swallow* eight weeks earlier at Cape Three Points. Upon August 6th, Captain John Tarleton's *Liverpool* galley was taken off Sestos, with Robert Hays joining up. Sometime in August, the *Martha*, Captain Lady's snow from Liverpool, was captured off Cape la Hou, and Joshua Lee joined Roberts' men.

Off Point Sestos in Liberia upon August 8th, the pirates took the Royal Africa Company frigate-slaver *Onslow*, bound for Whydah and Cape Coast Castle. A 410-ton ship, it carried 12 guns, with cargo valued at £9000, destined for Cape Coast Castle. Captain Michael Gee had stopped at Sestos on the pretext of taking on fresh food and water, but in reality pursuing his private trading interests. Anchored alongside was Captain Canning's *Robinson* from Liverpool. With many of the crew ashore, possibly trading for slaves, William Magness, Roberts' quartermaster, easily took the moored ships. Lord Sympson 'showed off' to the fifty or so merchant seamen and passengers, shouting that he was as bold a pirate as Roberts, and bullying the passengers with his cutlass. Mrs Elizabeth Trengrove was travelling to Cape Coast Castle to join her husband, and William Mead made advances to her, forcing off her hooped petticoat. Another pirate, John Mitchell, smashed Mead over the head with his flint-lock, and told her that she would be safe from pirate advances in the gun-room. The brutal 'Little David' Simpson followed her, leering and telling his fellow 'Lords' that he would stand sentinel and safeguard her honour. As was the practice of the time, the pirate who chose to carry out such 'guard-duties' expected something in return, and she was raped three times by him over the next few days. This awful event would come back to haunt Mrs Trengrove.

Roberts next came on board. Black Bart asked if anyone of the crew would join him, and stated that no-one would be forced. He mentioned to a by-stander 'I must oblige these fellows with a show of force.' After a mock show of being 'forced', many crewmen did join, such as Phillip Bill, William Petty, Abraham Harper, Peter Lesley, William Wood, Edward Watts, John Horn, James Crombie and John Stevenson, and he impressed two Royal Africa Company agents named Thomas Castell and Edward Crispe. (Castell survived to give evidence against the pirates in the Cape Corso trial). Abraham Harper, a cooper, now had the job of removing all the casks and cooper's tools from prizes. Some soldiers captured were going to serve in the castle garrison, on a wage of £13 a year in local currency only (so savings were useless), and could only look forward to a miserable native diet of plantain and 'canky'. They wanted to join the pirates, but Roberts' crew was reluctant to take on 'landlubbers'. Eventually they were allowed to join, but only with a 'quarter-share' of any plunder, compared to the usual one share for a pirate. The Reverend Roger Price, a Welshman, was also asked to join, and take a share of the booty. All in return that Roberts asked was that he said prayers and made punch. He refused, and the pirates returned his confiscated property. He also claimed goods belonging to other passengers, which were returned to them later. However, Roberts kept three prayer-books of Price's, and his corkscrew. Bart informed the minister that his men led a dissolute life but he tried to keep them in order on a Sunday, allowing no rowdiness, evil-doing or games.

The Onslow was a well-built 410-ton frigate, and became the fourth 'Royal Fortune' as the old one was leaking. It was mounted with 40 guns, the gunwales highered for extra protection, and its deck-houses pulled down. Johnson describes Roberts' carpenters 'making such alterations as might fit her for a Sea Rover, pulling down her bulkheads, and making her flush, so she became, in all respects, as complete a ship for their purpose as any they could have found; they continued to her the name of Royal Fortune and mounted her with 40 guns.' The bulkheads, or internal walls between decks were taken away, as there was no need to store cargo. A clear space was needed for working the guns, as in a man-of-war. Making her flush meant that the forecastle was removed and the quarterdeck lowered or removed, giving a flat weather-deck, suitable for fighting and boarding.

Captain Gee was given the old *Royal Fortune* when the work was completed. The new *Royal Fortune* hoisted French colours, as there was no knowing where the Royal Naval vessels were cruising, and moved on up the Bight of Benin to Jacquin for a short stay. (The frigates were still

"Roberts' crew carousing at old Calabar River".

at Principe, Prince's Island, at this time, careening. The crews were suffering from venereal diseases and malaria, and at least 50 had died from each ship. Captain Ogle was forced to press crewmen off local shipping and purchase slaves in order to get a full complement of crew.) The pirates forced the *Onslow's* surgeon, Hamilton to join them on the *Royal Fortune*, and took another surgeon, George Willson from Captain Tarlton's ship off Assinie near Cape Coast Castle, and put him on the *Ranger*. Willson and two others escaped from Sutton a few days later, by a subterfuge of pretending to get new drugs off one of the prize vessels. Their small sailboat made for the coast before Sutton could do anything.

The fleet moved on to Old Calabar in the Bight of Biafra (Nigeria) to careen. Roberts had gleaned from captured despatches that the two men-of-war were still at Principe. On Oct 1st Roberts boarded the *Joceline* under Captain Arthur Loane and made him pilot their ships up the tricky river with its 13 feet draught. Once up the Calabar River, they were out of sight of the Navy. Roberts generously paid Loane for his services. He could be useful again, so there was no point in plundering his ship. Robert Haws joined up with Roberts. Bart found two ships lying inland. From the galley slaver *Mercy* he impressed the musicians, and yet another surgeon, William Child. (Musicians were carried on slavers to while away the time of the slaves, and entertain the crew). Israel Hynde of Bristol joined him as did Cuthbert Gross, John Griffin (a much-needed carpenter) and Thomas Giles. He also captured Captain Rolls' slave galley, the *Cornwall*, and impressed some more men, including a hunchbacked musician, James White, the Welshman David Rice and the surgeon Peter Scudamore. This surgeon quarrelled with *Lord* Moody, who did not want him. However, Roberts had found a real friend in Scudamore, who was the only surgeon to voluntarily sign articles on record. Scudamore was arrogant, but intelligent, and Roberts came to enjoy his cultured company, while the surgeon took to the life of a pirate like a duck to water.

From captured despatches on these two prizes, Roberts now discovered that the men-of-war were over 200 miles away at Principe, so he decided to move on again to trade with another port. With goods to trade, Roberts moored his three ships and three prizes on October 1st off the native township of Calabar, and forty men went ashore under cover of his forty guns. 2000 hostile natives lined up to face them – they did not deal with white men in this part of modern-day eastern Nigeria, and were rightly suspicious of the pirates' motives. After a few fusillades of musket-shot and showers of spears, both sides had lost a few men, but Robert's men stayed their ground. The local tribe retreated, and the pirates kept on firing at them, then set fire to the town. There was now a stand-off – the pirates were not welcome on land, and the natives would not come near them. Several pirates were killed, and the natives retreated back into the jungle, with their much-needed goods and provisions. The attack was still being recounted 200 years later by locals in their tribal legends. From now on Bart sent a pinnace full of pirates on a regular basis to the mouth of the Calabar, looking for the opportunity to board merchantmen lying at anchor in the estuary, perhaps taking on water. It was now that Scudamore showed himself to be a '*true*' pirate, cursing Captain Rolls and hoping that he would drown as he was a '*great rogue*'. The surgeon took his medicines, scales and knives off the *Cornwell*, before that ship, the *Mercy* and the *Joceline* were returned to their captains. The unfortunate Elizabeth Trengrove left the clutches of Sympson to carry on her journey.

Roberts went off to careen 400 miles south at Cape Lopez, where John Jessup deserted and vanished. The squadron then moved on to a safer careening site at Annabon, a small island 200 miles from the Cape. Jessup had been a shipmate of Roberts when he had first been taken by Howell Davis, and was a proficient gunner, but was frequently so drunk that he had missed out on his share of plunder. When the *Summersett* had been taken in 1720, he had distinguished himself, but now was regarded by Roberts and his fellow-pirates as a hopeless sot. The aggrieved Jessup was picked up on the Gabon Coast by a Dutch trader, whose captain did not believe the story that he had been marooned. Unluckily for Roberts, Jessup was taken to the *Swallow* at Cape Coast Castle. Here, clapped in irons, he turned informer and told Captain Ogle all about the movements of Black Bart, and his intention to ravage the Gold Coast next. By now 280 men had died on the *Weymouth*, and the vast majority of its 240-man crew had to be press-ganged, for it to now accompany the *Swallow* towards the Gold Coast. On October 20th, both men-of-war left Principe, piling on full sail, to chase Roberts.

On Dec 14th, 1721 the Dutch galley *Gertrouycht*, under Captain Benjamin Kreeft was taken at Gabon, in a crazy drunken attack. The pirates strung sausages, which had been made by Kreeft's wife, around their necks. The men went ashore to hunt for fresh meat, hunting for buffalo, then reprovisioned and traded at Annabona Island (Palagula). Roberts now moved off to Cape La Hou (French Ivory Coast), with the more competent Welshman Skyrme now replacing *Lord* Sutton as captain of the *Ranger*, after Sutton resigned.

CHAPTER VI

1722 THE LAST DAYS OF THE GREAT PYRATE

On January 2nd, the *Elizabeth*, under Captain Joseph (or John) Sharp, was pursued and taken by the three pirate ships, off Jacquesville on the Ivory Coast. On board was the missing surgeon, Richard Willson. He managed to convince Sutton and Roberts that his boat had been blown onto the beach at Cape Mesurado. The pirates fortunately believed him, as he had been forced to live in miserable conditions there for five months, and they always needed surgeons. His old ship under Captain Tarlton had found him after a few weeks, feverish and starving, but refused to take him aboard. A French ship then picked him up, but abandoned Willson at Sestos, as they were afraid of his fever spreading to the rest of the crew. A negro trader took the starving, penniless Willson on as a bond-servant, working as a slave clearing land, until Captain Joseph Sharp ransomed Willson's indenture for £3 and 5 shillings. Willson was nursed back to health by the surgeon Adam Comrie on the *Elizabeth*. Willson and Scudamore now persuaded Roberts that Comrie should be forced to join the crew as another surgeon, as they were sure that Hamilton would desert as soon as he had a chance.

Willson now noticed on the *Royal Fortune* the forced mate Thomas Tarlton of Liverpool, the brother of the captain who had abandoned him at Mesurado. Captain Tarlton's slaver *Tarlton* had been taken four days before the *King Solomon*. Tarlton was therefore badly beaten up by Roberts and other pirates. This was unusual - but happened because he was a brutal mate according to his crew, some of whom had joined Roberts – usually Bart just threatened captains with '*I'll blow your brains out!*' Lords Moody and Harper wanted to shoot Tarlton, who was hidden under a sail by some fellow-Liverpudlians. With their constant success, Roberts was finding it increasingly difficult to restrain his crews - he seems to have become resigned to his fate from this time. Roberts had no escape - so many people knew him, that he could not retire anywhere in anonymity and safety. As a teetotaller and Christian, he must have

Roberts captains 11 merchantmen off Africa

despaired at the way his life was going - there was no escape *in the bottle* for Black Bart. With continued success, his crews were spinning out of control - they thought they were invincible, and at the same time he could not control their perpetual drinking, which made them far less efficient as seamen. Roberts was trapped in a web of his own making.

As the *Elizabeth* was being ransacked, the *Hannibal* of London, under Captain Charles *Ousley* was taken. The pirates virtually trashed it, because of the lack of plunder on the small ship, causing £2000 worth of damage. Lord Richard Hardy was so annoyed at the *'day's takings'* that he broke his cutlass on the Captain's head, who died soon after. Without Roberts' influence on the spot, the Lords were fast getting out of control. Roberts let Captain Sharp take the emptied *Elizabeth* away - Sharp was a good captain to his men, and had been kind to Willson. The *Hannibal* was to be used as a hulk to store loot as the pirate fleet was careened. Comrie signed articles and was voted to become the *Royal Fortune's* surgeon, and Willson served Skyrme as surgeon on the Ranger. The pirates did not vote for Hamilton as they knew he could not be trusted, and did not care for Scudamore's arrogance - he had even struck Lord

Moody when they had previously quarrelled. However, Roberts liked him and they needed Scudamore, as a surgeon who was not likely to try and escape. The *Ranger's* crew voted as a man for Scudamore to be transferred off their ship to join Roberts on the *Royal Fortune*.

Upon January 4th, the Dutch *Vlissingen*, (Flushingham), with Captain Gerrit de Haen was taken at Grand Bassam. Sixteen pirates boarded, and obliged the captain and mate to join them for a drunken feast, when they pretended to sing in Spanish and French out of a Dutch prayer-book. On the next day, the sloop *Diligence*, under Captain Stephen Thomas, was taken at Cape Appolonia. A second sailor named John Jessup joined Roberts, off the prize. Upon January 6th, the 200 tons *King Solomon* of London, a 12-gun slaver with a Welsh Captain, Joseph Traherne, was taken off Cape Appolonia. William Magness, quartermaster, again led a long-boat to take it, as the *Royal Fortune* could not tack near enough to it. Captain Traherne shouted *'Defiance'* and fired a musket at the approaching pirates, but his men were half-hearted in supporting him. The pirates called out that any resistance would meet with *no quarter*, the King Solomon's Welsh bosun, William Phillips, led the crew in asking for quarter against the captain's wishes. It was not worth sailors risking their lives for the Royal Africa Company, as the pirates knew full well – only the captain was a financial loser if the ship was seized. In 1723, partly because of Phillips' actions, an Act of Parliament was passed punishing seamen who would not defend their ship against pirates. John Lane, John King and Samuel Fletcher joined up from the *King Solomon*. Roberts was pleased with the booty, and asked Traherne *'How dared you fire? Didn't you see the two ships commanded by the famous Captain Roberts?'*

The pirate John Walden addressed the recalcitrant Captain Traherne *'Captain, what signifies this trouble of yo-hoping and straining in hot weather? There are plenty more anchors in London and, besides, your ship is to be burned'* – he then cut the anchor cable. Walden was a hot-headed and argumentative man, known as *'Miss Nanny'* by the crew. (One noted writer on pirates believes that 'Miss Nanny' was an 18th- century term for a homosexual, but this author cannot find any such reference. The writer uses this to make the connection that Walden was Robert's lover, but again there is nothing to prove this allegation. Surely this 'fact' would have been noted in the interrogations and trial transcripts of above 200 men if it was the case. To this author, it seems that Roberts was asexual, if anything). Phillips helped Scudamore, Walden and Magness ransack the boat and showed little love for his former captain, encouraging the pirates to hit him. What cargo they could not take, they threw overboard. More men had joined Roberts' crew, including more soldiers. Peter de Vine, who had sailed under Stede Bonnet on the pirate sloop *Revenge*, joined willingly. The drunkard Joe Mansfield found a beautiful crystal glass, which Lord Moody promptly seized. When Mansfield protested, Moody threatened to blow his brains out. Scudamore took the medical equipment and supplies, and argued with another pirate over a backgammon table. Magness was forced to intervene, and Scudamore took the table, before returning for Captain Traherne's quilt and bolster. Surgeon Willson was so preoccupied with looting that he omitted to dress a pirate's wound, and Roberts threatened to cut his ears off. The Welsh bosun Phillips was *forced* for his seamanship skills, and the ransacked *King Solomon* allowed to go free. Philips later testified that he signed Roberts' Articles because a pistol had been laid pointing at him on the table, as if to say that if he did not sign, he would be shot.

The pirates now heard that HMS *Swallow* had at last left Principe. Roberts realised that he had to sail on away from the vicinity of Cape Coast Castle, and headed for Whydah, the busy port where the Portuguese paid for slaves in gold. The Royal Africa Company's Williams Fort was 3 miles inland, and could not guard the port with its guns. The *Swallow* and *Weymouth* were very near at this time, but luckily for Roberts, had veered away to anchor off Cape Corso on January 7th. Ogle was disappointed that his provisions from England had not arrived. Some of these supplies had been looted off the *King Solomon* by Black Bart only the day before, unknown to him. Captain Ogle now heard that Roberts had just taken a French ship off Axim, and that three pirate vessels, presumably those of Roberts, had taken a galley off Axim Castle and another Royal Africa Company ship. The captains surmised that Roberts would leave the Gold Coast and head for Whydah (Ouidah) on the Bight of Benin, and set off from Cape Coast on January 10th to capture him there. Whydah was the richest port in West Africa. The King of Dahomey lived six miles inland with his hundred wives, and exacted a toll to the value of 20 slaves from each of the *blackbirders* who picked up slaves there. The corpulent king sent contingents of spearmen into the interior to raid villages and bring young men and women to the slave-ship captains. His avarice was such that he sold the slaves naked, without their '*arse-clouts*' (loin-cloths). Slaves were kept at Wydah in a stinking storehouse known as '*The Trunk*'. A Guinea slaver wrote '*the negroes were put into a booth, or prison, built for that purpose, near the beach, all of them together; and when the Europeans are to receive them, they are brought out into a large plain, where the surgeons examine every part of everyone of them, to the smallest member, men and women all being stark naked.'* Wounded, sick and those with venereal diseases were rejected, and the rest branded and replaced in cages. In the Niger Delta, slaves were herded into a huge cage known as a *barracoon*. However, the Royal Africa Company hoarded its slaves in huge stone castles along the shore, usually in rock dungeons.

On Jan 11th, 1722 Black Bart sailed into Whydah roadstead, flying his personal colours, and immediately took 12 slave ships. Hearing the drums and music, 5 Portuguese, 4 French and 3 English *blackbirders* struck their colours immediately when they saw Roberts' black flags. The French ships each had around 30 guns and 100 men. The ships included the *Carlton* of London, under Captain Allright, the *Porcupine* under Captain Fletcher and the *Hardey* under Captain Dittwitt. All the captains fled ashore in their tenders when they saw Robert's flotilla enter the harbour. The ships had been stripped to take maximum cargoes of slaves across the Atlantic, and had little to loot. However, Roberts knew that their captains had gold to pay for negroes. Only the *Carlton* had taken on its slaves, and its captain could only raise 40 ounces of gold dust to retrieve his ship. The Royal Africa Company's agent loaned him 100 ounces to release the ship. All except the *Porcupine* agreed to be ransomed for 140 ounces of gold each. The pirates even gave the captains of galleys such as the *Sandwich* receipts for the gold-dust, stating on one: *'This is to certify whom it may or doth concern, that we GENTLEMEN OF FORTUNE have received 8 lbs. of Gold-Dust for the ransom of the Hardey, Captain Dittwitt commander so that we discharge the said ship.*
Witness our hands this 13th January 1722

Batt. Roberts

Harry Glasby'

This may have been at the honest Glasby's request, but the Portuguese captains were given the identical dubious receipts but jokingly signed by Lords Sutton and Simpson as '*Aaron Whifflington*' and '*Sim. Tugmutton*'

The *Porcupine*, however, was an interloper, an illegal trader. Her slaves were already chained up, and her captain ashore settling his bills. Captain Fletcher refused to negotiate with the pirates. Roberts gave the order to unchain the slaves and transport them to his ships, then burn the *Porcupine*. In the boarding party was *Miss Nanny*, John Walden, who was furious at having to do this slow and tedious job of unshackling the leg and wrist irons, while the other freebooters were happily drinking themselves into oblivion after an easy day's work. To Roberts' horror, he set fire to the slaver before the unfettering was finished, and all eighty natives died. Some screaming negroes, chained in pairs, *'jumped overboard from the Flames, were seized by Sharks, a voracious Fish, in plenty in the Road, and in their Sight, torn Limb from Limb alive. A Cruelty unparalleled.'* Roberts' control was now extremely tenuous – success had bred contempt for any discipline among the harder members of his crews. He could not punish them, for the offence had not occurred in battle. Outside battle conditions, the quartermaster was in real control of the ship.

Now, some of Roberts' crew took the *Comte de Thoulouze*, although it had been ransomed, and mounted extra guns on her from the other French ships. (This seems to be another *Comte de Thoulouze*, as the ship captured in June was a naval warship). 18 French sailors were also put on her, to return to Whydah if it was not a fast ship. It was a former privateer from St Malo, so the pirates obviously liked *the cut of its jib,* and intended to test its suitability at sea. Thomas Diggle was among the men forced to join Roberts. On one of the English ships, Roberts' men found a letter from Director-General James Phipps of Cape Coast Castle. (He was on a salary of £2000 per year, plus bribes or *'dashees'* from illegal traders, *interlopers*). It was meant for The Royal Africa Company agent on Whydah, Mr. Baldwin, informing him that Roberts had been spotted off Cape Three Points, and that the man-of-war *Swallow* was chasing him towards Whydah. Black Bart addressed his crew, telling them that there was no point in risking anything by staying and fighting the *Turnip-man's* ship. The crew easily agreed with this sense, and the three ships sailed off towards Annanbona Island to hole up. (The turnip-man was King George).

The *Swallow* missed Roberts by just two days when it sailed into Whydah on the 15th. Surgeon Hamilton was left at Whydah, as the pirates had no need of a surgeon who hated being with them. Roberts sailed out in the *Royal Fortune*, Skyrme in the *Ranger*, Captain Bunce in the *Little Ranger*, and followed by the captured *Comte de Thoulouze*. On the day they left, Roberts took the sloop *Wida* of London, under Captain Stokes, off Jacquin. Stokes had tried to avoid Whydah because he had known the pirates were there and was unfortunate they caught up with him on his escape route to Grand Popo. The *Wida* was burnt and its crew taken aboard – they wanted no-one to inform the *Swallow* of their whereabouts. Roberts had by now lost many men to disease contracted at Calabar and elsewhere. A great proportion of his men had never encountered a serious battle. Many of the *Lords* were perpetual drunkards,

Captain Chaloner Ogle

perpetually quarrelling with their teetotal captain. Roberts had no way out.

Throughout November and December, the third-raters chased up and down the African coast, following up merchant reports regarding Roberts' whereabouts. The *Weymouth* then left to pick up some goods held illegally by the Dutch at Des Minas, while the *Swallow* returned to Cape Coast Castle. There, Chaloner Ogle read two despatches that three suspicious ships had been seen at Whydah. Ogle had been delayed in reaching Whydah because he had helped two local ships at Accra, and did some personal business with a trader called Little Betty Morris. General Phipps was furious at this because on the night of January 14th, the *Swallow* had nosed into Little Popo, to be told that Roberts was at Whydah, by a French boat. On the 15th Ogle found the burned hulk of the *Porcupine* and the other ships at anchor that Roberts had ransomed. Ogle and Hill were now given information that the pirates had gone to Jacquin, 7 leagues away, so moved there, before returning to Whydah to take on more men. Captains Ogle and Hill were now scouring inlets as they realised that the *Comte de Thoulouze* would need careening and refitting, and that the pirates needed water.

Ogle had been tardy in approaching Roberts thus far, but had been told of the fortune in gold aboard the *Royal Fortune*. Knowing that Roberts' ships were laden with booty changed the equation for Chaloner Ogle, aboard his 50-gun man-of-war. He directed the *Swallow* a thousand miles to Gabon, where he had captured Roberts' man, Jessup, but found no signs of Roberts. Ogle then interrogated the pirate prisoner, John Jessup, who was held in chains in the *Swallow's* hold. Jessup explained that he had not escaped from the Gabon estuary area, but from Cape

Lopez, a hundred miles south. Roberts' days were numbered. However, it had been a reasonably successful two or so years. A modern estimate of the fortunes earned by Roberts and his crews is over £100,000,000. The *Sagrada Familia* alone was worth over £5,000,000. He virtually stopped international trade wherever he went.

THE TAKING OF THE GREAT RANGER

The *Comte de Thoulouze* had proved a fine sailer, but needed further fitting out and careening, as the naval commanders had rightly ascertained. It was to join Roberts' fleet, renamed the *Great Ranger*, under Captain Skyrme who had been commander of the *Ranger*. The *Ranger* was now called the *Little Ranger*. While the refitting was being done, there were duels ashore. Discipline was now a major problem – Roberts could not keep his crew sober any longer, and quarrels kept flaring up in the three overcrowded ships.

On February 5th, at daylight, after tracking around Prince's Island, Roberts' ships were sighted at Cape Lopez. The informer Jessup had told Ogle that he had escaped at Cape Lopez, and that it was a favourite resting place for Roberts. The *Great Ranger* (the former *Comte de Thoulouze*) was on its side, ready to be careened, as was the *Royal Fortune*. From the cliffs, Roberts spotted Ogle's ship in the distance and judged that it was a Portuguese trader. The *Swallow* moved away to avoid a shallows known as Frenchman's Bank, so Roberts assumed it was a merchantman attempting to flee from them. Ogle had wanted to attack the pirates as they rested in a drunken stupor, and raged at his helmsman until the situation was explained to him. Ogle had been forced out to sea again, to make a long tack to run into the bay again. Roberts rapidly ordered the *Great Ranger* to be righted, and a party of 20 men from the *Royal Fortune* boarded it. The *Royal Fortune* needed more work on her keel, and the *Little Ranger* was a store-ship, not really equipped for chasing and fighting. Ogle could not believe his luck - he could pick off the ships one by one.

Skyrme was sent off to chase the 'merchant', hopefully to procure some sugar for making punch. Ogle cleverly kept up the deception, allowing the *Ranger* to slowly gain on him until the two ships were out of sight of Roberts and Roberts could not hear any cannon. (Three miles is the maximum distance of sight to the horizon, for anyone standing on a beach). Ogle closed off all his gun-ports, pretending to be a merchantman and put on all sail, but allowed Skyrme to slowly close on him. When Skyrme was in musket-shot, Ogle ordered the lower guns to be run out, and its 32-pounders raked the *Great Ranger* with cannon shot into its rigging and below the water line. Skyrme realised his mistake, and fired a broadside back. In the exchanges, Captain Skyrme had a leg shot off. The pirates, waved on by Skyrme and his cutlass, were encouraged to board the naval vessel. Their topmast fell down, so they had no option – they could not outsail it. However, the new crew members and forced men were unwilling to suffer any more casualties – the *Great Ranger* was almost dead in the water and being straddled with chain shot and musket shot. Surgeon Comrie worked desperately on the wounded and dying, while Lord Valentine Ashplant and boatswain Hynde urged on the less committed pirates. A forced man, Lilliburne, ran down to the powder-stores with a musket, determined that no pirate would blow the ship up to prevent their capture. Hynde's arm was blown off. After four hours of fighting, from 11 – 3, Skyrme was forced to ask for quarter as his men deserted their posts to escape the deadly hail of missiles. When promised quarter, Skyrme ordered the black flags to be thrown into the water. Ashplant weighted them and did so. The opinion among Roberts' men was that he would soon come and rescue them. Skyrme had lost ten men, and another 20 like himself were very seriously wounded. However, as the navy was preparing to board, there was a great explosion, tearing a hole in the *Great Ranger's* side.

As the boarding-party came across to the *Great Ranger*, an explosion ripped out the great-cabin. The Welshman John Morris, with other hardened pirates Roger Ball and William Main, had decided to blow up the ship. They overpowered Lilliburn, and Morris fired his pistol into the remaining powder, but there was too little left to hole the hull. Four pirates including William Main and Roger Ball were badly burned, and Morris and another died horribly. Ball had been blown through the side of the boat, and rescued from the sea. The boarding party found 23 negro slaves and 16 French prisoners on board. Around 30 pirates were dead or terribly wounded, leaving around 30 new and pressed crew members. Most of the battle-hardened '*Lords*' of Howell Davis were still on the *Royal Fortune*, with '*The Great Pirate*' Roberts. The Swallow's surgeon John Atkins, treating the blackened William Main, noted the silver whistle on a ribbon around his neck, and said '*I presume you are the boatswain of this ship*'. Main answered '*Then you presume wrong, for I am the boatswain of the Royal Fortune, Captain Roberts, commander.*' He averred that there were 120 'clever fellows' on the *Royal Fortune*, and he wished he was with them. Ball refused to be treated, and that night became delirious, shouting that Roberts would come and save them all.

Ogle's response was the typical naval one of the day - he ordered the terribly burned man to be flogged in the morning. During his flaying, Ball still shouted back, and was whipped again. He fell into a coma and died the next day.

Ogle thought about burning the disabled *Great Ranger*, but realised that he did not want the prisoners and wounded on the *Swallow*. He therefore spent the night repairing it, and sent it to Princes Island with the French prisoners and four of his own men. By evening on February 6th, he was ready to go for Roberts, with his crew in fine fettle – they had not lost a man. On February 9th, Captain Thomas Hill was sailing the Neptune off Cape Lopez, a 200-ton pink with 10 guns. Roberts, in the newly careened *Royal Fortune*, easily took her, with £4000 in goods and stores, and put the crew and passengers of the burned *Wida* (Jan 13th) on her. There was plenty of alcohol on the *Neptune*, and a drunken Captain Bunce of the *Little Ranger*, said that he would salute Skyrme on his return with a 13-gun salute. Roberts was waiting for Skyrme to return before he could take to the seas again.

THE END

On February 10th Black Bart was sitting down calmly in his great-cabin breakfasting with Captain Hill and no doubt wondering where Skyrme was. He was anchored in the lee of Parrot Island, off Cape Lopez on the Guinea Coast. Possibly, Skyrme was spending his time ransacking the prize at sea rather than towing it back with him. Eating salmagundy, there was tea for Roberts and beer for Hill. The crew was drunk on the liquor taken from Hill's ship, when a ship was seen to be approaching. Roberts probably thought it was Skyrme returning. As Ogle saw the third ship, the *Neptune*, he guessed that Robert's crew would be dead drunk, celebrating, and was again correct. Most were asleep with hangovers, except a few pressed men, Harry Glasby the reluctant sailing-master and Roberts the teetotaller.

Ogle approached carefully, so as to give the appearance of a merchantman, and flew a French flag. However, a deserter from the *Swallow*, Armstrong, rushed into the great cabin and told Roberts that it was his old naval man-of-war. The pirates from the *Little Ranger* were ordered to join the *Royal Fortune* immediately. Roberts was almost trapped, and his men were is a desperate condition. Lords Magness and Dennis rushed around, kicking senseless pirates awake and hurrying them on board the *Royal Fortune*.

Lord Simpson was instructed to find out from Armstrong the *Swallow's* firepower and its weaknesses in sailing, and the Royal Fortune hurriedly hove to, Roberts exclaiming '*it is a bite*' (deception). Roberts had very little time as the *Swallow* was almost upon her. It was on its second long and cautious tack through the shallows, and Black Bart managed to cast anchor by 10.30. He left the *Little Ranger* filled with treasure. He had decided to set all sail and pass next to the man-o-war, to assess her firepower. Armstrong had told him that the Swallow was a good ship going into the wind, but slow when sailing with the wind. Robert's men were not yet ready to return cannon fire, and Roberts could then assess whether to make a run for it into the open seas. He had to risk a full broadside, which unnerved the new helmsman Johnson. Roberts told Magness and Dennis that he would not try to board the Swallow, as his men were not fit for action. If the newly careened *Royal Fortune* passed the Swallow, the odds were that she could be outsailed. If the *Royal Fortune* was disabled, he could swing her onto the nearby cliffs and most of his men could escape into the forests. As the sails were set he went and dressed himself in his usual attire for battle. He finished dressing in his matching crimson coat and breeches, both with the same gold damask pattern, white ruffled lace shirt, and a long red feather in his hat. His expensive pistols were carried in a red silk shoulder strap, and he wore a great diamond-crusted gold cross.

On deck alongside Black Bart, the former 3rd mate on the *Princess*, was Stephenson, who had been the *Princess's* 2nd mate, and Roberts ordered his helmsman Johnson towards the oncoming man-of-war. The wind was from the shore, and the stratagem could work. At 11 in the morning the first broadside of the *Swallow* was fired from a pointblank range of 20 yards. Dennis had managed to reply with 20 cannon. The *Royal Fortune* passed, as the Swallow drifted towards the shore. However, the top of the *Royal Fortune's* mizzen topmast was felled and interfered with the mainsail. The panicking Johnson swung to starboard, disobeying Black Bart's instructions to keep a straight course. The *Royal Fortune* lost way, as it was directly behind the *Swallow's* stern. The *Swallow* tacked around to catch up with the almost becalmed *Royal Fortune*, taking its wind off the land. Black Bart cursed the helmsman and watched and waited as the *Swallow* inexorably made ground on him. He knew that his sails could not fill out until the *Swallow* came alongside him, and its 32-pounders smashed into his ship, and its other cannon, muskets and swivels destroyed his rigging and men on deck. He now knew that there would be several point-blank broadsides before the *Royal*

Fortune could shake off the Swallow. Dennis prepared his gunners, while Magness roared around the deck urging his men on. The scarlet-clad Roberts watched, not moving amongst the hysteria. He was the easiest target on deck - it was almost as if he was waiting for his death.

The first broadside did tremendous damage, but even worse was the constant bombardment of swivel guns sweeping chainshot and grapeshot across the decks. Marksmen in the Swallow's rigging picked off Roberts' crew. The scarlet captain fell over a cannon, killed instantly by grapeshot in his throat. Stephenson, who had taken over as helmsman from the cowardly Johnson, shouted at Bart to '*stand up and fight like a man*', then burst into tears when he found Black Bart was dead. '*Miss Nanny*' Walden's leg had been blown off. Black Bart's body was weighed down and thrown overboard, following his previous instructions. Only two more pirates were killed after Roberts' death - he was their only leader. One appears to have been his second mate from the Princess, Stephenson, as he was not tried at Cape Corso. As he had been made steersman instead of the useless Johnson, the fate of the *Royal Fortune* was probably sealed with his death. Harry Glasby took over as helmsman and urged the pirates to surrender, but confused and leaderless, they decided to sail off. The Swallow caught them, probably because of Glasby's deliberate bad steersmanship or poor winds. Roberts' body was hoisted overboard by Magness and Stephenson after his express wish, but no-one came forth to take his place. The *Lords* descended into a drinking frenzy as the *Swallow* raked their ship with fire for two hours. The main mast came down. A few leaderless pirates fought courageously, but were hampered by the drunks, cowards and forced men. At two o'clock Lord Magness asked for quarter, or else they would blow up the ship. Ogle agreed. Yet another Welshman on the crew, the boatswain James Philips, now tried to blow the ship up with a lighted taper, shouting '*Let us all go to Hell together!*', but was restrained by Glasby and Captain Stephen Thomas (captured with the Diligence on January 5th - he was later acquitted on piracy on the grounds that '*it was unlikely that a master of a vessel at £6 a month should be a volunteer amongst such villains*'). Magness threw the Ship's Articles into the sea, but Roberts' black flags were pinned to the deck by a broken mast. As the boarding party arrived, a deserter from HMS *Rose*, Joe Mansfield, temporarily woke up from his drunken coma and shouted for the pirates to help him board and capture the *Swallow*. On board the Royal Fortune, Ogle found '*an English ensign jack and Dutch pennant and ye black flag hoisted at the mizzen peak.*' Roberts had used captured Dutch flags when posing as a Dutch interloper and capturing 14 French traders at Martinique.

Charles Johnson, in his 1724 'A General History of Pyrates' noted: *'The Account of Roberts runs into greater length than that of any other Pyrate... because he ravaged the seas longer than the rest... having made more Noise in the World than some others.'* Roberts seemed to have kept his command longer than any other pirate captain, pillaging the Caribbean for eighteen months and the Guinea Coast for a further eight. From a £3 per month third mate on a slaver, he wreaked more havoc and made more money than any pirate before or since. His death ended *'the Golden Age of Piracy'*.

Howard Pyle, in his 1891 *'The Buccaneers and Marooners of America'*, wrote: *"He made a gallant figure," says the old narrator, "being dressed in a rich crimson waistcoat and breeches and red feather in his hat, a gold chain around his neck, with a diamond cross hanging to it, a sword in his hand, and two pair of pistols hanging at the end of a silk sling flung over his shoulders according to the fashion of the pyrates." Thus he appeared in the last engagement which he fought—that with the Swallow—a royal sloop of war. A gallant fight they made of it, those bulldog pirates, for, finding themselves caught in a trap betwixt the man-of-war and the shore, they determined to bear down upon the king's vessel, fire a slapping broadside into her, and then try to get away, trusting to luck in the doing, and hoping that their enemy might be crippled by their fire. Captain Roberts himself was the first to fall at the return fire of the Swallow; a grapeshot struck him in the neck, and he fell forward across the gun near to which he was standing at the time. A certain fellow named Stevenson, who was at the helm, saw him fall, and thought he was wounded. At the lifting of the arm the body rolled over upon the deck, and the man saw that the captain was dead. "Whereupon," says the old history, "he" [Stevenson] "gushed into tears, and wished that the next shot might be his portion." After their captain's death the pirate crew had no stomach for more fighting; the "Black Roger" was struck, and one and all surrendered to justice and the gallows. Such is a brief and bald account of the most famous of these pirates. But they are only a few of a long list of notables, such as Captain Martel, Capt. Charles Vane (who led the gallant Colonel Rhett, of South Carolina, such a wild-goose chase in and out among the sluggish creeks and inlets along the coast), Capt. John Rackam, and Captain Anstis, Captain Worley, and Evans, and Philips, and others—a score or more of wild fellows whose very names made ship captains tremble in their shoes in those good old times..*

And such is that black chapter of history of the past—an evil chapter, lurid with cruelty and suffering, stained with blood and smoke. Yet it is a written chapter, and it must be read."

AFTERMATH

Of the 152 men on board, 52 were negro slaves. Only 3 men were killed on the *Royal Fortune*, and none on the *Swallow*. Ogle stole a great deal of gold-dust from Bart's great-cabin. £2000 of gold dust was recovered from the *Royal Fortune*, and Ogle went to Cape Lopez on February 12 to raid the *Little Ranger's* gold dust, jewellery and cash. However, the *Little Ranger* was empty. All the pirates' chests had been broken open. Captain Hill had departed in the Royal Africa Company ship *Neptune*, and in August gave back 50 ounces of gold-dust, but the vast majority of Roberts' fortune disappeared. This seems to have been the origin of the persistent story that Roberts buried his treasure on the Ile de Los Idols, north-east of Sierra Leone. Some of Roberts' men appear to have escaped into the woods in the mayhem, having been left onshore, and operated in West Africa in the 1720's intermixing with the Kru tribe. 45 of Roberts' captured crew had been '*black saylors, commonly known by the name of gremetoes*', mariners from the Sierra Leone and Liberia region. The Kru were well-known for their skill in handling long canoes at sea, and for their independent leadership of slave revolts if captured. Intriguingly, it was noted in the early 19th century that '*a Kru makes a bad slave, because they know that if they are enslaved, they will commit suicide immediately.*'

The *Swallow* stayed to boot-top and take on water at Cape Lopez, and sailed with the *Little Ranger* on February 18 for Princes' Island to rendezvous with the *Great Ranger*, which they met on February 22. Ogle set course for Cape Coast Castle, but a tornado at St Thomas Isle meant that he lost his prize ships. Most prisoners were on the *Swallow*, and it became difficult to keep control of the ship. The *Swallow's* crew had been divided between four ships. The pirates were manacled and guarded night and day. Hungry, they shouted that they would not have enough weight on them to hang. Young Sutton, the master-gunner, complained bitterly about being chained next to a pirate who was praying to go to Heaven. Sutton responded '*Did you ever hear of any pirate going thither ? Give me Hell, it's a merrier place. I'll give Roberts a salute of thirteen guns at its entrance.*' Sutton then made a formal complaint to have the pirate removed from his side or his Prayer Book confiscated.

In this dark atmosphere, Lords Ashplant, Magness and Mayer plotted to take over the Swallow and kill its officers. A mulatto boy was used to carry messages, but two prisoners chained next to Lord Ashplant heard of the plot. The surgeon George Willson, who joined from the *Stanwich*, betrayed the pirates in an attempt for clemency. Guards were doubled on the prisoners, and it was discovered that several had already broken their shackles. Roberts had been a shrewd judge of men after the Walter Kennedy lesson, and had called Wilson a double-rogue and threatened to cut off his ears in the past. Off Cape Corso, a French ship from Nantes struck its colours upon sighting the *Swallow*, thinking that Roberts was in charge – he struck terror from beyond the grave. The prisoners were placed in the slave dungeons at Cape Coast Castle.

A report in *The Weekly Journal* on February 24th, 1722, reads: *'Tis computed that within five years past the pyrates have taken 140 English vessels on the Coast of Newfoundland and Africa. The report of the taking of the Weymouth man of war by Roberts the pyrate proves groundless.'* HMS *Weymouth* sailed into the Castle on March 26th, and the three prize ships rode out the storm and eventually made it to Cape Coast Castle upon April 3, two weeks after the *Swallow's* arrival. The *Royal Fortune* also survived the tornado and then took fresh food and water at St Thomas Isle before following on to the Castle. However, the pirate surgeons Scudamore and William Child had a free run of the ship to look after the wounded on board. Scudamore entreated the slaves on board to mutiny, using his smattering of their language, and the other prisoners willingly agreed to fight rather than be hanged. There was only a skeleton crew on board, but the day before the mutiny William Childs revealed the plan to an officer, and Scudamore was chained up.

Meanwhile, upon March 1st the Neptune moored at Cabinda (Angola) to take on 400 slaves, which were sold in August in Barbados. Captain Hill surrendered 50 ounces of gold here to the Governor, to avoid being prosecuted as a pirate, but still made a handsome profit from the affair. Both Ogle and Hill blamed each other for the disappearance of gold-dust. Ogle wrote that 300 pounds of gold-dust had been found. What was in the *Royal Fortune* and what was in the *Little Ranger* will never be known, but both Hill and Ogle profited enormously.

THE TRIAL AT CAPE CORSO CASTLE, THE BIGHT OF BENIN - THE GREATEST PIRATE TRIAL OF ALL TIME

This started on March 28th, 1722 with a Vice-Admiralty Court consisting of Captain Mungo Herdman, Lieutenant John Barnsley and Second-Lieutenant Charles Fanshawe, all from H.M.S. *Weymouth*, plus the Company agents Francis Boye, Henry Dodson and Samuel Hartease, Captain William Menzies of the Company ship *Chandos*, and The

Honourable James Phipps, Director-General of the Company. Interestingly, the Registrar of the Court was the Swallow's surgeon, John Atkins, who recounted the capture of the pirates to Daniel Defoe. Because of legal technicalities, the only charges proceeded with, concerned the attack on H.M.S. *Swallow*.

The court was then filled with sixty-nine prisoners taken from the *Great Ranger*, commanded by Captain James Skyrme, who was barely alive. Most pirates admitted that they had signed the Pirate Articles and taken plunder, but all stated that they had been 'forced' into the life by Captain Roberts. The Frenchmen, and sailors recently taken from the *Whydah* and *Porcupine* all denied taking Pirate Articles.

The prisoners were taken out, while the Court decided what actually constituted an act of piracy. It was decided that newly-entered men might be precluded if they had not shared any booty, nor voluntarily taken or robbed a ship. Then the prisoners from the *Royal Fortune* came into court, of whom eight-seven were charged with piracy. Thomas Castell, a Company agent forcibly impressed from the *Onslow* in 1721, gave evidence that all the pirates who boarded the *King Solomon* did so voluntarily.

Ninety-one pirates were found guilty and seventy four acquitted. Captain Skyrme and most members of the '*House of Lords*' were found '*Guilty in the Highest Degree*', and the President of the Court, Captain Herdman pronounced:

'*Ye and each of you are adjudged and sentenced to be carried back to the place from whence you came, from thence to the place of execution without the gates of this castle, and there within the flood marks to be hanged by the neck till you are* **dead, dead, dead.** *And the Lord have mercy on your souls'.............'After this ye and each of you shall be taken down, and your bodies hung in chains.' ('Records of the High Court of the Admiralty').*

Herdman sentenced fifty-two of Bart Roberts' crew to death, twenty men to an effective death sentence in the Cape Coast mines, and sent another seventeen to imprisonment in London's Marshalsea Prison. Of these seventeen, thirteen died in the *Weymouth* in passage to London, The four survivors were eventually pardoned while in Newgate Prison. Two 'guilty' sentences were 'respited'. Of the fifty-two pirates hung at Cape Coast, nearly half were Welsh or West Countrymen, and most of the others indentured servants or poor white colonists. Fifteen pirates had died of their wounds on the passage to Cape Corso Castle, and four in its dungeons. Ten had been killed in the *Ranger*, and three in the *Royal Fortune*. Thus ninety-seven of Roberts' crew had died. The seventy negroes on board the pirate ships were returned to slavery.

THE END OF THE HOUSE OF LORDS

Surgeon Atkins's account of the hangings is repeated in Defoe's *'History of the Pyrates'*. The first six to hang were the hardened 'Lords' Sutton, Simpson, Ashplant, Moody, Magness and Hardy. Atkins offered his services as a priest, but even Sutton, who had been suffering dysentery for days, ignored him. They called out for drinking water, and complained that *'We are poor rogues, and so get hanged while others, no less guilty in another way, escaped.'* Loosened from their shackles, they walked carelessly to the gallows. 'Little David' Simpson spotted poor Elizabeth Trengrove in the huge crowd, who he had ravished when the Onslow was taken in August 1721. He shouted *'I have lain with that bitch three times, and now she has come to see me hanged.'* The executioners did not know how to hang men, and tied their hands in front of the 'Lords'. Lord Hardy stated calmly *'I have seen many a man hanged, but this way of having our hands tied behind us I am a stranger to, and I never saw it before in my life.'*

Later hangings saw many of the men admit their sins, especially surgeon Scudamore, the only ship's doctor to have willingly joined any pirate ship. He asked for two days reprieve to read the scriptures, and was allowed to sing the 31st Psalm on the gallows before being swung off. A young man known as *'Captain'* Bunce also confessed to his sins, and blamed the liveliness and vivacity of his nature. He ended his speech from the gallows with the following words: *'I am now extremely afflicted because of the injuries I have done to all men, and I beg theirs and God's forgiveness. I exhort you here present to remember the Creator in the days of your youth and guard betimes so that your minds take not a wrong bias. I stand here as a beacon upon a rock to warn erring mariners of danger.'* (The gallows stood on a rock.)

Eighteen of the bodies were dipped in tar, encased in a frame of iron bands, and hung from gibbets in chains from nearby Lighthouse Hill, Connor's Hill and Catholic Mission Hill, so that they could be seen by ships as a warning to pirates. Others were simply left hanging for the birds to eat. In Robert Louis Stevenson's *'Treasure Island'* is the following passage:

'You've seen 'em, maybe, hanged in chains, birds about 'em, seamen pointing 'em out as they go down with the tide .... And you can hear the chains a-jangle as you go about and reach for the other buoy.'

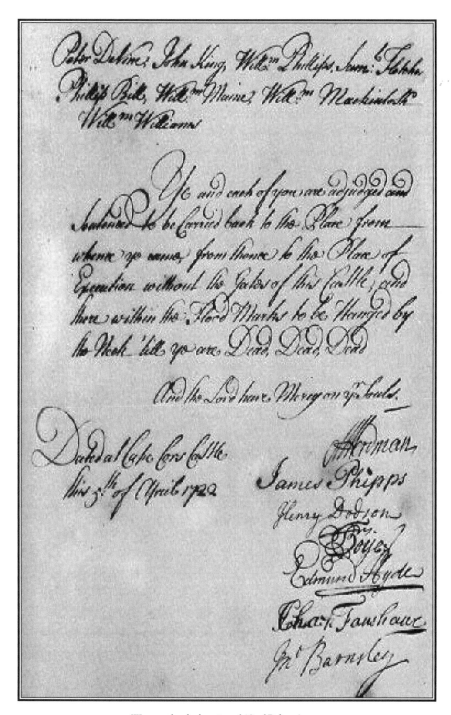

Warrant for the hanging of 19 of Roberts' crew

CAPTAIN CHALLONER OGLE

This architect of Roberts' defeat now took the HMS *Weymouth* and HMS *Swallow*, with their three prizes, back to Cape Lopez to clean the boats and take on water before heading across the Atlantic to Port Royal, Jamaica. However, lying at anchor there, they suffered a massive hurricane on August 28th, 1722. Only four men-of-war and two merchant-men survived, and about fifty other boats sank, including the *Royal Fortune* and *Little Ranger*. The town was itself devastated and around 300 people died there. This was almost exactly 30 years after the huge earthquake which tipped Henry Morgan's grave into the sea.

The naval ships were refitted and returned to England in April 1723, and Challoner Ogle was knighted by George I for killing Roberts, the only occasion any naval captain was knighted for such a deed. At the Admiralty Court, Ogle now petitioned for the *Great Ranger* to be the ship and effects of pirates, so he could partition its spoils. The prize and spoils were assessed at a value of just £5,364, of which the Court took £280 in expenses, Ogle was granted £3,144, and £1940 was to be distributed among the officers and crew of the Swallow as 'head-money'. The worth of the gold-dust and valuables was not assessed, but Ogle computed it at just a few pounds per man, which he refused to pay until ordered to do so a year later, with the 'head-money'.

On April 3rd, 1725, more than 3 years after the capture, the *'London Journal'* reported that the *Swallow's* officers and men had been paid the declared rate due to them under royal proclamation for taking of pirates. It noted *'it is remarkable that none of the Officers and crew of the said ship knew they were entitled to the said bounty, till the publishing of a book entitled "A General History of Pyrates", where the said Proclamation is taken notice of."* Thus Captain Johnson (Daniel Defoe) was responsible for them received their money off the arrogant Ogle. His men were furious with Ogle, who they rightly suspected of creaming off much of the booty, and unanimously petitioned Lord Berkeley, First Lord Commissioner of the Admiralty to intercede with King George. Ogle steadfastly refused to reapportion the shares, even when the Admiralty Secretary forwarded to him another letter stating that the King would be pleased to see a second distribution. Ogle finally responded by refusing on the grounds that he needed more money now that he had been made a knight of the realm by the King. The Admiralty tried once again in 1726 to force some money out of him, but Challoner Ogle repeated the same excuse. He wrote that he hoped that the Lords of the Admiralty would appreciate that the money which he had retained would be needed to help him keep up the dignity befitting his state. This rogue was made Commander-in Chief and sent to Jamaica in 1732, and promoted to Rear-Admiral of the Blue fleet in 1739. In 1742 he was in charge of the West Indies Fleet, then made Admiral of the White, retiring as a full Admiral and Commander-in-Chief of the Royal Navy. He died in 1750, one of the original London *'fat cats'*.

FOOTNOTE ON WALTER KENNEDY

On December 15th, 1719, the *Royal Rover* took the *'Sea Nymph'*. Off Barbados, it was spotted by Kennedy, and after a 7-hour chase Captain Bloodworth's New York snow was captured. It was kept alongside the *Royal Rover* for 8 days, until it was given back to Bloodworth, along with 16 forced men who wanted to return. Howell Davis's forced surgeon, Archibald Murray, was amongst those to receive their freedom. They reached Barbados on Christmas Day, 1719, and Murray testified against Kennedy's pirates at Edinburgh 11 months later. A mulatto who had served with Roberts was hanged in Virginia in March 1720, and was possibly one of Kennedy's deserters. This was a rare event, as usually black pirates were put into slavery at this time. Kennedy set course for Ireland for remaining the crew to disperse, but his poor navigation wrecked them in Scotland. Most of the crew were captured and executed, but Kennedy found his way to Dublin. Later, in London, he set up a brothel in Deptford, and also had a sideline in burglary. One of his dissatisfied harlots informed that he was a robber, and in prison he was recognised as a pirate and hanged.

FOOTNOTE ON THOMAS ANSTIS

Howell Davis, Thomas Anstis, Christopher Moody, Dennis Topping, Walter Kennedy and William Magness were all together on the *Buck*, and conspired to take that ship into piracy. Upon Davis' death, they all served under Black Bart, until Topping's death in battle, Kennedy's defection in October 1719, and Anstis' desertion on April 18th or 21st, 1721. Anstis had become tired of Roberts' increasingly autocratic manner, and had left Black Bart as their ships approached Africa. Anstis believed that there were better prospects in the West Indies. In the 18-gun brig *Good Fortune* he then captured several ships around Hispaniola, Martinique and Jamaica, increasing the size of the crew. During this time he *'abused and wounded'* a Captain Doyle of Montserrat, who had tried to prevent a female passenger from being raped. She was killed and thrown overboard. In Johnson's lurid writing, which may or may not be true, *'twenty one of them forced the poor Creature successively, afterwards broke her Back and flung her into the Sea.'*

After careening, the brutal Anstis made for Bermuda and captured the *Morning Star*, which was refitted with 21 guns and 100 men. John Fenn, a former member of Black Bart's crew, was given the captaincy of the captured ship, as Anstis was used to the handling of the *Good Fortune*. However, both crews wished to give up piracy as there had been little treasure taken, and Anstis and Fenn drew up a petition for pardon, claiming that they had been forced by Black Bart. They waited for a response to an island off the south-west of Cuba, and according to Johnson, for nine months *'they passed their time in Dancing and other Diversions'* including mock trials. When no answer had been received by August 1722, the *Good Fortune* and *Morning Star* went to sea, and found off a merchantman that there was no interest from the authorities in giving them a pardon. Anstis and Fenn thus returned to piracy.

Fenn wrecked his ship on the Grand Caymans, and the *Good Fortune* anchored while Anstis tried to recover the crew. Unfortunately for Anstis, two men-of-war, the *Hector* and *Adventure*, came across them. Anstis cut his cable and fled, but the Royal Navy was on the point of taking him when the wind dropped. The heavy warships were becalmed, while the *Good Fortune's* crew desperately rowed her to safety. Sailing to the Bay of Honduras to careen, Anstis took three more ships and burned them all to leave no trace of his whereabouts. With too many prisoners aboard, the merchant Captain Durfey attempted to take the *Good Fortune*, but was beaten off.

In early December, a large frigate was taken. Encumbered by prisoners and loot, Anstis decided to keep her, and mounted her with 24 guns, giving its captaincy to Fenn again. Fenn had been disabled fighting for Black Bart, with only a single hand, and a poor record in captaincy, having lost the *Morning Star*. More prizes were taken in the Bahamas, before the ships went to Tobago to careen and refit in April 1723. The man-of-war *Winchelsea* came across them, and burned all the ships except for Anstis' *Good Fortune* which escaped in the nick of time. John Fenn fled into the woods, but was captured a day later and hanged at Antigua. Soon after, several recent recruits and forced men mutinied, killing Anstis and his officers, and put the ship into Curacao.

PARTIAL LIST OF SHIPS TAKEN BY THE BLACK CAPTAIN

The following table gives us about 220 ships and 250+ fishing boats that were taken by Roberts - nearer 500 prizes than the 400 accorded in most textbooks.

Date	*Ship*	*From*	*Captain*	*Where taken*
Spring 1717	Dutch, taken by Davis			
Spring 1719	Davis killed at Principe			
Spring 1719	Roberts in command - attacked Principe - took French ship and two Dutch sloops			
Early July	Careened			Near Cape Lopez
2nd week in	Experiment			
July 1719	(renamed Fortune)	London	Cornet	Off Guinea Coast
1 day later	Merchantman	Portugal		
2 days later	Temperance	Bristol?	Sharman	
August 1719	Careened			Ferninandino off Brazil coast
Sept 1719	Attacked 42-ship Lisbon treasure fleet - took Sagrada Familia and two other Portuguese ships	Lisbon		Bahia de Todos, Brazil
Oct 1719	Sloop	Rhode Island	Cane	Surinam
Oct 1719	Careened Royal Rover			Islet near Devil's Island
Oct 1719	Royal Rover and Sagrada Familia disappear under Kennedy			
January 10, 1720	Philippa sloop		Daniel Greaves Trinidad	Laquary Roads,
Feb 1720	2 sloops			Off Guadeloupe
Feb 1720	10-gun trader	Bristol		Off Barbados
Before Feb 12 1720	Benjamin	Liverpool		
Feb 18 1720	Joseph sloop		Bonaventure Jelfes	
Feb 19 1720	Chased pirate Sea King		Joined La Palisse	
Feb 1720	Pink	French		Off Barbados
Feb 26 720	Roberts attacked by Summersett and Philippa			
Feb 1720	Repaired at Martinique, then careened at Cariacou	Picked up marooned pirates from Revenge		
May to mid-June 1720	about a dozen vessels' including a pink and a brig			Off coast of North America
May 1720	Expectation	Topsham		Newfoundland Banks

June 1720	Ferryland harbour, Newfoundland, looted one ship and burned Admiral's ship			
June 1720	Phoenix snow	Bristol	J. Richards	Newfoundland Banks
June 1720	Brigantine	Teignmouth, Devon	Peet	Newfoundland Banks
June 21 1720	Trepassey harbour - 22 sloops and 250 fishing boats, inc. Bideford Merchant	Replaced Fortune with Capt. Copplestone's brig	Admiral Babidge	Newfoundland
June 1720	St Mary's Harbour - took at least another 4 sloops and several fishing boats			Newfoundland
June 25 1720	Sidbury sloop	Bristol	William Thomas	Newfoundlandd Banks
June-July 1720	French fleet of 6 ships taken	French flagship renamed Good Fortune		North America coast
July 1720	4 more French ships			North America coast
July 1720	Brigantine Thomas	Bristol		Banks
July 1720	Richard pink	Bideford	Jonathan Whitfield	Banks
July 1720	Willing Mind	Poole		Banks
July 1720	Blessing	Lymington		Banks
July 1720	Happy Return sloop	William Taylor		Banks
July 1720	A ship of 26 guns and its consort sloop			Banks
July 14 1720	Samuel sloop		Cary	Off New England coast
July 15	Snow	Bristol	Bowles	Off New England coast
July 18	York, or Little York	Bristol	James Phillips	Off Virginia
July 18	Love brig	Lancaster	Thomas	Off Virginia
August 1720	Success sloop		Fensilon	Off South Carolina
August 1720	Storm, careened at Cariacou			
Sept 4 1720	Relief sloop		Robert Dunn	Cariacou, Grenadines
Sept 19 1720	French sloop			
Sept 1720	sloop	Rhode Island (captured again)	Cane	
Sept 1720	Thomas brigantine			
Sept 26-27 1720	Mary and Martha, plus 6 ships at Basseterre inc. Capt. Cox's Greyhound sloop, Capt. Hingstone's ship, M. Pomier's French ship, Capt. Cox's Greyhound and Capt. Henry Fowles' ship	Liverpool	Wilcox	St Kitts

Sept-Oct 1720	Sheltered at St Bathelemy			
Oct 1720	22-gun brig captured	Renamed Royal Fortune	Tortola,	Virgin Islands
Oct 25	English brig			St Lucia, near Martinique
Oct 25	sloop	As storeship	M. Courtel	St Lucia
Oct 23-26	14 English and French ships			Off Martinique
Oct 1720	Dutch interloper with 30 guns, plus 15 ships looted in harbour	Interloper became new Royal Fortune		St Lucia harbour
Dec 1720	Mary and Martha (again)	St Kitts	Wilson	
Dec 1720	Thomas Emanuel		Thomas Bennett	Bermudas
Dec	Aborted transatlantic crossing near Cape Verde Islands, returned to Surinam after a 4000 mile round journey			
Jan 13 1721	Sea King sloop (Capt. Richard Simes Barbados sloop, the Fisher, caught fire)	Rhode Island	Benjamin Norton	Off St Lucia
Jan-Feb	Several sloops to replace the crew lost in the Atlantic crossing			
Jan 1721	Saint Anthony sloop		John Rogers	
Jan 1721	flyboat			Basseterre harbour
Jan-Feb 1721	Boot-topping in Hispaniola, then careening in Bennet's Cay			
Feb 1721	Mayflower sloop			Off Martinique
Feb 1721	sloop			Off Guadeloupe
Feb 18 1721	Dutch interloper			St Lucia harbour
Feb 1721	14 Martinican traders	Martinique - 13 were burned		St Luce Bay, Martinique
March	Rested on St Barthelemy			
March 26	Lloyd galley		Hingston	Off Antigua
April 1721	Roberts fights with Thomas Jones			
Apr 9 1721	Jeremiah and Anne			West Indies
Apr 1721	French man-of-war with 41 guns and 140 crew	Roberts is said to have hung the Governor of Martinique		Off Leeward Isles
April 1721	merchantman	Virginia		
April 17	Prince Eugene	Dutch	Bastian Meake	mid-Atlantic
April	small snow			mid-Atlantic
April	Set course for Africa, Anstis deserts April 18			
May 1721	Dutch snow Christopher		Thomas Heindrich	mid-Atlantic
May 1721	Norman galley			Off Cape Verde

June 1721	St Agnes warship and Comte de Thoulouze warship	French, guarding the Senegal gum trade		Off Senegal River,
Sierra Leone				
June 1721	Merchant ship	French		Frenchman's Bay, Senegal
June 12	A French ship, three other ships looted and several burned			Brent Island
End July	Semm Galley	Dutch		Off Axim
August 1721	Robinson	Liverpool	Canning	Off Grain Coast
August 6	Stanwich galley	Liverpool	Tarlton	Off Sestos
August 8	Onslow	London	Gee	Off Sestos
August	Martha snow	Liverpool	Lady	Off Cape la Hou
August 1721	Ship?	Dutch?		
September	Careened in Old Calabar			Bight of Biafra
Oct 1 1721	Joceline		Loane	Calabar River
Oct 2 1721	Mercy galley			Calabar River
Oct 5	Hannibal	London	Charles Ousley	Calabar River
Oct 1721	Cornwall galley		Rolls	Calabar River
Oct 1721	Running battle with Calabar natives			
Dec 14 1721	Geetruyt, or Geertrouycht galley	Dutch	Benjamin	Gabon Kreeft
Jan 2 1722	Elizabeth		Joseph Sharp	Jacque Jacques
Jan 2 1722	Tarlton	Liverpool	Thomas Tarlton	Assinie
Jan 3	Hannibal		Ousley	
Jan 4	Vlissingen (Flushingham)	Dutch	Gerrit de Haen	Grand Basaam
Jan 5	Diligence sloop		Stephen Thomas	Cape Appolonia
Jan 6	King Solomon	London	Joseph Traherne	Cape Appolonia
Jan 11	Porcupin Carlton (Charlton)	London	Fletcher	Whydah
	Hardey On Jan 11, apart from the 3 English slave ships, 5 Portuguese and 4 French were also taken		Allright Dittwitt	
Jan 11	Comte de Thoulouze	French privateer	There may have been two ships of this name - see June 1721	Whydah
Jan 13 or 15	Whydah (Wida) sloop	London	Stokes	Off Jacquin
Feb 5-6	The Ranger is taken by Ogle at sea			
Feb 9	Neptune		Thomas Hill	Cape Lopez
Feb 10	The final battle - Roberts dies			

PRISONERS TAKEN FROM THE RANGER and GOOD FORTUNE - THEIR FATE

R = taken from the Ranger. RF = taken from the Royal	Place of Birth	Taken from	With Bart from	Age at Trial	Verdict
Michael Mare (Maer) R	Ghent	In the Rover when Dutch from 1717	1718	41	Guilty - hung at Cape Corso Castle April 11th 1722
Martin (or Marcus) Johnson RF	Smyrna (Greece)	Rover when Dutch like Michael Mare	1718	21	Guilty - hung at Cape Corso Castle April 11th 1722
'Lord' Richard Hardy R	Wales	With Howel Davis	1718	26	Guilty - hung in chains at Cape Corso Castle April 3rd 1722
'Lord' Henry Dennis R	Bideford	With Howel Davis	1718	–	Guilty - but reprieved and sentenced to 7 years working in a plantation for the Royal Africa Company.
'Lord' Valentine Ashplant R	Minories, London	With Howel Davis	1719	32	Guilty - hung in chains at Cape Corso April 3rd, 1722
Robert Birdson R	Cornwall	With Howel Davis	1718	30	Guilty - died in prison?
'Lord' William Magness (Magnus) R	Minehead	With Howel Davis	1718	35	Guilty - hung in chains at Cape Corso April 3rd, 1722
'Lord' Christopher Moody RF	–	With Howel Davis	1718	28	Guilty - hung in chains at Cape Corso April 3rd, 1722
'Lord' David Sympson RF	North Berwick	Capt. Greaves Philippa of Trinidad	Jan 10th 1720	36	Guilty - hung in chains at Cape Corso April 3rd, 1722
'Lord' ThomasSutton RF	Berwick	With Howel Davis	1718	23	Guilty - hung in chains at Cape Corso April 3rd, 1722
John Jessup (1)	Wisbech	Taken with Roberts by Howel Davis	Feb 1719		Surrendered at Princes Island - Guilty - petitioned successfully for Royal Africa Company Indenture
Hag. Jacobson RF	Bristol	Dutch ship at Surinam	1719	30	Guilty - hung in chains at Cape Corso April 11th 1722
Joseph Moor(e) RF	Mere, Wiltshire	May Flower sloop	Feb 1720	19	Guilty - hung at Cape Corso Castle April 11th 1722
Josecph Nositer (Nossiter) RF	Sidbury, Devon	Expedition of Topsham	May 1720	26	Guilty - hung at Cape Corso April 16th, 1722
Joe Mansfield	Orkneys	Deserter from Rose, picked up at Dominica with Philips and Butson	June		Guilty but reprieved as he gave information on Scudamore's plot, although other sources state he was hung on April 16th at Cape Corso
James Philips (Phillips) RF	Antigua	Revenge pirate sloop Dominica	June 1720	35	Guilty - hung in chains at Cape Corse April 20th , 1722
Robert Butson	Ottery St. Mary, Devon	Revenge pirate sloop	June 1720	30	Guilty - hung at Cape Corso April 16th, 1722
William Williams (1) RF	Plymouth	Sidbury of Bristol Capt. William Thomas, at Newfoundland	June 25th 1720	40	Guilty - hung April 9th, 1722 although he had previously tried to escape from Roberts at Sierra Leone
William Williams (2) RF	Holland	Sidbury sloop	June 1720	30	Guilty - hung April 16th, 1722
William Fernon RF	Somerset	Sidbury	June 1720	22	Guilty - hung in chains at Cape Corso Castle April 11th, 1722
Roger Scot(t) RF	Bristol	Sidbury	June 1720		Guilty - reprieved to serve the Royal Africa Company for 7 years

William Main R	–	Capt. Peet's Brigantine	June 1720	28	Guilty - hung at Cape Corso April 9th, 1722
Richard Harris (Harries) R	Devon or Cornwall	Capt. Richards' Phoenix snow of Bristol	June 1720	45 the oldest	Guilty - hung at Cape Corso April 16th 1722
D. Littlejohn R	Bristol	Capt. Richards' Phoenix snow of Bristol	June 1720		Guilty - reprieved to serve the Royal Africa Company
Thomas How R	Barnstaple Devon	Joined from Trepassey fishing boat Newfoundland	June 1720		Guilty - reprieved to serve the Royal Africa Company for 7 years
John Phillips (Philips) RF	Alloa	Fishing boat Newfoundland	July 1720		Guilty - hung in chains at Cape Corso Castle Aprill 11th, 1722
James Harries RF	Jersey	Capt. Jonathan Whitfield's Richard pink	July 1720	28	Sent for trial at Marshalsea
Harry Glasby		Capt. Cary's Samuel sloop off New England	July 1720		Acquitted
Hugh Menzies RF		Capt. Cary's Samuel	July 14th 1720		Acquitted
Thomas Owen RF	Bristol	Capt. Phillips' Little York of Bristol	July 18th 1720		Guilty - reprieved and sold to the Royal Africa Company
William Taylor RF	Bristol	Little York of Bristol	July 18th 1720		Guilty - reprieved to serve the Royal Africa Company
James Greenham R	Marshfield Gloucester	Little York of Bristol	July 18th 1720		Guilty - successful petition to Royal Africa Company indenture
John Jaynson R	Lancaster	Love of Lancaster	July 18th 1720	22	Guilty - hung at Cape Corso Castle April 11th, 1722
James Clements RF	Brisol	Capt. Fensilon's Success sloop	July 1720	20	Guilty - hung at Cape Corso Castle April 11th, 1722
Herman Hunkins R		Success sloop	July 1720		Sent for trial at Marshalsea
John Parker RF	Dorset	Willing Mind of Poole	July 1720	22	Guilty - hung at Cape Corso Castle April 11th, 1722
Hugh Harris R	Corfe Castle, Devon	Willing Mind sloop	July 1720		Guilty - reprieved to serve the Royal Africa Company
William Mackintosh R	Canterbury	On Newfoundland Banks	July 1720	21	Guilty - hung at Cape Coast Castle April 9th, 1722
Thomas Willis R		Richard of Bideford	July 1720		Acquitted
George Smith RF	Wales	Mary and Martha	July 1720	25	Guilty - hung at Cape Corso April 20th, 1722
John Walden (1) R	Whitby	Mary and Martha	July 1720	24	Sent for trial at Marshalsea
John Walden (2) RF	Somerset	Blessing of Lymington	July 1720	24	Guilty - hung in chains at Cape Coast Castle April 23rd, 1722
Robert Crow RF	Isle of Man	Capt. Williams Taylor's Happy Return sloop	July 1720	24	Guilty - hung at Cape Corso
Christopher Lang R		Thomas brigantine	Sept. 1720		Sent for trial at Marshalsea
James Skyrme R	Somerset	Greyhound sloop of Bristol	Oct. 1720	44	Guilty - hung in chains at Cape Corso Castle April 13th 1722
John Mitchel R	Shadwell, London	Norman galley	Oct. 1710		Guilty - reprieved and sold to the Royal Africa Company
T. Withstandenot R		Norman galley	Oct. 1720		Acquitted
Peter la Fever R		Jeremiah and Anne	April 9th 1721	20	Acquitted

William Shurin R	Wapping, London	Jeremiah and Anne	April 1721	20 ind efoe	Guilty - reprieved to serve the Royal Africa Company
Robert Wilbourne RF		Capt. Whitby's Jeremiah and Anne	April 1721		Acquitted
Robert Johnson RF	Whydah	Jeremiah and Anne	April 1721	32	Guilty - hung at Cape Corso April 20th, 1722
William Darling RF		Jeremiah and Anne	April 1721		Acquitted
William Mead RF		Jeremiah and Anne	April 1721		Sent for trial at Marshalsea
Thomas Diggles RF		Capt. Thomas Heindrich's Christopher Dutch snow - mid Atlantic	April 1721		Acquitted
Ben Jeffreys (Jeffries) RF	Bristol or Devon	Norman galley of Cape Verde	May 1721	21	Guilty - hung at Cape Corso April 20th 1722
John Francia RF		Sloop at St Nicholas	April 1721		Acquitted
Dan Harding RF	Congresbury Somerset	Dutch interloper, El Puerto del Principe, St. Lucia	April 1721	26	Guilty - hung at Cape Corso Castle April 11th 1722
John Coleman RF	Wales	Adventure sloop	April 1721	24	Guilty - hung in chains at Cape Corso April 20th 1722
Charles Bunce RF	Exeter	Dutch galley Semm	April 1721	26	Guilty - hung at Cape Corso April 16th, 1722
R. Armstrong RF	London	Dutch galley, deserter from HMS Swallow	April 1721	34	Guilty - hung as a deserter from the foreyard on HMS Weymouth
John du Frock RF		Capt. Hingston's Lloyd galley off Antigua	May 1721		Sent for trial at Marshalsea
William Champnies RF		Lloyd galley	May 1721		Acquitted
George Danson RF		Lloyd galley	May 1721		Acquitted
Isaac Russel RF		Lloyd galley	May 1721		Sent for trial at Marshalsea
William Watts R	Irish	With Capt. Josse at Sierra Leone	July 1721	23	Guilty - hung in chains at Cape Corso April 20th 1722
William Davis (Davies) R	Welsh	With Capt. Glynne at Sierra Leone - deserter from the Ann Galley	July 1721	23	Guilty - hung in chains at Cape Corso April 20th, 1722
Abraham Harper RF	Bristol	Capt. Gee's Onslow at Sestos	Aug. 1721	23	Guilty - hung at Cape Corso Castle April 11th, 1722
Peter Lesley (Lashley) RF	Aberdeen	Onslow at Sestos	Aug. 1721	21	Guilty - hung at Cape Corso April 16th, 1722
Thomas Watkins RF		Onslow at Sestos	Aug. 1721		Acquitted
Philip Bill RF	St. Thomas Isle	Onslow at Sestos	Aug. 1721	27	Guilty - hung at Cape Corso Castle April 9th, 1722
Joseph Stephenson (Stevenson) RF	Whitby	Onslow at Sestos	Aug. 1721	40	Guilty - hung at Cape Corso Castle, April 16th, 1722
James Cromby RF	Wapping London	Onslow at Sestos	Aug. 1721		Guilty - petitioned to indenture at Royal Africa Company
Thomas Garret RF		Onslow at Sestos	Aug. 1721		Acquitted
George Ogle RF		Onslow at Sestos	Aug. 1721		Sent for trial to Marshalsea
Thomas Stretton R		Onslow at Sestos	Aug. 1721		Acquitted
William Petty R	Deptford	Onslow at Sestos	Aug. 1721	30	Guilty
Michael Lemmon R		Onslow at Sestos	Aug. 1721		Acquitted
William Wood R	York	Onslow at Sestos	Aug. 1721	27	Guilty - hung at Cape Corso April 20th, 1722
Edward Watts R	Dunmore	Onslow at Sestos	Aug. 1721	22	Guilty - hung in chains at Cape Corso April 20th, 1722

John Horn R	St. James London	Onslow at Sestos (a soldier)	Aug. 1721		Guilty - reprieved to serve the Royal Africa Company
Robert Hays RF	Liverpool	Capt. John Tarleton's Liverpool galley	Aug. 1721	20	Guilty - hung at Cape Corso April 20th, 1722
James Barrow R	Liverpool	Capt. Lady's Martha snow of Liverpool off Cape la Hou	Aug. 1721		Sent to Marshalsea for trial
Joshuah Lee R	Liverpool	Martha snow	Aug. 1721		Guilty - reprieved to serve the Royal Africa Company
Roger Gorsuch RF		Martha snow	Aug. 1721		Acquitted
John Watson RF		Martha snow	Aug. 1721		Acquitted
Robert Hartley (1) R		Capt. Canning's Robinson of Liverpool off Grain Coast	Aug. 1721		Acquitted
James Crane R		Robinson of Liverpool	Aug. 1721		Sent for trial to Marshalsea
George Smith R	Wales	Capt. Tarleton's Stanwich galley of Liverpool of Sestos	Aug. 1721	24	Acquitted
Roger Pye R		Stanwich galley	Aug. 1721		Acquitted
Robert Fletcher R		Stanwich galley	Aug. 1721		Sent for trial to Marshalsea
Robert Hartley (2) R	Liverpool	Stanwich galley (a gunner)	Aug. 1721		Guilty - reprieved on petition to serve a Royal Africa Company Indenture
Andrew Rance R		?	Aug. 1721		Sent for trial to Marshalsea
Cuthbert Goss R	Plymouth	Dutch ship	Aug. 1721	21	Guilty - hung within the flood-marks at Cape Corso Castle April 20th, 1722
Thomas Giles R	Minehead	Mercy galley of Bristol at Calabar	Oct. 1721	26	Guilty - reprieved to serve the Royal Africa Company
Israel Hynde R	Aberdeen or Bristol	Mercy galley	Oct. 1721	30	Guilty - hung in chains at Cape Coast Castle April 13th, 1722
William Child RF		Mercy galley surgeon	Oct. 1721		Acquitted
John Griffin RF	Blackwall London	Mercy galley carpenter	Oct. 1721		Guilty - reprieved into 7 years slavery for the Royal Africa Co.
Peter Scudamore RF	Welsh but 'of Bristol'	Capt. Rolls' slave galley Cornwall at Calabar	Oct. 1721	35	Guilty - hung in chains at Cape Corso Castle April 13th, 1722
Christopher Granger		Cornwall galley at Calabar	Oct. 1721		Acquitted
Nicholas Brattle RF		Cornwall galley at Calabar	Oct. 1721		Acquitted - a musician
James Whittle RF		Cornwall galley at Calabar	Oct. 1721		Acquitted - a musician
Thomas Davis RF		Cor wall galley at Calabar	Oct. 1721		Acquitted
Thomas Sever RF		Cornwall galley at Calabar	Oct. 1721		Acquitted
Robert Bevins RF		Cornwall galley at Calabar	Oct. 1721		Guilty
T. Oughterly RF		Cornwall galley at Calabar	Oct. 1721		Guilty
David Rice RF	Welsh but 'of Bristol'	Cornwall galley	Oct. 1721		Guilty - sentenced to 7 years in the Royal Africa Company Plantations

Name	Origin	Ship	Date	Age	Verdict
Robert Haws RF	Yarmouth	Capt. Loane's Joceline on the 1721 Calabar River	Oct. 1st	31	Guilty - hung at Cape Coast Castle April 11th, 1722
William Church R		Gertruycht of Holland	Dec. 14th 1721		Acquitted - a musician
Phillip Haak R		Flushingham of Holland	Jan. 1722		Acquitted - a musician
William Smith R		Capt. Joseph Sharp's Elizabeth	Jan. 2nd 1722		Acquitted
Adam Comry R		Elizabeth	Jan. 2nd 1722		Acquitted - the surgeon testified against George Wilson and Scudamore
William May RF		Elizabeth	Jan. 1722		Acquitted
Edward Thornden RF		Elizabeth	Jan. 1722		Acquitted
Peter de Vine R	Stepney	Capt. Trahern's King Solomon off Cape Appollonia	Jan. 6th 1722	42	Guilty - hung at Cape Corso Castle April 9th, 1722
John Johnson R	Near Lancaster	King Solomon	Jan. 1722	22	Acquitted but Gosse says hung
John Stodgill R		King Solomon	Jan. 1722		Acquitted
John Lane (Line) RF	Lambert St. London	King Solomon (a soldier)	Jan. 1722		Guilty - indentured for 7 years to Royal Africa Company
Sam Fletcher RF	East Smithfield	King Solomon	Jan. 1722		Guilty - indentured to Royal Africa Company on petition
William Phillips RF	Lower Shadwell London	King Solomon	Jan. 1722	29	Guilty - hung at Cape Corso Castle - April 9th, 1722
Jacob Johnson RF		King Solomon	Jan. 1722		Acquitted
John King RF	Shadwell London	King Solomon	Jan. 1722	20	Guilty - reprieved to serve the Royal Africa Company
Benjamin Par RF		Capt. Kanning's Robinson	Jan. 1722		Acquitted
Josiah Robinson R		Capt. Thomas Tarlton's Tarlton at Cape la Hou, Assinie	Jan. 2nd		Acquitted
John Arnaught R		Tarlton	Jan. 1722		Acquitted
John Davis R		Tarlton	Jan. 1722		Acquitted
Henry Graves R		Tarlton	Jan. 1722		Sent for trial to Marshalsea
Thomas Howard R		Tarlton	Jan. 1722		Acquitted
John Rimer R		Tarlton	Jan. 1722		Sent for trial to Marshalsea
Thomas Clephen R		Tarlton	Jan. 1722		Acquitted
George Wilson RF		Tarlton	Jan. 1722		Guilty - execution witheld on the King's pleasure, as he informed
Edward Tarlton RR		Tarlton	Jan. 1722		Acquitted
John Jessup (2) RF	Plymouth	Capt. Stephen Thomas' Diligence sloop	Jan. 5th 1722	20	Guilty - hung at Cape Corso April 20th, 1722
Hugh Riddle RF		Diligence sloop	Jan. 1722		Acquitted
Stephen Thomas RF		Diligence sloop	Jan. 1722		Acquitted
Henry Dawson R		Whydah sloop at Jacquin	Jan. 1722		Acquitted
William Glass R		Whydah sloop	Jan. 1722		Acquitted
James Cosins R		?	Jan. 1722		Sent for trial to Marshalsea

William Guineys R		Capt. Fletcher's	Jan. 11th		Acquitted
		Porcupine	1722		
Richard Wood RF		Porcupine	1722		Acquitted
Richard Scot RF		Porcupine	1722		Acquitted
William Davison RF	Wales	Porcupine	1722	23	Acquitted
Sam Morwell RF		Porcupine	1722		Acquitted
Edward Evans RF		Porcupine	1722		Acquitted
Thomas Roberts RF		Capt. Allwright's	Jan. 11th		Acquitted
		Charlton (or Carlton)	1722		
John Richards RF		Charlton	1722		Acquitted
John Cane RF		Charlton	1722		Acquitted

'Lords' Hardy, Moody, Magness, Ashplant, and Sutton had served with Howell Davis. It is significant that these were the first six men hung, all on April 3rd, and all six were then displayed in chains. They showed contempt for the hangings, and complained that the inexperienced hangmen tied their hands in front of them, instead of behind, as was the custom. In the mass hanging of 14 pirates upon April 11th, Jacobson, Philps and Fernon were transferred into chains. The next batch of prisoners to be hung in chains were the one-legged Skyrme, 'Nanny' Walden and Israel Hynde, both of whom had lost arms in the final fight, and the rogue surgeon Scudamore. These four were the only executions on the 13th of April. In another mass hanging of 14 men on the 20th, another 5 men were hung in chains - Edward and William Watts, William Davies, James Phillips and John Coleman. Thus a total of 18 pirates in chains was the grim sight for ships entering the harbour, for several months after. Stevenson may refer to the sight in *Treasure Island* - '*You've seen 'em, maybe, hanged in chains, birds about 'em, seamen pointing 'em out as they go down with the tide … And you can hear the chains a-jangle as you go about and reach for the other buoy.*'

Thomas Jones had returned to England and was incarcerated in the Marshalsea, where he died. Of the 17 men committed to the Marshalsea Prison in Southwark, 13 died on the homeward trip on HMS Weymouth. Of the two respited, George Willson died soon after on the Cape Coast, and the other received the King's Pardon.

18 impressed men from the French ship at Whydah in February 1722 were taken off the *Ranger* and acquitted. The acquitted musicians had '*served as Musick on board the Royal Fortune, being taken out of several merchant ships, having had an uneasy life of it, having sometimes their Fiddles, and often their Heads broke, only for excusing themselves, as saying they were tired, when any Fellow took it in his Head to demand a Tune*' (trial transcript)

Roger Ball died of burns caused by John Morris exploding gunpowder in the Royal Fortune. Another William Main in the crew was blown up on the Royal Fortune. 10 men were killed in the Ranger and 3 in the Royal Fortune.

Fate	No. of men	Notes
Executed	52	In 1722 at Cape Corso Castle: 6 on April 3rd; 6 on April 9th; 14 on April 11th; 4 on April 13th, 8 on April 16th, 14 on April 20th
Guilty, and sentenced to Death, reprieved on petition to 7 years' **Servitude** for Royal Africa Company	20	All seem to have died before their 7 years were completed
To **Marshalsea** Prison	17	13 died on the voyage
Respited	2	1 died, 1 pardoned
Acquitted	74	
Negroes	70	52 on Royal Fortune, 28 on Ranger - some were slaves and some were seamen
Died en route to Cape Corso	15	
Died in Cape Coast Castle	4	
Killed on Ranger	10	
Killed on Royal Fortune	3	
TOTAL Crew Members	267	

Footnotes:

1. Among Roberts' pirates captured by Challoner Ogle was John Place in 1722. Not far off Cape Coast Castle, in October 1748, he led a mutiny on the HMS *Chesterfield*, wishing to settle a colony. He was hanged. (see *Mariners' Mirror*, 47, 1961). When the captain and most of the officers were ashore, the first lieutenant took the ship to sea, to turn pirate. However, the *Chesterfield* was recovered by the boatswain, who sailed it to the West Indies. The first lieutenant and lieutenant of marines were shot, and the carpenter, his mate and three others hanged.

2. The nature of equality aboard pirate ships, with blacks being treated as equal, was known in the early 18th century. In 1715 the ruling Council of the Colony of Virginia worried about the 'connections' between the "*Ravage of Pyrates*" and "an *Insurrection of the Negroes.*" They were right to be concerned. By 1716 the slaves of Antigua had grown "*very impudent and insulting*" and reportedly many of them "*went off to join those pirates who did not seem too concerned about colour differences.*" These connections were trans-Atlantic; stretching from the heart of Empire in London, to the slave colonies in the Americas and the 'Slave Coast' of Africa. In the early 1720s a gang of pirates settled in West Africa, joining and intermixing with the Kru—a West African people from what is now Sierra Leone and Liberia, renowned both for their seamanship in their

long canoes and when enslaved for their leadership of slave revolts. The pirates were probably members of Bartholomew Roberts' crew who had fled into the woods when attacked by the Navy in 1722. This alliance is not so unusual when you consider that of the 157 men who did not escape and were either captured or killed on board Roberts' ship, 45 of them were black — probably neither slaves nor pirates but "*Black saylors, commonly known by the name of gremetoes*" — independent African mariners primarily from the Sierra Leone region, who would have joined the pirates "*for a small demand of wages.*" We can see the way these connections were spread and the how the pirates' legacy was disseminated even after their defeat in the fate of some of those captured on Roberts' pirate ship. "*Negroes*" from Black Bart's crew grew mutinous over the poor conditions and "*thin Commons*" they received from the Navy. "*Many of them*" had "*lived a long time*" in the "*pyratical Way*", which obviously for them had meant better food and more freedom.

3. The remnants of Roberts' pirates who intermarried with the Kru Tribe, may have some connection with *Palm Wine* music, which is believed to have its origins in the *Kru* tribe of Liberia, and combines elements from Caribbean Calypso with local melodies and rhythms. *The music was so called because the music could be largely heard in clubs where palm-wine was usually served without limitation. The music could be heard in bars along marina areas enjoyed by sailors and crewmen. Palm Wine guitarists had a tremendous impact on most African guitarists of today and their influence can be heard in both Highlife and Soukous guitar players. Presently Pine Wine music is on the decline, the last well known artist being S.E. Rogie who died in 1994. However Palm Wine music originated, it is an expression of the day-to-day life of ordinary people, the music of their hearts. It tells of people's joys and sorrows, pleasures and displeasure, success and disappointments. The word Palm Wine is used to describe a milky white liquid tapped from the Palm tree. It has 2 percent alcohol, it is cheap and it makes a mellow natural high. When people gather around the fire to share life experiences, some are shy and bashful, but after drinking a few glasses of Palm Wine, it brings them out.*

America's formula-driven music industry has been unkind to most African musicians. It beckons with the promise of enormous riches, then rebuffs with a calculated closed-mindedness. Palm Wine guitar music is like folk music or blues. In Palm Wine music people sing heart-to-heart songs, what they feel. They drink a little to feel happy, and what they drink is Palm Wine. The wine is a sweet milky sap from a variety of palm tree plentiful in West Africa. The music is a blend of rural tradition and urban acculturation. Fortified by the arrival of cheap acoustic guitars, and the musical exchange fostered by sailors plying the waters along the Gulf of Guinea and Sierra Leone who staffed the apparatus of colonialism up and down the coast, it took root in the twenties and thirties. The sailors, many of whom were from the Kru tribe of Sierra Leone and Liberia, brought sea shanties and records from other lands. Krios, the comparatively well-educated descendants of an amalgam of Africans of varying ethnicity, freed from slavery and repatriated to the colony of Freetown (now Sierra Leone's capital), carried music from post to post throughout British West Africa. Freetown in the fifties and sixties was a particularly good place for musicians. There were always parties to play for in the bustling capital, and a variety of bars competed for customers with the lure of live music. Recording, too was becoming a means of generating both income and a measure of fame. European record companies had representatives roaming West Africa in search of talent; the British company Decca even had a mobile studio, which periodically visited Freetown.

4. 'The Black Captain' should be made into a Spielberg movie. 'Black Bart' was a film starring Dan Duryea and Yvonne de Carlo. Unfortunately, it was a Western about a stagecoach robber who termed himself Black Bart, Charles Bowles, from Norfolk, England. He served the Union Army at Vicksburg and was wounded before the Siege of Atlanta. For eight years he plagued Wells Fargo with a string of at least 28 robberies. Boles operated on foot with an unloaded shotgun and never robbed stagecoach passengers or drivers. Between robberies he lived in San Francisco, and disappeared from the Palace Hotel, Visalia, California in 1888 and was never heard of again. The 1996 book 'Black Bart, Boulevardier Bandit: The Saga of California's Most Mysterious Stagecoach Robber and the Men who Sought to Capture Him', by George Hoeper, recounts the story.

CHAPTER VII

JOHN PHILLIPS (PHILIPS) d. 18th April 1724

John Phillips was probably forced from the *Inven,* the first prize captured by Thomas Anstis in the *Good Fortune,* a day after he and Thomas Jones deserted Bart Roberts (-see the footnote on Anstis in the entry on Howell Davis. Another source says that this John Phillips had originally been captured along with Bart Roberts by Howel Davis). Anstis had not wished to sail for Africa, and Jones had been involved in a brawl with Roberts. Phillips was needed by the pirates as a carpenter. Soon the pirates took the *Two Sisters,* under Captain Richards, and headed for Martinique. However, narrowly escaping from two French men-of-war off Montserrat, the next we hear of the *Good Fortune* is in the *Weekly Journal* of January 13th, 1722:

'*Our merchants have received the following advice from St Christophers dated October 15th, 1721, that they were in daily expectation of the arrival of the new governor, with some men-of-war along with him which they very much wanted. That the Hector man-of-war, Captain Brand, having buried most of her crew could then do but little service. That several pirate ships infested the coast where one carrying thirty guns and 400 men some days before had engaged two French men-of-war. She carried a black flag at her top-mast-head. The action took place off Montserrat but she got away from them and bore away from Antigua. That five men newly come in there that did belong to the Inven, Captain Ross, from Cork in Ireland, having on board 600 barrels of beer besides other provisions which ship was taken off Martinico by a pirate sloop well mounted with 140 men. That Colonel Doyley of Montserrat with his family was on board the said vessel and was very much cut and wounded by the pirates. That 21 of these brutes had forced a woman passenger one after another and afterwards broke her back and threw her into the sea.*' Doyley had been attacked for trying to defend the woman - the story shows how remarkable the discipline of Captain Bart Roberts was, regarding the safety of women.

Anstis and Jones next captured Captain Marston's ship carrying alcohol and provisions, and five men joined the crew, before taking

Captain Smith's *Hamilton* in late June 1722. At Mohair Key, the crew laid up for a few weeks, to drink their way through the liquor and careen the *Good Fortune*. They returned the looted and stripped *Hamiton* to its captain, and headed for the Gulf of Campeachy, taking two Spanish ships on the way, with meagre returns. One was driven ashore at Campeachy and one was burned. Strangely, the next ship they encountered was Captain Smith's *Hamilton* again. It had been captured by a Spanish privateers, and was being taken into Cuba when the Spaniard ran aground. Jones asked Smith if he had been looking for his empty bottles, before he was put into an open boat with his remaining crew, and the *Hamilton* was burnt. On October 21st, the rich *Don Pedro* was looted off Hispaniola, the first decent prize since Anstis and Jones had deserted Roberts. £3000 in goods was taken, and its surgeon forced, after a short battle when two of its crew were killed. A few days later, the *Morning Star* was captured, 32 guns were transferred to her, and the one-handed John Finn was elected captain. The *Morning Star* and *Good Fortune* took Captain Lubbock's *Portland* in December, then two more small prizes before taking Captain Ellwood's *Nightingale*, at anchor of Tortuga. This was April 1722, and while the pirates careened, Montigny la Palisse and those former members of Roberts' crew must have mused upon the poor 'luck' of Anstis as a leader. Roberts concentrated on specific areas to hunt, whereas Anstis seemed to have no strategy but to rely on ships passing at sea. Some wanted to steal the *Good Fortune*, and Anstis was replaced in an election as its captain by Bridstock Weaver. The unhappy pirates allowed Ellwood to sail off in the *Nightingale* upon condition he took the following petition for pardon to Governor Lawes of Jamaica and return with an answer:

To His Most Gracious majesty, by the Grace of God, of Great Britain, France, and Ireland, Defender of the Faith

The Humble PETITION of the Company, now belonging to the Ship Morning Star and Brigantine Good Fortune, lying under the ignominious Name and Denomination of Pyrates, Humbly sheweth:

That we your Majesty's most loyal Subjects have, at sundry Times, been taken by Bartholomew Roberts, the then Captain of the aforesaid Vessels and Company, together with another Ship, in which we left him, and have been forced by him and his wicked Accomplices, to enter into, and serve, in the said Company; as Pyrates, much contrary to our Wills and Inclinations: and we, your loyal Subjects utterly abhorring and detesting that impious Way of Living, did, with a unanimous Consent, and contrary to the Knowledge of the said Roberts or his Accomplices, on, or about, the 18th Day of April, 1721, leave, and ran away with, the aforesaid Ship Morning Star and Brigantine Good Fortune with no other Intent and Meaning than the Hopes of obtaining toy Majesty's most gracious Pardon. And that we, your Majesty's most loyal subjects, may with more Safety return to our native Country and serve the Nation, unto which we belong, in our respective Capacities, without Fear of being prosecuted by the Injured, whose Estates have suffered by the said Roberts and his Accomplices, during our forcible Detainment, by the said Company. We most humbly implore your Majesty's most royal Assent, to this our humble Petition. And your Petitioners shall ever pray etc.

The forced carpenter, John Phillips, and Thomas Jones, sailed with Ellwood with the petition, as they were both confident of a reprieve. Jones had fought against Roberts and escaped from him, and Phillips had been forced as an *'artist'*. Governor Lawes sent the petition to London, having received it on July 6th. By the time the various authorities in London had decided to pardon the pirates, the August deadline given by the pirates had passed, and they returned to piracy. Phillips managed to return to England on the *Nightingale*. Learning that some of his co-pirates under Anstis had been taken to gaol in Bristol, he panicked and quickly decided to try to sail to Newfoundland, leaving Topsham harbour. Having failed to gain a pardon, Phillips had remained *'under cover'* in Bristol, as he felt that his story of being 'forced' would not be believed. (Thomas Jones, the old comrade of Howell Davis, who had personally fought Bart Roberts, and had deserted with Anstis, was one of those arrested - he was sent to the Marshalsea Prison in London, and later executed). Upon landing at Peter Harbour Phillips deserted his ship, and became a splitter in a cod-fishery. The work was terribly hard, in freezing conditions, but was safer and easier than being a merchant seaman in those days. Roberts had easily recruited such men in his raids on neighbouring Trepassy, and Phillips soon grew tired of an honest life. He had tasted the fruits of the easy life of piracy, and it beckoned him stongly.

On August 29th, 1723, with William White he stole a small schooner belonging to a William Minors (or Minott), off Saint Pierre Island. White was one of Minors' crewmen. Sixteen disaffected men had plotted the capture, but only four turned up, so they sailed away with three others, Phillips being chosen as captain. White had no position, but John Nutt was sailing-master, James Sparks the gunner, and Thomas Fern the carpenter. Articles were drawn up, and in the absence of a Bible, they swore them over a hatchet. Defoe enumerates Phillips' articles on board the *Revenge*:

1. *Every Man shall obey civil Command; the Captain shall have one full Share and a half in all Prizes; the Master, Carpenter, Boatswain and Gunner shall have one Share and a quarter*

2. *If any Man shall offer to run away, or keep any Secret from the Company, he shall be marooned, with one Bottle of Powder, one Bottle of Water, one small Arm and Shot.*

3. *If any Man steal any Thing in the Company, or game to the Value of a Piece of Eight, he shall be marooned or shot.*

4. *If at any Time we should meet another Marooner (that is, Pyrate) that Man shall sign his Articles without the Consent of our Company, shall suffer such Punishment and the Captain and Company shall think fit.*

5. *That man that shall strike another whilst these Articles are in force, shall receive Moses' Law (that is, 40 Stripes lacking one) on the bare Back.*

6. *That man that shall snap his Arms, or smoke Tobacco in the Hold, without a Cap to his Pipe, or carry a Candle lighted without a Lanthorn, shall suffer the same Punishment as the former Article.*

7. *That Man that shall not keep his Arms clean, fit for an Engagement, or neglect his Business, shall be cut off from his Share, and suffer such other Punishment as the Captain and the Company think fit.*

8. *If any Man shall lose a Joint in Time of an Engagement, he shall have 400 Pieces of Eight, if a Limb, 800.*

9. *If at any Time we meet with a prudent Woman, that Man offers to meddle with her, without her Consent, shall suffer present Death.*

By taking several small fishing boats, Phillips added to his crew. A former pirate named Burrill became boatswain. One of his prisoners from a merchantman was the ex-pirate John Rose Archer, who had served under the infamous Blackbeard, Edward Teach, in 1718. Archer was quickly made quartermaster. Phillips called his ship the *Revenge*, and in October 1723 captured another Welshman, William Phillips. In that month, the brig *Mary*, another brig, a Portuguese brig and the sloop *Content* were taken, with reasonable takings off each prize. From the *Content*, its first mate John Master, William Phillips, William Taylor and James Wood were 'forced'. The crew holed up and careened in a small bay on Barbados for several weeks, but ran desperately short of provisions, so returned to sea.

Phillips spotted a large 12-gun Martinican ship with 35 crew, and was forced to attack it for much-needed supplies. It tried to outsail the *Revenge*, which took almost a day to overhaul her, and after bitter fighting it was taken. Four of the survivors, one a surgeon, were impressed as pirates, and the ship reprovisioned. Two more ships were taken, then the *Revenge* was careened again, in Tobago. Anstis had careened there with Phillips, and Phillips wanted more men for his crew. Some pirates had hidden there in the recent past, members of the crews of Anstis and Finn when they were attacked. However, he only found one marooned negro, Pedro, who said that the other men had been taken off by a man-of-war. The *Revenge* now beat a hasty retreat when a man-of-war was spotted by Burrill, taking on water nearby, and the four French prisoners were left behind.

Several more ships were taken, with more violence than was necessary. They included a sloop from New York, a Virginia ship under Captain Haffam, three Jamaican sloops, a snow and a Portuguese ship bound for Brazil. In February 1724, John Phillips put William Phillips and four others on board Captain Laws' captured snow, with Thomas Fern as captain, ordering them to sail in consort with the *Revenge*. One night, the consort attempted to elude the *Revenge*, but was chased for several hours and taken in a savage battle. James Wood was killed. William Phillips had to have his left leg amputated. There was no ship's surgeon, so John Rose Archer, with some experience of these matters, sawed Phillips' leg off. He then used a red-hot axe to cauterise the stump. However, he burned too much of Phillips' body away from the wound area, leaving terrible injuries. William Taylor had also been injured in the leg. Heading north from Tobago, a Portuguese ship and three sloops were taken, and Fern again tried to escape in one of the sloops. He was shot by Captain Phillips, in accordance with the ship's articles, and another seaman a few days later for the same offence. Over 30 French, English, American and Portuguese ships were taken in nine months in the West Indies and along the Atlantic Coast.

On February 7th, 1724, Captain Huffan's ship was taken off North Carolina. The navigator Harry Gyles was forced, as was Charles Ivemay, but John Masters was allowed to leave, as he had a wife and children who would starve without his income. On March 25th, another two ships were taken, one under another John Phillips, and one under Captain Robert Mortimer. On March 27th, Mortimer struck Phillips with a hand-spike in the shoulder, while trying to lead a mutiny. But his men stood by and Phillips slashed him with his sword three times, then Nutt and

Archer hacked at his prostrate body before Burrill kicked it and ordered Mortimer's crew to throw his body overboard. John Salter's sloop off the Isle of Sabloes was next taken on April 4th, and kept as a prize. Captain Caldwell's schooner was also captured and Phillips was about to scuttle it when he discovered that it was owned by the Mr Minors who had 'supplied' him with the *Revenge*, so he let it go. A ship under Captain Dependance Ellery was taken, but it had tried to out-run the pirates, so they forced the unfortunate master to dance until he dropped with exhaustion. Ten vessels were shortly taken, with the following masters, Joshua Elwell, Samuel Elwell, Mr Combs, Mr Lansley, James Babston, Edward Freeman, Mr Start, Obadiah Beal, Erick Erickson and Benjamin Wheeler. In early April 1724, Phillips took two ships travelling from Virginia to New York. From the *Dolphin*, Edward Cheeseman and John Filmore, (the great-grandfather of President Millard Fillmore) were forced to become pirates. Phillips replaced his ship with the *Dolphin*, which was a better sailer, a sloop out of Cape Ann.

Phillips sailed back up to Newfoundland, intending to take on more crew from the disaffected cod-splitting fraternity, and off Nova Scotia took Andrew Harradine's brand-new sloop on April 17th. Harradine quickly discovered that over half the crew were forced men, and were anxious to be rid of Phillips. A day later, Harradine, Fillmore, Cheesman and some other forced men attacked the pirates with axes and hammers. The desperate Phillips tripped over, and was killed by Captain Harridan's hatchet. Phillips' head was cut off, pickled and tied to the mast-head. Archer and the few pirates were overpowered. The gunner James Sparks and John Nutt were thrown overboard by Edward Cheeseman in the mutiny. The remainder of John Phillips' crew were chained up, and Harridan took the ship to land in Boston on May 3rd. Cheeseman and Fillmore were tried in Boston on May 12th and acquitted, while Archer and White were found guilty. Phillips and Burrill's heads, pickled in Newfoundland, were exhibits at the trial. Some of Phillips' personal treasures were awarded by the court to Fillmore, including silver knee-buckles, shoe buckles, a tobacco box, a silver-hilted sword and two gold rings.

Archer, William Phillips and William White were hung on Bird Island in Boston Harbour on June 2nd. They were ministered to in their last days by a fierce Boston theologian, of whom John Jameson remarked in 1923 that '*Cotton Mather ministered to them in their last days, adding, one would think a new horror to death*'. The amputee William Phillips was somehow reprieved after conviction, as was William Taylor. The negro

Pedro was acquitted, as was another impressed negro known as Pierro, and three impressed Frenchmen, John Baptis, Peter Tafferey and Isaac Lassen.

Books

The following are representative of the books consulted for this publication.

Clinton Black 'Pirates of the West Indies' Cambridge 1989

F.B.C. Bradlee 'Piracy in the West Indies and its Suppression' Essex Institute 1923

Aubrey Burl 'That Great Pyrate' Alun Books 1997

James Burney 'History of the Buccaneers of America' 1816 Aberdeen University Press reprint 1949

Calendar of State Papers, Colonial Series, Eyre and Spottiswoode

Chappell 'History of the Port of Cardiff'

Barry Clifford and Paul Perry 'The Black Ship' Headline 1999

David Cordingley 'Under the Black Flag', Random House 1995

David Cordingley 'Pirates: From the Americas to the Far East' Salamander 1996

Captain A.G. Corse 'Pirates of the Eastern Seas' Frederick Muller

E.A. Cruickshank 'The Life of Sir Henry Morgan' Macmillan of Canada, Toronto 1935

George Francis Dow and John Henry Edmonds 'The Pirates of the New England Coast 1630-1730' Marine Research Society, Salem Massachusetts 1923

Charles Ellms 'The Pirates' Own Book' Portland 1844

J. Esquemeling 'The History of the Buccaneers' first published in English 1684

Robert Falconer 'Falconer's Marine Dictionary' 1780

Peter Gerhard 'Pirates of the pacific' University of Nebraska 1995

Philip Gosse 'The History of Piracy' Cassell 1932

Philip Gosse 'The Pirate's Who's Who' Burt Franklin 1924

C.H. Haring 'Buccaneers in the West Indies in the 17th Century' Methuen 1910

Captain Charles Johnson (Daniel Defoe) 'A General History of the Pyrates' 1724

Peter Kemp 'The Oxford Companion to Ships and The Sea' Oxford University Press 1979

Peter Kemp and Christopher Lloyd 'Brethren of the Coast' The Windmill Press 1960

James Lydon 'Pirates, privateers and Profits' Boston 1971

G.E. Mainwaring 'Life and Works of Sir Henry Mainwaring' Navy Records Society 1920

David Marley 'Pirates and Privateers of the Americas' ABC-CLIO 1994

Jennifer Marx 'Pirates and Privateers of the Caribbean' Krieger 1992

David Mitchell 'Pirates: An Illustrated History' Dial Press 1976

P. Pringle 'Jolly Roger' Museum Press' 1953

Marcus Rediker 'Between the Devil and the Deep Blue Sea' Cambridge 1987

Stanley Richards 'Black Bart', Christopher Davies, 1966

Jan Rogozinski 'A Brief History of the Caribbean' 1992

W. Adolphe Roberts 'Sir Henry Morgan' Hamish Hamilton 1933

Frank Sherry 'Raiders and Rebels' Henry Morrow 1986

Dava Sobel 'Longitude – the True Story of a Lone Genius Who Solved the Greatest Scientific Mystery of His Time', 4th Estate paperback edition 1998

Captain William Snelgrave 'A New Voyage to Guinea, and the Slave-Trade' 1744

Spencer 'Annals of South Glamorgan'

L.A.G. Strong 'Dr Quicksilver 1660-1742 - the Life and Times of Dr Thomas Dover' Andrew Melrose 1955

W. Llewelyn Williams Sir Henry Morgan, the Buccaneer, Transactions of the Honourable Society of Cymmrodorion, Session 1903-1904, published 1905.

Neville Williams 'Captains Outrageous' Weidenfield and Nicholson 1962

Alexander Winston 'No Purchase, No Pay' Eyre and Spottiswoode 1970

George Woodbury 'The Great Days of Piracy' Elek Books 1954

George Wycherley 'Buccaneers of the Pacific' The Bobbs-Merrill Company 1924